Levinas Studies

Levinas Studies: An Annual Review

Series Editor:
Jeffrey Bloechl

Editorial Board:
Marie L. Baird
Leora Batnitzky
Bettina Bergo
Robert Bernasconi
Richard A. Cohen
Edwin E. Gantt
Claire E. Katz
Jeffrey Kosky
Philippe Nemo
Adriaan T. Peperzak
Michael Purcell
Jill Robbins
Anthony Steinbock
Andrew Tallon
Rudi Visker

Levinas Studies
An Annual Review

Volume 10

Jeffrey Bloechl, ed.

Duquesne University Press
Pittsburgh, Pennsylvania

Levinas Studies: An Annual Review is published annually by Duquesne University Press as a forum for Levinas scholarship. Essays submitted for publication may focus on any aspect of Levinas's thought and writings. Manuscripts should conform to *The Chicago Manual of Style* and be approximately 8,000–12,000 words in length. Authors should include a written statement that the manuscript is being submitted exclusively to *Levinas Studies*. We encourage electronic submissions in Microsoft Word format, sent to dupress@duq.edu, followed by hard copy (printout) of the essay sent by regular mail to Jeffrey Bloechl, Editor, *Levinas Studies,* Department of Philosophy, Boston College, 140 Commonwealth Avenue, Chestnut Hill, MA 02467.

Copyright © 2016 Duquesne University Press
All rights reserved

Published in the United States of America by
Duquesne University Press
600 Forbes Avenue
Pittsburgh, Pennsylvania 15282

No part of this book may be used or reproduced, in any manner or form whatsoever, without the written permission of the publisher, except in the case of short quotations in critical articles or reviews.

Levinas Studies: An Annual Review
Volume 10

ISBN 978-0-8207-0496-8
ISSN 1554-7000

∞ Printed on acid-free paper.

Contents

Editor's Introduction   vii
Jeffrey Bloechl

Abbreviations   xv

The Transcendence of Words   1
Akos Krassoy

Tracing a Traumatic Temporality: Levinas and Derrida on Trauma and Responsibility   43
Cathrine Bjørnholt Michaelsen

"Flipping the Deck": On *Totality and Infinity*'s Transcendental/Empirical Puzzle   79
Jack Marsh

The Recurrence of Acoustics in Levinas   115
Roberto Wu

Bearing the Other and Bearing Sexuality: Women and Gender in Levinas's "And God Created Woman"   137
Deborah Achtenberg

Interpreting from the Interstices: The Role of Justice in a Liberal Democracy—Lessons from Michael Walzer and Emmanuel Levinas   155
Nicholas R. Brown

Otherwise than *Laïcité?*: Toward an Agonistic Secularism in Levinas   187
Mark Cauchi

Ethical Dwelling and the Glory of Bearing Witness 221
Hanoch Ben-Pazi

About the Contributors 249

Index 251

Editor's Introduction
Jeffrey Bloechl

Already long before Emmanuel Levinas's death ten years ago, his work had been the subject of thousands of essays, book-length studies, and doctoral dissertations in dozens of languages.[1] In the meantime, there are also several international associations dedicated to the proliferation of that work, bringing scholars together for seminars, symposia, and full-scale conferences. This torrent of scholarship seems not to have slowed, though it has certainly diversified. One thus hears talk of waves in the reception of Levinas: after (1) an early concern to situate him in relation to the phenomenological tradition he proposes to redefine in light of modes of intentionality that it will have hitherto suppressed, there was (2) a range of work somewhat more absorbed in questions raised mainly by Derrida, though also to some extent by Ricoeur, Lyotard, and others, and most recently there is (3) a growing effort to bring his thinking to bear on questions and problems in the way of concerted social action.[2]

In fact, we have not been able to decide whether Levinas ought to be read first in relation to phenomenology and fundamental ontology, deconstruction and hermeneutics, or social and political theory, and this is because those distinctions, which to be sure have their own importance, can seem to harbor others that Levinas would surely reject. Let us recall that it is the self-declared task of phenomenology to investigate the appearing of things but also to include the non-appearing of what transcends being and appearing. Let us also recall that deconstruction exposes the unthematized infrastructures by which meaning is expressed and order is projected. And let us simply note that it is the business of social and political theory to describe, and where necessary criticize, the limits within which desired action between citizens either occurs or fails to occur. For Levinas, the positive transcendence that expresses itself in a human face that is more than its appearing has gone unnoticed and excluded by a Western tradition that has not held in question the powers of the subject, so that we fail to catch sight of a responsibility that precedes any attempt to submit it to a perspective or an order. In short, the argument in favor of radical responsibility for the other person opposes, together and at once, any primacy for being and appearing, seeing and interpreting, and even freedom and self-determination. The critique of line and light is always and already in solidarity with the critique of law and institution, and a claim for the priority of the stranger over oneself has evident moral and political stakes that cannot be without considerable reservations about any thought of universal principles or foundations.

This is certainly not to suggest that there is no use in reading Levinas from any number of perspectives, but rather that each such reading can and probably should take into account what is learned from the others. Perhaps it is true that we have all but exhausted the results of approaching *Totality and Infinity* mainly as a response to Heidegger and Sartre. But in some cases that sort of engagement has in turn opened the way to a deeper understanding of Levinas's interlocutors' own works—who has not been led by careful work on *Totality and Infinity* more deeply than before into the guts of *Being and Time?*—whereupon one may well expect a more penetrating sense of what truly divides the great texts. Likewise, it may be true that we have read and re-read Levinas straightforwardly on justice and plurality until there is little more to be said about the matters themselves. But again, in the meantime what has been learned there has shed new light on the real implications of positions taken by modern liberals and communitarians. Nothing prevents us from expecting a renewed conversation with them that might yield a sharper sense of what Levinas's thinking truly offers modern politics, and vice versa.

One could no doubt repeat this call with regard to virtually every author and theme that has held Levinas's attention, and even a number that he gives no sign of recognizing. This comes down only to asking that one read carefully within a space opened up by earlier scholarship. The essays appearing in this tenth volume of *Levinas Studies* are representative of this manner of work. Not that the *manner* itself is of primary importance. Instead, one greets with appreciation the advances made along lines already laid down, or else in directions well marked but too little explored. The essays appear in chronological order as regards the central text or theme that each takes up, though we have long gotten used to the idea—and I have invoked it here—that to a considerable extent Levinas's central claims and key concepts inform, support, and sometimes even supplement the meaning of one another. His full conception of language, for example, matures only in the late 1950s and early 1960s,[3] yet as Akos Krassoy shows in "The Transcendence of Words," the essay that opens this volume, the status of words is submitted to careful consideration already nearly a decade earlier, and moreover with concerns about image and expression that presage and continue to inform Levinas's later critique of image as projection and violence.

In the second essay, "Tracing a Traumatic Temporality: Levinas and Derrida on Trauma and Responsibility," Cathrine Bjørnholt Michaelsen returns to the Derrida-Levinas encounter often identified as the source of multiple refinements between *Totality and Infinity* and *Otherwise than Being*. However, her interest is not with exploring that well-worn theme, but instead with pursuing an undeveloped remark by Derrida that attracted considerable attention only much later. What really separates the Levinasian conceptions of temporality and trauma from those of Freud? And what are the implications of each position for an ethics of call and response? For Michaelsen, breaking with Levinas without siding entirely with Freud, responsibility rescinds from the thought that the suffering of the other person calls for infinite commitment, since finite commitment necessarily imposes meaning on it. Infinite commitment, it is reasoned, fails to let the suffering of the other person be precisely what it is: *his* suffering, thus in an important sense his *secret*, since it cannot be truly known by anyone else. But responsibility does not therefore stand mute before the suffering that is secret. Responsibility testifies to the secret as secret, and thus to suffering as suffering.[4]

Derrida is also among the first to have caught sight of deep tension between the transcendental and empirical conditions for Levinas's proposal that the face of the other is the self-expression of an otherness that is absolute.[5] In "'Flipping the Deck': On *Totality and Infinity*'s Transcendental/Empirical Puzzle," Jack Marsh revisits this site with particular interest in identifying the methodological justification for claims that often seem to rest precisely on mutual confirmation between extraordinarily forceful claims about the subject and about the Other. "Flipping the deck" is, as many will know, an expression from card play: a skilled dealer can overturn an entire range of cards first to last and last to first—likewise, a skilled apologete can reverse an entire argument from the premise immediately at hand all the way to its antipode—in a single move that skips the labor of moving laboriously from each single step to the next one. Marsh proposes that we find this sort of gesture at work in Levinas's text, and he wishes to disrupt it in order to pause over details many have thought are passed over too quickly.

In "The Recurrence of Acoustics in Levinas," Roberto Wu rejoins the theme of words and transcendence explored in Akos Krassoy's essay, but this time prompted, like Michaelsen and March before him, by remarks found in Derrida's "Violence and Metaphysics." In this case, the crucial remark simultaneously illumines Derrida's nascent philosophy of contamination and trains important light on Levinas's apparent strategy of purification throughout *Totality and Infinity:* in order to make ethics originate from an absolute call, it will be necessary to place sound above light (and indeed time above space). Has Levinas integrated this point in his subsequent work? The question opens a new reading of *Otherwise than Being, or Beyond Essence* (including its relation to earlier texts) in which hearing and the metaphor of sonority remain crucial even for our understanding of being and beings, but where they are no longer developed as if apart from or strictly overcoming sight and vision.

Yet another strand of Levinas's philosophy that has elicited early and ongoing attention is its implication for sexuality and gender. Deborah Achtenberg's "Bearing the Other and Bearing Sexuality" offers us the instructive reminder that this theme can also be probed in Levinas's Jewish writings. One would be hard put to find a text that reaches more deeply into ancient sources than Levinas's 1972 talmudic commentary, "And God Created Woman." At first glance, the central claim of that text contains no surprises for Levinas's reader: our humanity precedes our sexuality and gender, which, as forms of being human, thus are equal. But Achtenberg is keen to read the Torah itself with or alongside Levinas, and in doing so she comes to a question of considerable importance for anyone interested in a justice that would be more than an abstraction from the concrete experience of suppression or marginalization. It is one thing to say that women and men are fundamentally equal; it is another thing to insist on social practices in which that equality is realized. This of course prompts reflection, as it were, back on *Totality and Infinity*, which by the time of the talmudic commentary was already a decade old. Perhaps the later text amends some of what is most controversial in the earlier one.[6]

Working in a more robustly sociopolitical vein, Nicholas Brown's "Interpreting from the Interstices: The Role of Justice in a Liberal Democracy" brings Levinas into dialogue with the work of the American political theorist Michael Walzer. The two share considerable discomfort with the modern liberalism of someone like John Rawls. The latter is commonly understood to take the view that, as regards political action, it is to be expected that good government will insure that all citizens have sufficient freedom and thus sufficient equality to exercise their rights and pursue their interests. As regards political theory, modern liberalism engages in the project of formulating a universal account of inalienable rights, permissible interests, and proper governance. Those who are familiar with Levinas's conception of ethical plurality will recognize the basis for significant hesitation at any notion of a justification that does not originate in concrete responsibility, and those who are familiar with his occasional political writings will also anticipate serious misgivings about prolonged confidence in the institution. Walzer's position, itself explicitly critical of modern liberalism, is consonant with this much. But Walzer is also intent on grounding concrete responsibility in practices that are promoted by a community that draws on a shared tradition. Walzer's difficulty is also that of communitarians like Stanley Hauerwas and Alasdair MacIntyre: after all, in the meantime liberalism is, at least in the North Atlantic, the order of the day. How then to open a society that is by and large liberal to a richer sense of what counts as morally and politically acceptable? And why do so? As Brown shows, Levinas is far from deaf to these questions, and, interestingly, he responds to it in a manner close to that of Walzer — by probing the resources of the Jewish and talmudic tradition for signs of a means to redefine normativity in a manner that is closer to the real conditions for practice.

The final two essays in this volume take up the importance of Levinas's philosophy for ongoing reflection on religion. It is well known that in France the question of religion is closely related to the question of politics, and that few serious French religious thinkers fail to also address themselves to the latter at some length (Jean-Luc Marion being perhaps the most prominent exception). In Mark Cauchi's "Otherwise than *Laïcité*?" we are shown that the two themes are woven together in the very fabric of Levinas's thinking. Historically, this has been a matter of the emergence of a dimension of life that either detaches itself from the religious or only is set apart from overtly religious action and consciousness within a composite way of life. In the Anglophone world, we know something of this development under the heading of what is called "secularism" or, at the existential level, our "secularity" — which perhaps corresponds with what in *Totality and Infinity* is defined as the "atheism" of the subject. In (post-)Christian France, the rise of *laïcité* has been a generally Catholic and Protestant concern. It has also been alloyed with the broadly liberal current of French politics. Readers of Levinas are accustomed to the thought that his philosophical works open a way to reflection on the existential problem. According to Cauchi, it is to his Jewish writings that we must turn for help with the social and political problem. Here of course his essay passes close to some features of what is argued by Nicholas Brown's essay on the promise of Levinasian ethics for enriching the premises of liberal democracy. But whereas Brown finds something of an ally for Levinas in Michael Walzer, Cauchi puts Levinas in discussion with Chantal Mouffe and William Connolly. Mouffe, Connolly, and Levinas have in common an insistence on plurality as the irreducible condition of human community, and thus the original source of every moral and political demand. But whereas for Mouffe and Connolly this defines politics by agonism, Levinas underwrites the political with ethics. Cauchi asks us to consider whether the agonism of modern democracy is an essential feature of what Levinas is willing to recognize as the secular.

In "Ethical Dwelling and the Glory of Bearing Witness," Hanoch Ben-Pazi closes this volume with an exploration of the religious dimensions of Levinas's own philosophical work. Heidegger remains an important reference even in the late works, which oppose to the authenticity of a Dasein that has taken up a resolute relation with its own finite being, the sincerity of a subject that takes responsibility for the infinite otherness to which it is always already open. The datum of this responsibility is, as Michaelsen has shown, a suffering beyond the comprehension of the one who catches sight of it. Responsibility is thus a bearing witness and, Ben-Pazi adds, "sincerity" is a name for the fact that this is also a living out of what one truly is. For Levinas, I am the impossibility of understanding my neighbor's suffering *and* the ineluctability of nonetheless attending to it. But then, "sincerity" is also a name for what is altered in one's consciousness and in one's being in the world by an honest reckoning with it. It means to be called to a responsibility that one cannot fully execute: one is guilty before an accusation, and one's home in the world is first and essentially a place of hospitality for the other in need.

Notes

1. One knows that the standard bibliographies, despite valiant efforts to the contrary, are somewhat less than comprehensive. See first Roger Burggraeve, *Emmanuel Levinas: Une bibliographie primaire et secondaire (1929–1985), avec complément 1985–1989* (Leuven: Peeters Press, 1990); and, more recently, Joachim Duyndam et al., "The Levinas Online Bibliography: Primary and Secondary Sources," accessed January 10, 2016, http://www.duyndam.demon.nl/Levinas/Online_Bibliography.html.

2. See Peter Atterton and Matthew Calarco, "Editors' Introduction: The Third Wave of Levinas Scholarship," in *Radicalizing Levinas*, ed. P. Atterton and M. Calarco (Albany: State University of New York Press, 2010), ix–xi.

3. Indeed, the recent appearance of previously unpublished works has given us an improved understanding of this theme. The second volume contains a number of texts dedicated specifically to the relations between speech and silence, written and spoken language, and words and transcendence. See Emmanuel Levinas, *Oeuvres complètes*, vol. 2, *Parole et silence et autres conférences inédites* (Paris: Grasset/IMEC, 2009), 65–104, 199–229, 323–47.

4. There is undoubtedly important work still to be done here. Michaelsen's essay stakes out a somewhat different position than that of Rudi Visker in a number of essays exploring much of the same terrain. See, e.g., R. Visker, "The Price of Being Dispossessed: Levinas's God and Freud's Trauma," in *The Face of the Other and the Trace of God*, ed. Jeffrey Bloechl (New York: Fordham University Press, 2000), 243–75.

5. It did not take long. Derrida's review essay "Violence and Metaphysics" appeared in 1964, barely three years after the original French text of *Totality and Infinity*. And indeed, already before Derrida, Jean Wahl had raised the issue in public discussion after Levinas's early 1962 lecture, "Transcendence and Height." The discussion (and the lecture itself) appear in Emmanuel Levinas, *Liberté et commandement* (Paris: Fata Morgana, 1994), especially 77–78.

6. The possibility is suggested, but without further development, in Diane Perpich, "From the Caress to the Word," in *Feminist Interpretations of Emmanuel Levinas*, ed. Tina Chanter (University Park: Pennsylvania State University Press, 2001), 49n10.

Abbreviations

The following abbreviations of Levinas's primary works are used in this volume. Any other abbreviations used in individual essays for non-Levinas works are indicated at the beginning of the endnotes for those essays.

Works in English

- AT *Alterity and Transcendence.* Trans. Michael B. Smith. New York: Columbia University Press, 1999.
- BPW *Basic Philosophical Writings.* Ed. Adriaan T. Peperzak, Simon Critchley, and Robert Bernasconi. Bloomington: Indiana University Press, 1996.
- BV *Beyond the Verse: Talmudic Readings and Lectures.* Trans. Gary D. Mole. Bloomington: Indiana University Press, 1994.
- CPP *Collected Philosophical Papers.* Trans. Alphonso Lingis. Pittsburgh: Duquesne University Press, 1998.
- DF *Difficult Freedom: Essays on Judaism.* Trans. Seán Hand. Baltimore: Johns Hopkins University Press, 1990.
- EE *Existence and Existents.* Trans. Alphonso Lingis. Pittsburgh: Duquesne University Press, 2001.
- EI *Ethics and Infinity.* Trans. Richard A. Cohen. Pittsburgh: Duquesne University Press, 1985.
- EN *Entre Nous: Thinking-of-the-Other.* Trans. Michael B. Smith and Barbara Harshav. London: Continuum, 2006.

GCM *Of God Who Comes to Mind*. Trans. Bettina Bergo. Stanford, CA: Stanford University Press, 1998.

GDT *God, Death, and Time*. Trans. Bettina Bergo. Stanford, CA: Stanford University Press, 2000.

HO *Humanism of the Other*. Trans. Nidra Poller. Chicago: University of Chicago Press, 2006.

IR *Is It Righteous to Be? Interviews with Emmanuel Levinas*. Ed. Jill Robbins. Stanford, CA: Stanford University Press, 2001.

LR *The Levinas Reader*. Ed. Seán Hand. Oxford: Basil Blackwell, 1989.

NT *Nine Talmudic Readings*. Trans. Annette Aronowicz. Bloomington: Indiana University Press, 1994.

OB *Otherwise than Being, or Beyond Essence*. Trans. Alphonso Lingis. Pittsburgh, PA: Duquesne University Press, 1998.

OE *On Escape*. Trans. Bettina Bergo. Stanford, CA: Stanford University Press, 2003.

OS *Outside the Subject*. Trans. Michael B. Smith. Stanford, CA: Stanford University Press, 1996.

PN *Proper Names*. Trans. Michael B. Smith. Stanford, CA: Stanford University Press, 1996.

TI *Totality and Infinity*. Trans. Alphonso Lingis. Pittsburgh: Duquesne University Press, 1969.

TIH *The Theory of Intuition in Husserl's Phenomenology*. 2nd ed. Trans. André Orianne. Evanston, IL: Northwestern University Press, 1995.

TO *Time and the Other*. Trans. Richard A. Cohen. Pittsburgh: Duquesne University Press, 1987.

UH *Unforeseen History*. Trans. Nidra Poller. Urbana-Champaign: University of Illinois Press, 2004.

Works in French

AQE	*Autrement qu'être ou au-delà de l'essence.* The Hague: Martinus Nijhoff, 1974.
CC	*Carnets de captivité, suivi de Écrits sur la captivité et Notes philosophiques diverses.* Ed. Rodolphe Calin and Catherine Chalier. Paris: Grasset/IMEC, 2009.
DEE	*De l'existence à l'existant.* 2nd ed. Paris: Vrin, 1998.
DMT	*Dieu, la mort et le temps.* Paris: Grasset, 1993.
DSS	*Du sacré au saint: Cinq nouvelles lectures talmudiques.* Paris: Éditions de Minuit, 1977.
PS	*Parole et Silence et autres conférences inédites au Collège philosophique.* Paris: Grasset/IMEC, 2009.
QLT	*Quatre lectures talmudiques.* Paris: Minuit, 1968.
TeI	*Totalité et infini: Essai sur l'extériorité.* The Hague: Martinus Nijhoff, 1961.

The Transcendence of Words

Akos Krassoy

Levinas's central contribution to aesthetics and the philosophy of art is his well-known and provocative attempt to *ethicize* art. Yet, there is hardly any certainty regarding the nature of this ethicization. As far as the realization of Levinas's program is concerned, readers usually remember its harmful effects.[1] On the other hand, there are equally appreciative tones in his reading of art. It might be more correct to say that the derogatory side is part of a fundamentally ambiguous attitude. It is almost as if Levinas's radical ethical thinking, the job of which is to tackle totalizing Western thought, should speak in two voices when it comes to the aesthetic and the arts.

Most of the commentaries run into, and then set out to resolve this weird situation marked by pejoration and ambiguity in one way or another. This is no easy task to accomplish; there is surely no single way out of this labyrinth. An element of irony is definitely required on the side of the interpreter. Arguably, my text may be no exception in the long line of attempts. In the following, I shall try my hand at these complexities and, similarly to other readers, deal with the contradictory remarks and implied but underdeveloped ideas by putting them into a meaningful framework. Like others before me, I shall do my best to provide a narrative as coherent as possible in which the letter and the spirit of Levinas are followed and the relevant (phenomenological) aesthetic context is taken into account. In my case, this will mean siding with those interpreters who see a fixed set of problems dominating—that is, a single consistent path winding—in Levinas's difficult itinerary. In more concrete terms, I shall join the camp of those who show sensitivity to the introduction of the critical act and argue that the shortcomings of the aesthetic are, to some extent, reversed in its recontextualization in human communication.[2] Yet, unlike these authors who touch upon the issue of criticism to varying degrees, I shall concentrate fully on placing critical activity in the center of Levinas's aesthetic thought and thus treating art as an important segment of ethical signification. My focus will be on the reintegration of the disengaged image into reality; I shall try to determine what this development in art implies in Levinas's ethical phenomenological project. Concerning the particular course of my text, I shall concentrate mostly on the issue of ambiguity and, gradually working my way through it, deal with pejoration at the same time. I shall first analyze what is at stake in this ambiguousness, then attempt to establish its governing logic, only to prepare the ground on which criticism as a way out of the maze can be seen in its entirety.

A REAL HEADACHE: AMBIGUOUSNESS

Anyone interested in Levinas's aesthetic thought arrives at a truly interesting but nebulous field. By nebulousness I primarily mean the overly ambiguous character of Levinas's position. What Levinas has to say is indeed quite difficult to pin down or, at least, it is highly equivocal: the noise of critique is balanced by the sound of quiet but all the more patent affirmation. In every phase of his thinking there is a suspicion felt toward artistic expression, which may on occasion reach the level of derogation; all this is nevertheless accompanied by clear-cut support. This can be sensed in chance remarks, such as, in "Reality and Its Shadow"—the essay mostly responsible for the bad reputation of

Levinas in aesthetics—where Levinas discusses the plasticity of literary works and mentions a "particularly admirable page" in Proust's *The Captive* (RS 10). In spite of the anti-aesthetic logic and philistine-like rhetoric of the essay, the art-loving character of the author—who is beyond a doubt an affectionate reader—is revealed for a second.

Remarks like this are quite suggestive with respect to Levinas's appraisal of the arts—as are many other details of Levinas's work. Of all these, his apparent knowledge and use of artworks in his philosophical work stand out; they are obviously not easy to square with the critical environment. Besides spending energy on a minute phenomenological analysis of the negativity of aesthetic experience (e.g., in *EE* 45–51, or in RS), his sympathies are equally undeniable, particularly when it comes to backing up a philosophical point by way of an artistic example. While he is quite intent on rejecting the arts in a theoretical fashion, he often makes use of them in his line of reasoning. To support his argument throughout his oeuvre, Levinas invariably relies on the expressive capacity of literary pieces or plastic works. It is as though it were acceptable to take advantage of the otherwise heavily criticized powers of the arts on occasion, when *not thematically* addressing them. As long as the arts are not the subject of Levinas's investigations, they have a jolly good role to play: to assist the line of argument relying on their rich, intuitive base. The vision necessary for phenomenological-existential analysis in his texts is often provided by artistic examples.

What is most interesting is that this assistance is not limited to the type of support in which works are exclusively used for articulating a philosophical idea, while they themselves, as artistic entities, are ignored. Certainly, most of Levinas's encounters with art cover such merely *referential use*, in which the specifically artistic ways of expression of works are not considered important. For example, Oblomov's "radical and tragic indolence" (*EE* 17) in Goncharov's novel is briefly mentioned with reference to the existent's difficulties in contracting existence, a key interest of the early Levinas. There are countless examples of such referential connection to artworks in which there is no attention paid to the work of art itself.³ Levinas is most of the time not interested in the "artfulness" of these and other examples; he does not examine the distinctness of the realization of the literary theme. A given issue is basically taken from the work and rented out to philosophy, where it is then interpreted in the light of the ongoing analysis. However, there are other, really eye-opening examples surpassing the merely referential treatment of the arts. Occasionally, Levinas pays tribute to the artwork and its unique modes of expression. For instance, in his mentioning Rodin's sculpture in *Existence and Existents*, the reference is carried out in such a way that it is not only a corresponding theme identified in the texture of the work but also the artistic realization of the theme that attract his curiosity (70).⁴

Aesthetic versus Ethical Events

The brief reference to Rodin in *Existence and Existents* may deserve more attention, as by studying this particular example one may put one's finger on exactly what is going on in the equivocation of art. Here Levinas, it seems, pays attention to what art can say in its own language as well as to what a certain artwork can do in comparison to other artworks. It is emphatically Rodin's pedestals that give the impression of a theme Levinas is working on in his elaboration of hypostasis. The focus is on the style of Rodin's works; as Levinas specifies, these are not conventional or abstract bases but *idiosyncratic pedestals*. There is something in the way they are worked out that reminds the beholder of the event currently under analysis in the philosophical work. This distinguishing quality is located in the organic relation between the sculpted body and its supporting pedestal. In the forming of the bases, Levinas identifies a special manner of *weighing* on the support, which allows him to establish a connection with a few freshly developed existential categories, that is, the event identified in the body, position, and consciousness.⁵ What is more, the connection is established between two events: the event of hypostatic manifestation and *the event of the artwork*. As Levinas intimates, these statues are not to be taken referentially, the work of art as it were standing for a certain soul or idea.[6] On account of the special relationship with the base, there is an event realized (not expressed) in the work; and in this sense the work of art brings to fruition Levinas's existential phenomenological sensitivities about the status of the body: his endeavor to try and take it simply "the way a man engages in existence, the way he posits himself" (*EE* 70) rather than positing it in the categories of being, substantive, experience, etc. As Levinas underlines on the same page, to take the body as an event means that it *is* itself an event, just like—it could be added—the sculptures of Rodin *are* the event of position.

Without a doubt, this disclosure of the phenomenological problematic directly in a work of art is surprising in the light of the critical remarks. Given the above parallel between Rodin's idiosyncratic pedestals and the event of position, one wonders why a few chapters earlier in the same book Levinas classifies Rodin's statues as essentially limited artwork in which "reality is posited...in its exotic nakedness as a worldless reality, arising from a shattered world" (*EE* 49). This thesis matches perfectly well with (what seems to be) his overriding sentiment toward art in the early works, in which the claim is about a marvelous schematism at work over and against the reality of the world,[7] whereas it surely does not match with the abovementioned elaborate reading of the organic relationship between body and base. It makes the reader ask in disbelief: *Just how could an essentially plastic work put forward the event of position through its own means?* The limits of art fly in the face of the event expressed in art. Levinas invested a great deal of energy into detaching the aesthetic event from its ethical counterpart. In *Existence and Existents* and "Reality and Its Shadow," he gave a thorough description of the peculiarities of aesthetic experience, discussing how it falls outside of the world into the realm of anonymity owing to the intermediation of the image, the independence and materiality of sensation. Yet, he somehow manages to find basic themes of his existential phenomenology (localization and the body) in the framework of an artwork, in the language of a competitive and adversary ontological structure. The event of the existent as advent is revealed in the course of an aesthetic event.[8]

THE AMBIGUOUSNESS OF ART IN LATER WORKS

As far as later positions on the business of art are concerned, the equivocation is further confirmed. After studying the entire span of arguments in Levinas's oeuvre, it is still quite difficult to tell if he is for or against the arts; there is only a curious amalgam of positions presented. There is obviously no shortage of positive remarks: depending on the context, Levinas may occasionally maintain the ethical event in art, and, what is more, in a *theoretical* fashion this time, not merely hinting at his affirmative stance as is done most of the time in the early writings.[9] Levinas's thinking after "Reality and Its Shadow" is particularly interesting because of the thawing out of the harsh critique and his efforts to elaborate at length on the ethical capacities of the arts.

This reconciliation with the arts is felt, above all, in the realm of literature, such as in (what turns out to be) the ethical rereading of Blanchot's project on the idleness of literary space.[10] The presence of Blanchot, and particularly his critique of Heidegger's understanding of art as a discloser of truth, is strongly felt in Levinas's thinking. Levinas is very much in favor of an uncovering taking place in art that is emphatically not about truth; he welcomes the proposition on the work as not aiming at setting up a world (and letting the world *world,* as is done in Heidegger) (PV 136).[11] In these texts, too, Levinas acknowledges his friend's insights into the work of exteriority in writing and subscribes to his ideas on the world not being secured but going astray, becoming uninhabitable in the space of neutrality, thus uncovering the fundamental errancy of being (134).[12] Yet he ventures to attribute an ethical significance to this slackening of the world in the *outside* of literary eternity.[13] Although there are differences between Levinas's various Blanchot texts, the basic idea is to be seen in this breakdown language liberated from exercising power over things, that is to say, free from totalization and, as such, nurturing the opening of the same toward the Other. In the event of literature, utterances are not limited to their content: they lead one beyond the horizons of the world, and stage the *unthinkable* (134).[14] Somewhat surprisingly, Levinas now sees a possibility for a flight toward the transcendent in the invasion induced by literary space. The change is indeed quite baffling. Whereas previously declarations of the immanence of art would have sparked dread and served precisely as the engine behind the critique, now they tend to initiate the ethical opening of thought (e.g., "Only art would let us 'take off' — but for the fact that in that conquest of exteriority, we must remain for ever excluded; for, if it did offer shelter to the poet, exteriority would have lost its very strangeness" [134]). In 1966, Levinas ponders whether it would be wrong to take art and poetry for the event, "which frees language from its servitude towards the structures in which the *said* prevails" (SM 153).

In this way, one is certainly invited to recognize the hidden reserves of literary saying here and elsewhere, such as in Levinas's encounters with Celan. Still, before leading ourselves on to thinking that there is a real climax in Levinas's narrative, a few moments of cautioning should be indicated. First, it has to be kept in mind that in these "progressive" texts Levinas never reaches a final stance. Relying on a refined use of language, he toys with ideas, asks himself questions, reflects on what he is doing and delineates the limits of his own moves — he marks out paths without ever walking all the way down them. At best, he vacillates about an inviting option of seeing the ethical output of art.[15] Second, there is a significant amount of fluctuation taking place in his thinking as far as the textual contradictions are concerned. For instance, the abovementioned advances of the text on Blanchot from 1956 are nowhere seen in *Totality and Infinity,* where art functions as one of the objects of his critique of ontology, offering a fruitful contrast between the immanence of the image, the plastic, participation, etc., and the transcendence of the face. The 1961 book (written five years after "The Poet's Vision") is generally in line with the conclusions of "Reality and Its Shadow."[16]

The Logic of Rapprochements

There is a need to understand the logic of these rapprochements in depth. Levinas's suggestive approval of the transcendence of literature needs to be studied exhaustively and put in its appropriate place. As far as his later, increased interest in poetry is concerned, a few things stand out, such as, above all, the distinctiveness of the notion as used by him. In the essays on Blanchot and Celan, he relies on a completely novel version of poetry and literature diverging greatly from the one he uses on account of Sartre in "Reality and Its Shadow," dominated by the reification of the word, plasticity, and materiality. One of the novelties of Levinas's art essay is the adoption of Sartre's *eidetic* scheme, which—in a rather Hegelian fashion—defines the majority of the genres in terms of their art-immanent qualities and stresses the role of plasticity in their (dis)ability to convey meaning. Levinas accepts Sartre's dictum on disengagement and then again, contra Sartre, extends it to all the genres, including even prose writing, which enjoyed an exception in *What Is Literature?* because of its capacity for successful communication (*WL* 10–22).[17] For Levinas, *all art* is plastic, that is to say, dominated by the materiality of the medium: in the case of literature, this thesis would mean that the words are never used transparently, as successful means of communication, since the animating intention does not go through but gets held up in the image, in the words themselves, including—on Sartre's suggestion—their sonority, male or female endings, visual aspects, etc. Essentially, literature is treated as *art* in the pregnant sense by Levinas here, including even more fluid structures such as the time-novel (RS 10). Of course, at the end of the essay, Levinas takes something back from this thesis on the *defeat* of all art: he acknowledges the capacity of modern literature to interpret its own myths and intellectually mediate the fundamental insufficiency of the plastic (whereby he reinstates *to a small degree* Sartre's thesis on the exceptional standing of prose). Shakespeare's, Molière's Goethe's, and Dostoyevsky's pieces are just a bit more successful in saying what they want to say than other, fully plastic works.[18]

My point is that Levinas's readings of Blanchot and Celan have to be seen in the light of this line of modern literature attempting to contain the idolatry of art. Blanchot's conversation with Hegel in "The Servant and Her Master" may be proof of this (SM 152–53, 159). Levinas's interest in poetry reflects a confirmation as well as a pronounced rejection of Hegel's legacy. On the one hand, he joins the tide of poetry that is primarily intent on communicating something and surpasses the stage of self-sufficient art. This is quite obvious as, on these pages, Levinas is clearly interested in the themes of poetry beyond the musicality of words; in the works of these authors, the material side is not in focus, but diminished or even, perhaps, crossed out. Further, this impression is confirmed by his explicit willingness to release poetry from the order of art closely defined.[19] At the same time, however, he does not want to install the rule of the prose of the world. Surpassing plasticity is exercised in ways that do not pave the way for philosophical speech "gathering together above and beyond the language of poetry" (153). Surpassing art in poetry is done in a unique manner, not by locating a certain meaning in poetry and giving way to philosophy. The poetry favored by Levinas calls into question the seemingly indisputable claim that logos is the sole carrier of meaning. What is important for him is—as he says on the same page—that the meaningful is expressed beyond Hegel's completed discourse.

Levinas's later investigations are fueled by an interest in poetic language that belongs neither to the order of philosophy nor to aesthetics. His interests lie in the explosion of language and its capacity to *signify* nevertheless, which takes effect in the work of certain poets and writers. Closely defined, it is not so much poetry the genre that stirs his curiosity as the disruption of immanence this use of language uncovers best: one could "call it poetry or whatever" (SM 153).[20] The poetic word, as Levinas sees it, goes against the closure that takes place in the orders of knowledge and the cultural product.[21] In it, words are transformed; they are no longer signs standing for something, maintaining semantic content. This disruption of the order uncovers the original event of signification: giving a sign, that is, introducing meaning into Being by going out from Self to the Other (156–57). There is not much difference between a handshake and a poem, as Levinas likes to say based on Celan's theoretical writings ("Paul Celan: From Being to the Other," *PN* 40).

On the other hand, the surpassing carried out in the realm of poetry over and against the systems of ontological-aesthetic order will naturally leave *literature in the traditional sense* intact. One wonders if all these progressive insights have any bearing whatsoever on works permeated with plasticity to any degree, read as eminently sonorous, visually stimulating entities. As I suggested above, the issue in Levinas's aesthetics is about exceeding the rule of form and content in such a way that the problematic of art is exceeded, too. The ethical critic aims to surpass the problematic of plastic form (the totality of matter) and interpretative thought dealing with the plastic (the totality of content) in *the poetic* which is being—in this very move—lifted out of art. Curiously enough, this attempt of surpassing will confirm the system to be left behind. Or, the other way around, Levinas's efforts to excavate the ethical saying in literary works are, in a strange way, still in a dialogue with the logic of the *eidetics* of genres. It is as if, by locating—in a most audacious way (SM 153)—a unique sense in a poem (which cannot be accessed by the aesthetic and interpretative habits of the mind), the ancient, previously antiquated order of art would only get reinstated. Surpassing art in the ethical transcendence of the poetic only confirms the art-immanent order: this impression is further confirmed seeing Levinas's other, major references to art (e.g., *Otherwise than Being*), where he keeps on struggling with the issue of *meaning within matter*. Levinas's substantial encounters with art reflect a similar grappling with the problem of signifying despite the materiality of the work, not to mention the looming prospects of interpretative thought eager to render plastic sense.[22] It seems the fluctuation in Levinas's oeuvre has a coherence: the positive appraisals of literature lead outside of the realm of *art as we know it,* and as such are still in line with earlier and later accounts in Levinas's philosophical career, which are dominated by a wariness of plasticity and argue for the ambiguousness of art.[23]

SOLUTIONS TO THE PROBLEMS: A RETURN TO THE EARLY WORKS?

The overriding sentiment in Levinas is, it appears, that of surpassing toward the nonsensuous where ethical alterity blinks. As is well known, Levinas is after the unapparent phenomenon,[24] and when it comes to art this interest apparently runs into two obstacles: plastic form and content corrupting what is by definition nonfinite. Neither of these moves of totality fares well with his project to demonstrate the undermining of the intentionality of consciousness by a nonintentional, ethical relation. In a similar vein, Levinas's attraction to art seems to run along two lines of excess. He is primarily interested in the dissolution of aesthetic sense in the development of form, and, also, in the obliterations of philosophical content; yet—somewhat unfortunately for the philosopher of art—these moves lead him straight outside of the realm of art. Bluntly stated, there is no chance for a theory of art that would be truly intent on maintaining the ethical in an artwork; the option of realizing the ethical event in the texture of the aesthetic is not established in these later pieces.

It seems to me that this option is, nevertheless, given in "Reality and Its Shadow" and its focus on criticism: even though Levinas maintains a similarly dubious approach toward art, this particular statement of ambiguity comes closest to a full-fledged theory acknowledging the arts and their capacity for ethical signification. Levinas's art essay is the only comprehensive and—in terms of a philosophical aesthetics— significant account of art in his entire oeuvre. It is also worthy of note because the necessary points are given just here in terms of the above-mentioned struggle with artistic form and philosophical thought aiming to grasp the sense revealed in this form. As I argued above, Levinas engages in an intense conversation with Sartre (and Hegel), which unmistakably leaves its mark on his aesthetic thought in his later years: all this comes to the fore in "Reality and Its Shadow." In this mature theory, the *ambiguousness* of art is apparently replaced with a highly suggestive structural *ambiguity:* while Levinas condemns the aesthetic, he saves it in the critical act of art. This move is particularly interesting as it involves the *ethicization* of the previous statement on the negativity (wordlessness and exoticism) of the aesthetic event in *Existence and Existents* in such a way that the arts in the proper sense are, however, let go. Contrary to what is widely believed, Levinas is not satisfied with mere pejoration, ethically disparaging the aesthetic. Apart from the downside, he invests his energies in revealing the more promising, ethically meaningful side of art; a noteworthy theoretical effort is made to demonstrate the forces of reintegration present in the arts (rather than uncovering ethically favorable moments and then exposing their limits in the next move, as is done in later works). It may be the right choice to return to the problematic of the early works for anyone who wants to make sense of this aesthetic scheme wrestling with yet never resolving the same set of problems over the years.[25]

Critical Discourse

Of course, to understand its ethical significance, one has to close out even the slightest possibility of taking critical practice *in a corrective sense*. This insight is not easy to attain considering the sharply disapproving course of the essay, whereby criticism does not come into full view until the finale.[26]

Knowing the preceding discussion seems indispensable to understanding Levinas's sudden turn to criticism in its entirety. After analyzing in detail the aesthetic consciousness, the ontology, and the temporality of the image in the three main sections of the essay, Levinas calculates the total of his assessment, which leads to a reformulation of his thesis on irresponsibility as the most characteristic feature of art. In his view, the overriding aspect of aesthetic enjoyment is evasion: the experience of art "charms as a lightness and grace" (RS 12). The point is that in the rhythm of the peculiar reality of a book or painting one experiences a certain appeasement on account of which basic functions that are at work in philosophy, science, and action will be abandoned. Reception is, categorically speaking, not about comprehending. "Do not speak, do not reflect, admire in silence and in peace—such are the counsels of wisdom satisfied before the beautiful" (12). This statement on disengagement, incomprehension, and irresponsibility provides a lasting phenomenological aesthetic position, particularly when read in line with the first few paragraphs of the essay, where it is evident that the primary intention is to challenge theories in which art serves as a unique means of cognition, knowledge of the ineffable, the absolute, etc. prevalent in aesthetic theory and the everyday understanding of art. Levinas denies that an artwork could provide metaphysical access to reality, managing to speak where, as he says, common language fails (1). Instead, he is (hand in hand with Blanchot) bent on defining art in terms of exteriority, providing access to anonymous Being; his legacy is arguably about bringing to light the consequences of this situation in a fundamentally ethical subjectivity.

On the face of it, the turn to criticism at the end of the essay fits well into this scheme and is meant to confirm the essential exoticism of art. Levinas says, "But all this is true for art separated from the criticism that integrates the inhuman work of the artist into the human world. Criticism already detaches it from its irresponsibility by envisaging its technique. It treats the artist as a man at work. Already in inquiring after the influences he undergoes it links this disengaged and proud man to real history" (RS 12). This is just to suggest that the job of criticism is to regulate the obscuring of Being, in a subsequent move, separate from the practice of art. This means, as he phrases it on the same page, *choosing and limiting,* in other words, using the nontruth of the image eluding cognition in ways that it serves as the source of philosophical truth. Whatever is expressed in the shadows of art (in its allusions, suggestions, equivocations, and enigmas) gets clarified in the exegetical activity. When the aesthetic event is over and the rhythmic enchainment is gone, one returns to the world. The lights are on and one is *on the way out* of the cinema or concert hall to breathe some fresh air; one gathers in a sober-minded activity what happens in the work. Sooner or later, one writes down what happens in the work; one tries to make sense of the event in a critique. All this can reasonably appear as some sort of a rectification of the aesthetic, considering the distance that separates the elusiveness of the saturated aesthetic from the linguistic and temporal certainty of interpretation that characterizes reality. This corrective reading of criticism, whose main job is to *fix* image-sense, is also supported by the clearly intellectual nature of interpretation: as Levinas underlines, criticism relies on concepts and as such functions in a safe mode, in full self-possession—without, it could be added, based on the above, spilling half of the water brought to readers, to use Levinas's image. The "muscles of the mind" (13) are strained, once again working out something real as the course of enjoyment is over. The functions of philosophy, science, and action abandoned in the event are reestablished here.

On this view, Levinas's main objective in introducing criticism into the discussion is to confirm that there is no knowledge in art, except in its critical rendition. Art could, even as heavily distanced, have an application in reality; it will be included among human intellectual practices thanks to the interpretative efforts of criticism.[27] *At the same time,* it is clear that the role of criticism cannot be entirely corrective. There can be no doubt about the incomprehension of the arts in Levinas; yet, more questions should be raised concerning the *type of knowledge* released in the critical act. Even if there is a tendency to straighten out the peculiarities of the aesthetic, it is just not adequate to describe this amendment as primarily intent on fixing aesthetic sense (as I was suggesting above, for rhetorical purposes).

Certainly, the situation is quite complicated in the sense that, no matter what, the qualities of this critical move as essentially counter-aesthetic have to be recognized. At the end of the day, Levinas is dedicated to turning art-immanent sense into philosophical significations, which is a highly important phenomenon considering that the roots of his scheme lie so deeply in anonymity and exoticism. I mean that this proposal for reintegration and partial return to the Hegelian-Sartrean paradigm may prove to be very important in the final analysis, before—as one would be inclined to do—tying Levinas's aesthetic thought too closely to Blanchot. The introduction of criticism indicates one thing for sure: Levinas does not want to anchor art in the exotic for good, inaccessible to the rationality of the world. Levinas is aware of the fact that the experience of art does not end there but continues "once fever has subsided and day has dawned."[28] This has to be appreciated as a move for complexity and signaling an original stance in phenomenological aesthetics.[29] Still, it is important to understand that the development of the immanence of the aesthetic toward the riches of the world is done in a unique fashion in Levinas; that is, the critical intervention is not meant as a Hegelian totalization of plastic sense in reflection and conceptuality. Much in line with what was seen in Levinas's Blanchot essays, Levinas is not interested in the translation—the fixing—of the aesthetic in philosophical *thought*. Instead, he is attracted by tendencies of art where the totalized ways of knowing fall into doubt. In this sense, the real difference in the amendment is made by his novel, ethical reading of rationality and reintegration through this rationality preserving an element of openness.

Indeed, for Levinas, reintegration into language, conceptuality, and the world can sustain this disruptive, de-totalizing appeal because the critical activity unfolds in an essentially *oral* form, face to face with the Other.[30] This is an important point that may not come across in "Reality and Its Shadow"; it is only intimated there. There is much left in Levinas's pen upon finishing up his essay. Owing to the "intentionally limited perspective" (RS 13) of his study, he only manages to announce the importance of the task of criticism with its own consistent logic—to be worked out some other time. As an important segment of this logic, he names in advance the "perspective[s] of the relation with the other without which," he adds, "being could not be told in its reality, that is, in its time" (13). "The Transcendence of Words," written a year later (1949) and, in many ways, a sequel to the art essay, seems to expand on these vague remarks. In this essay, the abovementioned logic of the exegesis of art is developed at length and it becomes clear why there is a need to broaden the phenomenological aesthetic project in the direction of these two points. The insight is a simple one. It demonstrates quite well how these shorter texts from the late forties and the fifties serve as a field in which Levinas is working out the basic categories of his mature thinking, on the way to the Other.[31] In this case the outlines of the work of language (a central thought of Levinas's ethics, developed at length in *Totality and Infinity*) are discernible in his advocating of criticism. Firstly and most importantly, the logic of the philosophical exegesis of art is basically the logic of oral discourse, with all its novelties now identified in the field of art. Exegesis gathers the confidential aesthetic event upon *expressing* it to someone. In the critical activity one is placed in contact with the Other in verbal discourse (i.e., in the "perspective[s] of the relation with the other") on the margins of which the ethical relation returns. As one is confronted with the nudity of the interlocutor's face, the rule of ontology, in which the other is reduced to the same, is challenged and "the marvel of exteriority" returns (*TI* 42). And, as a second point of interest, this introduction into transcendence in the relation with another reveals pathways of reintegration understood for the most part as a return from the seemingly self-sufficient realm of the aesthetic into an ethical reality where Being is given in its most full-blown form (an insight that I dare to locate in the above line, "without which being could not be told *in its reality*").

Critique and Criticism

This might need some clarification. Although the link is more than obvious, it has to be assembled from a mixture of sources; insights from various texts need to be combined in order to show how the ethical relation surfaces in criticism. The following quote from "The Transcendence of Words" seems quite informative:

> The use of the word wrenches experience out of its aesthetic self-sufficiency, the here where it has quietly been lying. Invoking experience transforms it into a creature. *It is in this sense that I have been able to say elsewhere* that criticism, which is the word of a living being speaking to a living being, brings the image in which art revels back to the fully real being. The language of criticism takes us out of our dreams, in which artistic language plays an integral part. Certainly, in its written form, it in turn generates new criticism. Books call up books—but this proliferation of writings halts or culminates at the moment when the living word is installed and criticism blossoms into teaching. (TW 148; my emphasis)

In this quote, the ins and outs of Levinas's thinking on art are given. As far as the oral and discursive side of criticism is concerned, Levinas clearly states that he has in mind "a living being speaking to a living being"; the ever growing and multiplying body of criticism is predominantly a means to initiate face-to-face discourse and the transcendence inherent to it. Criticism *in a written form* is only important in as much as it gives rise—be it in a natural continuation of the text or in rejecting textuality—to speech and the opening up of the immanent in between speakers.

The quote also mentions—what I have described as the second major insight in Levinas's scheme—the self-sufficiency of the image transformed into fully real being on account of the use the word. To see this point in depth, it might be useful to recall the ethical functions assigned to discourse in general in *Totality and Infinity*. As is well known, Levinas rebels against the ontological imperialism dormant in Western thought, by which he refers to the process in which knowing being does not respect the difference of the known Being. On his argument, there are no limits to the freedom of spontaneity depriving things of their alterity: as a result of these tendencies, along comes a neutral Being, which totally matches the work of cognition. The other is reduced to the same by the use of a neutral term, which ensures the comprehension of Being, things appearing in light, as intelligible. This situation is *critiqued* in discourse, where he perceives a "non-allergic relation with alterity" (*TI* 47). In this anonymous community with the Other, he spots a desire for exteriority unfolding in which — as he argues on the same page — the "murderous" powers aiming to grasp are defeated as the impossibility of "killing" is realized and the consideration of the Other is promoted. I quickly discover that I have no power over the interlocutor. In the ethical relation freedom is questioned; as Levinas puts it, the tyrannical powers of the ego are tackled in it by a *violence that is beyond all violence*. As such, the eminence of the signification of the Other is recognized and justice is reinstated in the linguistic society.

This critique of totality is well on its way a decade earlier in "The Transcendence of Words," although with a special concentration on the rule of vision as opposed to sound. The above quote from this text reflects the nascent critique of the rule of the same and exchanges the order of givenness (the phenomenon) for that of *expression*. Naturally, as the main narrative of the essay is aesthetic (it was written as a review of Leiris's *Biffures*), the development of *critique* stands most of the time for the *criticism* of art, and, vice versa, in the text. Levinas develops his thoughts on the primacy of teaching via the ontological closure tangible in art. The parallel is certainly no surprise: while the essay takes vision for the main principle of the reduction of alterity (on account of which Being gives away its essence too hastily and the other is suppressed), the universality of art — as Levinas underlines — also rests on this primacy of vision (TW 147–48).

There certainly exists a larger narrative of this parallel: reference should be made to the overall affinities that persist in Levinas's critical undertaking between the widely acclaimed, immanent structures of everyday and scientific cognition *and* the arts, where the rule of this immanence is manifested in a compelling way. Once the prime areas of ontological closure, such as science and history, are censured, it will be inevitable to critique the aesthetic where the shine of ontology *culminates*. Naturally, the rule of a panoramic existence is discovered in the aesthetic, too. Of course, here the focus falls on the reduction inherent to the aesthetic and art as an autonomous activity. It is important to note that—much in line with the German aesthetic tradition tangible in his aesthetic thinking—Levinas does not draw the parallel with beauty as it is found in nature, but with the mechanism of *art* that singles out beauty from nature. As he says, "By creating beauty out of nature, art calms and quietens it. All the arts, even those based on sound, create silence" (TW 147). There is something to the way art presents the world that is reminiscent of the silent, self-reliant world of objects. Apart from letting the world appear (in Levinasian jargon: "letting it be"),[32] contemplation in aesthetic consciousness focuses on the mode of appearing, centering attention on the phenomenalization of the world itself. Art throws the spotlight on manifestation and even what Levinas calls the *manifestation of manifestation*.[33] In this special sense, art is part of the canon whose work consolidates ontological freedom and the conquest of Being. The knowledge of an ever-neutral Being is established in science and history; in its own way, the spectacle of art serves this knowledge, conveys it. On these grounds, by recognizing the link between panoramic Being and the *ostentation* of art, it is perhaps no exaggeration to talk about ontological-aesthetic violence as a whole as the prime target of the critique.

To return to the issue of vision in "The Transcendence of Words": on Levinas's view, it gives the order within which things can be seen and make sense; it is the primacy of vision over other senses that is responsible for establishing what is *given* at all (whereby his later assessment, terming vision as that which "grasps before the grasp," is prefigured [*TI* 302]). All this is felt in the credit given to sound and its merits in tackling ontological closure in return. In comparison with the codified, self-complete order of vision and art, sound stands out as, in Levinas's word, scandalous.[34] Whereas in vision form meets content in such a way that it appeases it, in the case of sound form cannot contain its content because the perceptible overflows. Conversion into vision and control fails; the given is surpassed. Certainly, this championing of sound has to do with the fact that, for Levinas, sounds are ultimately human sounds, "failed words" (TW 148), which cover a transcendent, and maybe even a transcendental origin in this system. It is quite evident that, on account of the critique of visibility and intentional thematization, Levinas is making room for the eminence of the Other as the new source of signification.[35]

Apart from the critique of totality, the outlines of Levinas's proposal for an epistemic game change is prefigured in this essay. Much is learnt about the limits of knowledge on account of the distinction given to sound over vision. In a sense, verbal activity implies replacing the episteme of self-completeness with an *ethical* one: the issue is not about an *experience* of reality anymore, but, emphatically, about an exposure to the presence of the Other and his or her words in which meaning is ultimately born. As Levinas argues, one understands that one is a creature, that is, the basic insight that "the first fact of existence is neither being in-itself nor being for-itself but being *for the other*" is apprehended (TW 149; emphasis in original). The reasons for this overwhelming change can be found in one's giving way to transcendence in expression: when using the living word the subject's mastery is eradicated, as it is impossible to remain within oneself, maintaining control over an idea. Speaking is very unlike the silent, self-sufficient order of the spectacle, where a subject can act as a master over exteriority. There is an "inexhaustible infinite exteriority" (*TI* 296) at work where thematization is refused. In speaking to the Other, one's existence as a subject is interrupted and a complicated situation takes effect where one is both a subject and an object. The privilege of the Other is introduced: in offering a word, one puts oneself forward—one teaches and one is taught. In Levinas's words, "The subject who speaks does not situate the world in relation to himself, nor situate himself purely and simply *at the heart of his own spectacle,* like an artist" (TW 149; my emphasis).

These insights on critique also give useful recommendations concerning what is happening in the criticism of art: it is clear that in critical discourse the world of the spectacle goes through a significant ontological transformation. As it is stated in the above quote, criticism, practiced in living speech with another living being, manages to dissolve the completeness of the aesthetic and redirect the image "in which art revels" to "fully real being" (TW 148). This ethical reality of teaching is defined here in detail as *more real* than the aesthetic-phenomenal reality also fostered by the sciences, and this is where the oral critical act returns.

THE RENEWAL OF WORKS

Totality and Infinity's characterization of discourse, directly in the context of works, provides an opportunity to observe the ontological transformation in its deeper implications. This may imply retelling the above story, yet this time with a focus on the underlying metaphysical motivations of the critique.

Speaking of works of art and their reality, the limitations of knowing, as Levinas sees them, need to be studied in further detail. This is a global phenomenon and goes with the knowledge of objects. For Levinas, there is a limitation in objective knowledge per se. On his view, any attempt to attain disinterested truth is doomed to failure as, from a wider metaphysical perspective, this truth will not surpass the status of an incomplete act of knowing, limited to the horizon of one who discloses. There are certain restrictions that go with the relation in which knowledge unfolds: whatever happens, however adequate to the object knowledge is, it still bears the mark of the way the knowing being approaches the known (*TI* 64). Knowledge is relative to us knowers.[36] From the radical perspective of the metaphysical, "truth" does not lie in the realm of *disclosure,* within the collection (*rassemblement*) of Being, but beyond, and that is where Levinas is looking: "The 'objectivity' sought by the knowledge that is fully knowledge is realized beyond the objectivity of the object" (67). The priority attributed to discourse is ever so visible from this angle: discourse is kept in high regard by Levinas precisely because it provides this much sought-after *kath'auton* manifestation of Being. Levinas is concerned with the singularity of the object from an ethical perspective, which is quite well reflected in his choice of words: he wants to trace the thing without its being "betrayed" as a theme, "oppressed" by a totalizing gaze, and "burgled" in its intimacy (64–67). As he sees it, being telling itself provides this type of absolute experience. It is found in the discourse of the face, where form—which constantly betrays manifestation and ends up as the *plasticity of the same*—is continually undone. For Levinas, the interlocutor is the holder of pure experience as he or she *does not appear in the light of other things, but in his or her own*. This can be seen in the style of appearance: the interlocutor *presents* him or herself to me while being irreducibly *foreign*. The Other's essence is in the vocative: even when called upon by me, he or she maintains radical heterogeneity. "The invoked is not what I comprehend" (69).[37]

What would this *kath'auton* manifestation of Being in the face-to-face mean with respect to the work and the words written or pronounced over the work? Interestingly, this question arises not only in our investigations focusing on the ethics of art criticism but also on these pages of *Totality and Infinity*, where Levinas defines the advances of discourse precisely in contrast to works.[38]

What is really striking here is Levinas's decision to position works in the heart of a metaphysical scheme, assigning an important role to them. Levinas's major undertaking is to reveal the *rending of totality:* the first step in this story is located in the ontological event of egoism, where control is exercised over anonymous alterity in labor, possession, enjoyment, and the corresponding time-consciousness (*TI* 175). This is an important step despite the fact that the mastery of the world leads to a somewhat lamentable reduction of otherness to the same (if by "lamentable" is meant an element of closure that does not stand in an antithetical relationship but is necessary to the surfacing of ethical exteriority, the key player in this dialectic). There is a need in the emerging subject to come outside of this separation, understood as a source of integrity and isolation at the same time. Levinas is, as I indicated above, highly interested in the manifestation of the intimate interiority of economic existence, and it is here that he refers to the work and its unsuccessful project to properly bring about this manifestation. As he underlines, "through works alone the I does not come outside" (176). As it seems, the work is qualified as carrying an important ontological alternative for a subjectivity locked up in its interiority, but it *fails* to live up to these expectations and ends up being a poorly understood subjectivity.

The reason for this is to be found in Levinas's problematic of plasticity: the *absence* with which the objectified work is inevitably impregnated. The subject can come out only in a rudimentary sense in an essentially complete entity, having the destiny of a sign to be appropriated—or, better, "surprised" and "raided"—by the reader. As Levinas reasons, the I tends to cherish a certain comfort and intimacy in the work, whereby, on the other hand, it petrifies in an essentially ambiguous *form*. The lines of meaning animated by the reader's intentionality are full of equivocations. "In undertaking what I willed I realized so many things I did not will: the work rises in the midst of the wastes of labor" (*TI* 176). Doubtless, Levinas is ready to acknowledge the positives of this *working out* of the interior: signs, as he underlines, feed and protect my intimacy. Even so, in the final analysis, he takes expression in works as the direct rejection of *expression*. In the artwork, he identifies the case example of the phenomenon constituting a flow of symbols and calling for endless psychoanalysis—as Levinas likes to characterize the opposite of the straightforwardness of expression (181). Levinas is—to continue this line of dualisms—not interested in appearing being remaining absent but rather in an absence that signifies despite the lack of appearance (the inapparent phenomenon).

As one would expect, the absence is overcome in the word, emphatically not to be taken in the sense of a linguistic product or work. Apparently, Levinas's ontology has place, other than the same of separated being (1) and its surrogate, the revealing-covering of this separation in works (2), for the actual expression of separated being and its reintroduction into alterity (3). On Levinas's view, discourse carries the ontological significance of introducing an order onto the scene where the equivocations of *interiority and its symbolism* are overcome in absolute reality. Actual existence takes effect with the presence of the idea of Infinity in me. All this is orchestrated not by exchanging the contentment of economy with discontent, but — overthrowing the system of totality — by exteriority completely shattering interiority in my attentiveness to the Other. Levinas's suggestion is that in the strange intimidation felt in front of the face, in Desire, one as it were discovers the limits of one's phenomenality and is invited to actual existence: "as responsible I am brought to my final reality" (*TI* 178).[39]

This ontological scheme holds the answer to the question raised above: it seems the possibility of introducing *kath'auton* Being arises in discourse in the wake of the separated being's appearance in works, which is also to suggest that the absolute can be introduced via the critical discourse of works. Criticism is — now we can see the above insight in its ontological implications — a principal area of the critique. Levinas's thoughts on the priority of expression are partly concentrated on the opening of the surrogate, the verbal deciphering of works. Works, together with the discourse above works, offer a meaningful possibility for implementing the rule of ethical transcendence.

The difficulty of grasping this thought might have to do with Levinas's depreciation of the critical *profession* whose job consists in invading the work, taking it in its phenomenality.[40] However, the depreciation of *oral* criticism does not follow from these premises; it is possible to argue for critical discourse while bringing down critical engagement as such. Levinas does precisely this in "Reality and Its Shadow": in the beginning of the text, he describes the critic as someone who ventures to translate the ineffable and as such contributes to the industry of the aesthetic; then, in the concluding section, he attributes a dignified role to philosophical criticism (RS 1–2, 13).[41] In the mature Levinas, there seems to be judgment passed on *criticism in its written form*.

Levinas describes the most common handling of the work as guessing someone's intentions, yet essentially in the absence of the author, on account of which the activities of the reader as well as the reader-critic invading the work in its completeness come to mind. "One has penetrated into his interior, but in his absence" (*TI* 181). Still, this is not the end of the story. Although works awaken in reception and, in their written critical appropriation, do not surpass the world of the phenomenon and invite the violence of the reader and the critic, critical discourse above works will bring the author back into his or her actual existence. As Levinas argues, the higher levels of objectivity, being as absolute, present themselves in *society*. Unlike the phenomenon that remains hidden despite its ostentation, its shine, the thing in itself is posited in discourse. In a somewhat Platonic move, Levinas stresses the importance of *assistance*, in which the interlocutor's absence in the reified words of the work is turned into a presence, the presence of the ethical. Via words, being gets to help itself: "the word alone [assists] the judges and render[s] the accused present, as though by the word alone the multiple concurrent possibilities of the symbol, which symbolizes in silence and in twilight, could be sorted out and give birth to the truth" (181).

Certainly, it could be argued that Levinas has in mind the speaking subjectivity assisting its *own* revelation here, and that the critical discourse on another's work only breaks into an interior in the author's absence, which is why it should enjoy no distinction whatsoever from the reception of works steeped in the phenomenon. The word *I* could be taken literally in statements like "from my speech-activity I absent myself, as I am missing from all my products. But I am the unfailing source of ever renewed deciphering. And this renewal is precisely presence, or my attendance to myself" (*TI* 182). Without a doubt, for Levinas *the author is not dead* by any means, and, along these lines, any critical intervention—except for the one where I can help myself, that is, interpret my own work—may be loaded with aggression. In simple terms: if it is another's work, we simply raid it. This might be a valid interpretation, particularly when one follows the text very closely, reading it verbatim, turning a blind eye to the secondary levels of meaning in Levinas's rich lingo.

Yet, this point on self-assistance may just hold because of a general, ethically more comprehensive role attributed to assistance. Levinas's texts with a focus on aesthetic issues seem to confirm this suggestion. In the light of "Reality and Its Shadow" and its link to "The Transcendence of Words," as well as other remarks in his oeuvre,[42] I would argue that Levinas talks about *renewal* precisely in the ethical phenomenological—rather than in a closely Platonic—sense here. In other words, absence is meant more globally, inhering in the problematic of plasticity, and the stress in Levinas's text on the work of language covers the possibility for one being to exist for another being and to exist in a way that is more than the author's fixed "interior" existence one tends to call to life in the silent course of the reception of works (see *TI* 182). The emerging subject needs to come out of its separation and be integrated into the reality of the world: this is all done in *expression*. This is the only way that the I is *expressed* in the context of works, that the ontological event of separation escapes totalization. In a word, it does not petrify in its plastic image. Even so, this is not to say that the main intention is to locate a particular person behind the work, at the other end of the line. Critical work is not so much about excavating the author from the vestiges of his or her work as fleshing out the Other of the text in a more ethically real fashion than the aesthetic allows. This is a general, textual Other, awakened as a *creature* in the face-to-face, not an identity. The excess that language carries over and against works of art and action covers a real development in the saturated aesthetic structures, and it is on this suggestion for renewal in *kath'auton* Being that the analysis should concentrate in Levinas's aesthetic thought. Levinas's stance responds to far more challenges than those of the caricature of the philistine ethicist concerned with the breakdown of communication and the misapprehension of ethical identity (*my face*!) in the arts. The objective of interpretation is to assist the image and reestablish the Other in his or her alterity in *an ethical plenitude* of discourse.[43]

HOPE FOR A THEORY OF ART: CRITICAL ARTICULATION

Once the potential for renewal and development implied in the critical activity has been recognized, a whole new realm opens up. In the light of the ethically comprehensive role of critical discourse, the path seems to be marked out for this aesthetics. As it appears, the distinguishing feature for Levinas's aesthetic project is to be located in the critical act's capacity to bring out the ethical event from the depths of the aesthetic, which implies ethically *liberating and enriching* in discourse what goes on in the intimacy of reception. "Such an enterprise is not the same as a simple reconstruction of the original from the copy" (RS 13). From its completion in form, image sense is introduced into the infinite realm of significations. This is to suggest that, while the arts as aesthetic are incapable of providing ethical reality, in a critically developed form they very much do so. In a sense—the argument goes—art runs a double agenda: as the holder of the image it *cannot*, however hard it tries, provide ethical knowledge (only an *experience* of the ethical); at the same time, in its critical realization it definitely constitutes an ethical event and provides knowledge.

I would like to stress the beneficial side of this intervention: just like in his philosophical work, Levinas is employing *a fine limit* on account of which a dogmatic ethicization of art is out of the question. The reference to the ethical is in no way doctrinaire, having, as it were, as its objective to annex artistic presentation. Without a doubt, artworks are addressed in this context in view of the ethical capacity they possess; still, this is a highly fluid realm of the ethical within which the framework of art, raised in the course of exegesis, is not alienated but distinguished. It has to be borne in mind that art in the Levinasian critical sense provides a unique opportunity in which the work of exteriority presents itself in the ethical relation. If Levinas's proposal for critical development holds, the arts prove to be a prime area where the ethical event comes to the fore. This is clearly a favorable situation: it is about the *drama*—and not the action, as Levinas argues on account of Nietzsche—of the exterior producing itself in the work, in a highly refined, nonontological fashion, never really appearing yet motivating appearing.[44] There is a heightened sense of the event unfolding strictly in the face-to-face, never visible from the side perspective, and this has become a concern of art now.

To illustrate this point, recourse could be taken to Rodin's case. It is clearly not in the framework of the aesthetic event—as was inferred above, in the case of his pedestals—that the ethical event and its context are revealed, but through the ethically developed, integrated rendition of art, in which the closed and static intentional structures of the aesthetic are bygone phenomena and the conditions of an ethical event are fully met. *Closely considered,* the event of localization and body is not manifested in the rhythmically dominated, restricted sphere of the aesthetic: an ethical event would be thwarted in the closure of the aesthetic—its distinguishing feature, openness and freedom, would be reduced in the framework of the image. Rodin's pedestals manage to embody the event of position-taking (and, emphatically, not *express* an idea) as, in the critical act, the force of the aesthetic gets deranged and an air of openness is established. The fancy of the image is ruptured in the course of discourse; whatever was condensed in the thick intentionality[45] of an artwork is now released in the conceptuality of the world. In Levinas's scheme, a critically conscious, fluid language (impregnated with the transcendence of the face-to-face) is by definition better suited to singularity as such than the fixed realm of the aesthetic. The philosophical can develop Rodin's theme to the extent that the event is understood in its entirety, in its full-blown version, yet not finalized in any sense of the word.[46]

But here my terminology is already giving away my incentives—where my analysis is headed and where, I believe, the real hope for this aesthetic scheme lies. Seeing these tendencies for renewal, one wonders to what extent the critical appropriation of the event is to be treated as *separate* from art. I have advanced this conclusion in my use of language: indeed, the issue is whether this ethically developed, integrated rendition of *art* that I have talked about is still seen in detachment from its image-base. In the wake of the subversiveness of the change, the emergence of significations—"worlds"—to which the aesthetic of art is subjected in discourse, the least one could say is that art does not end with the aesthetic event but, in one way or another, encompasses critical integration. The ultimate goal is to develop the saturated image into fully real being: how could all this be outside of art? At a minimum, the critical must be part and parcel of artistic *practice*, understood in a larger sense, with equal room in it for the work received and the ensuing work interpreted. Yet, I would venture even further and argue for unity, rather than any kind of separation, of steps following each other, in the work. As far as the inception of ethical meaning is concerned, it seems to me more adequate to talk about a genetic connection between the core and its articulation, whereby one arrives at *the aesthetic of art* and *art proper* bound up with one another in the model of ethical signification. This complex duality may just be the reason for Levinas's *doublespeak:* the ethical critic torn between disparaging the ostentatious aesthetic and welcoming the ethical saying in art at the same time.

Among others,[47] there are phenomenological-aesthetic motives present in Levinas that call for tying the critical close to its fertile ground, even if at the cost of seeing—what seemed unimaginable before—an ethical moment already in the mute reception. The point is to notice, subsequent to the anonymous core, the opening that will eventually occasion the ethical reduction in oral discourse. *The critique cannot be severed from the spectacle, for it stands deeper in the spectacle than expected.* To see this, it suffices to address the formal logic of Levinas's art essays and what is said about the exigency of criticism there. (Arguably, Levinas may need the critic to unwrap what is said here *in nuce.*) "The Transcendence of Words" talks about a heavy silence, a certain dread, and even bad conscience, despite the harmony of the beauty, and sees the necessity of the critique in "this need to enter into a relation with someone" (TW 147). Similarly, "Reality and Its Shadow" evokes an "an irresistible need to speak" (RS 1) on account of the aesthetic reduction and locates the source of the critical word *in the mind*. Levinas wants to rehabilitate criticism contra the critical profession and he does so by demonstrating how the reader-critic experiences an urge to speak in the presence of the image *completed* by the artist. The justification—the very source—of the critical is that it is impossible to contemplate in silence, that there is always something to say "when everything has been said" (2). As it appears, the exigency to speak arises in the midst of the intentional fulfillment of the image, facing anonymity. The transcendence of words is induced, first and foremost, in the insularity of the image. There is an inclination to integrate the inhuman into language and society—our lips are, as it were, starting to move already in the theater. Yet, to uncover this curious phenomenon one would have to look at the genesis of the ethical event in reception in detail, without which the story of the ethical signification of art could not be told in its reality.

Notes

In addition to the abbreviations at the front of this volume, the following are also used: Emmanuel Levinas, "The Poet's Vision (PV)," in *Proper Names*, trans. Michael B. Smith (Stanford, CA: Stanford University Press, 1996), 127–39; Emmanuel Levinas, "Reality and Its Shadow (RS)," in *Collected Philosophical Papers*, trans. Alphonso Lingis (Dordrecht: Martinus Nijhoff, 1987), 1–13; Emmanuel Levinas, "The Servant and Her Master (SM)," in *The Levinas Reader*, ed. Seán Hand (Oxford: Blackwell, 1989), 150–59; Emmanuel Levinas, "The Transcendence of Words (TW)," in *The Levinas Reader*, ed. Seán Hand (Oxford: Blackwell, 1989), 144–49; Jean-Paul Sartre, *What Is Literature?* (WL), trans. Bernard Frechtman (New York: Philosophical Library, 1949), 10–22.

1. Levinas's texts tend to give way to a rather off-limits reading of the arts with the reader often left in incredulity. In 1948, he writes, "There is something wicked and egoist and cowardly in artistic enjoyment. There are times when one can be ashamed of it, as of feasting during a plague" (RS 12).

2. See, for example, Richard Cohen, "Some Reflections on Levinas and Shakespeare" and "Uncovering the 'Difficult Universality' of the Face-to-Face," in *Levinasian Meditations: Ethics, Philosophy, and Religion* (Pittsburgh: Duquesne University Press, 2010), esp. 153–55, 159–60, and 244–45; Guy Petitdemange, "L'art, ombre de l'être ou voix vers l'autre?," *Revue d'Esthétique* 36 (1999): 88–93; and Tanja Staehler, "Images and Shadows: Levinas and the Ambiguity of the Aesthetic," *Estetika* 47, no. 2 (2010): 134–39.

3. In Hamlet's "to be or not to be," the impossibility of an exit in death (Levinas's "impossibility of possibility") is recognized (*TO* 73). In *Totality and Infinity*, Pushkin's Onegin is taken to exemplify man's ultimate relation to being and its objects: the case of the dandy, who "enjoys possessing the possession of the world," supports the redefinition of this relation along the lines of enjoyment and the elemental (contrary to the analyses of Heidegger's *Zeuglichkeit*) (*TI* 132–33).

4. The example of Rodin seems to be the right means of demonstration for the appreciative side because, apart from its phenomenological resonances, it proves that Levinas has an eye for plastic art. That is to say, Levinas's appreciation for art is not restricted to literature. This might be quite obvious and needless to point out, seeing, among others, the author's numerous encounters with plastic artists Sosno and Atlan in his later work. Emmanuel Levinas, *De l'oblitération: Entretien avec Françoise Armengaud à propos de l'oeuvre de Sosno* (Paris: Éditions de la Différence, 1990); Emmanuel Levinas, "Jean Atlan et la tension de l'art," *Cahier de L'Herne: Emmanuel Lévinas* (Paris: L'Herne, 1991), 509–12. At the same time, it is undeniable that his ethical ideal is firmly rooted in the literary cultures of the Bible and the Greeks, in the light of which "everything else is dancing" (*IR* 149). For Levinas, humanity cannot be based in aesthetic being and the enchantment that goes with it — that is, in Heidegger's pagan world. (*De l'oblitération*, 26–28.) The concluding section of "Reality and Its Shadow" seems to confirm the "insufficiency of artistic idolatry" (RS 13) characteristic of the majority of the arts precisely by distinguishing the intellectual capacity of modern literature to handle its own images ("interpret [its] myths" [13]). To a certain extent, the literature of Shakespeare, Molière, Goethe, and Dostoyevsky complies with Levinas's penchant for ethical-religious reality: they are capable of communicating transcendence in a primarily nonaesthetic fashion. As I shall demonstrate below, Levinas's reading of art has a strong affinity toward a concept of literature surpassing the sensuous, including — and this is an important point — even the sensuousness of literature *in the traditional sense*. To advance my conclusion, the difficulty with any distinction given to literature in Levinas is that it is restricted to an ethically privileged, unique sort of writing (Celan's poetry, prose, confession, prayer?); literature that can in any way be made liable for its materiality will not be saved. The plastic issue of literary works — also affecting the works of the classical authors mentioned above — is very much a concern for Levinas (10–11). Despite their fluidity, the images of literature are not exempt from idolatry — even literature qualifies as art for Levinas. On the aesthetic level, works belong uniformly to the order of ontology for Levinas — which is also to say that, if there is a possibility for

redeeming these works on the critical-linguistic level, it should apply to plastic and literary-plastic art equally. (See section titled "The Logic of Rapprochements.")

5. Levinas's main undertaking here is to substitute the substantive with hypostasis in which consciousness is maintained rather than given (*EE* 64–70). By looking into the disruption of the substantive when facing anonymous being in experiences like insomnia, he argues for the *advent* of the subject, trying to separate from anonymous Being. One of the key moments of this separation is consciousness's ability to retreat: to forget and interrupt the *there is* in sleep. The possibility of interrupting itself, of having recourse against itself, is indispensable for consciousness to maintain itself. Along these lines, Levinas realizes the potential and develops the theme of localization as an existential category in the life of the subject. What he is most touched by is the exceptional ontological status of *the here*, which serves as a base to being and consciousness. Being the very support of thinking, this position cannot presuppose a thought behind it that would grasp a here in objective space. "It is not first thought and then *here*" (66). He recognizes an event in this moment of subjectivization; in his eyes, the here is exempt from all universality and eternity. Certainly, in a common-sense view, the sleeping body is situated somewhere, as some kind of a presence in abstract extension. Yet, Levinas wonders, this presence may have to do with the original situation simply covered over by our relations with things, with habit and utility. Localization gets detached from its atmosphere. On the other hand, "sleep reestablishes a relationship with a place qua base" (67). From here, it is just one step further to the body, which also belongs to this supportive basis of life, ungraspable in the language of the scientific and the majority of the philosophical tradition. The body has to be approached through similar perspectives to those of an emerging being. The body clearly comes out as something nonsubstantive: not *posited* in space but a *position* itself. As Levinas phrases it, "it is the irruption in anonymous being of localization itself" (69).

6. For Levinas, the body is, as you would expect, not to be interpreted based on external experience; and, more importantly, neither will it do to take it in the context of internal experience. As he explains it, even *being* a body rather than *having* a body will not suffice, because it still suggests that the body is on the level of a being, an experience *not* an event by which man engages in existence, a position in which "the very transformation of an event into a being" (*EE* 70) is effectuated.

7. I am alluding to a well-known footnote of *Otherwise than Being* directly referencing "Reality and Its Shadow" and reaffirming the conclusions of the philosophy of art of his early work:

> The immemorial past is intolerable for thought. Thus there is an exigency to stop: *anagkè stenai*. The movement beyond being becomes ontology and theology. And thus there is also an idolatry of the beautiful. In its indiscrete exposition and in its stoppage in a statue, in its plasticity, a work of art substitutes itself for God. (Cf. our study "La réalité et son ombre," in *Les Temps modernes,* November 1948.) By an irresistible subreption, the incomparable, the diachronic, the non-contemporaneous, through the

effect of a deceitful and marvellous schematism, is "imitated" by art, which is iconography. The movement beyond being is fixed in beauty. Theology and art "retain" the immemorial past. (*OB* 199n21)

8. I almost said an ethical event, as the issue here in Levinas is *nearly* about ethical events getting revealed in the aesthetic. As Levinas explains it, hypostatical manifestation (with the *here* in it) still involves a threatening return of the *there is*, whereby an inclination for liberation is effected, eventually leading to a redemptive reading of time and the introduction of alterity in the book. For the early Levinas, the event of taking position is part and parcel of the economy of being, in which an existent arises, gets stuck with itself (in solitude and chained to its own ego), and is subsequently redeemed by a temporality that is suggestive of ethical transcendence. The event occasions the taking up of being in the instant, in the present, which will also bring in focus the hope implied in the evanescence of time.

9. As I shall argue, the discussion of criticism at the end of "Reality and Its Shadow" should be also seen as a theoretical appreciation of the ethical work done in art. Still, this contribution of art is only realized in retrospect, on account of scholarly insight. Arguably, the turn toward the "positive" ethical contribution of the arts only takes effect in a patent fashion with the Blanchot texts.

10. Levinas's texts on Blanchot were collected in the final section of *Proper Names* (*PN* 127–70): "The Poet's Vision" (1956), "The Servant and Her Master" (1966), "A Conversation with André Dalmas" (1971), and "Exercises on 'The Madness of the Day'" (1975).

11. For Heidegger's conception of the world set up in the work, see "The Origin of the Work of Art," in *Poetry, Language, Thought*, trans. Albert Hofstadter (New York: Harper, 1971), 43–44.

12. For Blanchot, writing stages complete desubjectivization. In *The Space of Literature*, it is taken in the sense of "what is being written" or "what writes itself" (*ce qui s'écrit*), and behind it there lies an endless, substanceless speech that renders impossible the subject's taking repose in language and collecting itself when starting or interrupting speech on whim. "To write is to break the bond that unites the word with myself," argues Blanchot, through which he envisages a complete reversal, where *language withdraws from the world*, that is, a detachment from the sense of exercising power over things in language, from declaring the world as light and action in speech. *The Space of Literature*, trans. Ann Smock (Lincoln: University of Nebraska Press, 1982), 25. Cf. PV 132.

13. Péter Bokody evocatively terms Levinas's interpretative move as the slow hijacking of Blanchot's position. Péter Bokody, *Érdeknélküliség és felelősség* [*Disinterestedness and Responsibility*] (PhD thesis, Eötvös Loránd University, 2011), 31.

14. "The Servant and Her Master" says the following about the transcendence of the poetic word in Blanchot's reading: "The poetic word itself can, however, betray itself, become engulfed in order and take on the appearance of a cultural product, a document or testimony.... This can be explained by the precise place in which it surfaces (and there is no other), between knowledge which embraces All and culture with which it identifies, two pincers which threaten to close around

it. It is precisely that moment between seeing and saying, when the pincers have not quite closed, that Blanchot watches out for.... It preserves the movement located between seeing and saying, that language of pure transcendence without correlative, like waiting which nothing awaited has yet destroyed, noesis without noema" (SM 157).

15. As far as ethical insight into art on account of Blanchot is concerned, this vacillation is totally acceptable and, what is more, firmly grounded in the thinking of the author. As Levinas says of his friend's work, "We find ourselves at grips with densities and masses which extend through dimensions and belong to an order peculiar to them, giving rise, as in delirium, to problems which are scarcely communicable once fever has subsided and day has dawned. That is the sole relief to Blanchot's literary space. The meaning of his world concerns our own. But interpretation is something this kind of work resists.... Everything here must be said in the mode of a '*perhaps*,' after the fashion of Blanchot himself when he wants to explain what has been said in his books" (SM 158n1; emphasis in original).

16. In a similar way, it is difficult to square the partial rehabilitation of art in *Otherwise than Being* with the footnote from chapter 5 of the same text (quoted above at note 7) still speaking about the "idolatry of the beautiful" and heavily steeped in the early essay's critical take on the arts.

17. Sartre conceives of a truly *dynamic* eidos of art. He is certainly conscious of the complexity that surrounds the various forms of art: for him, all poetry carries an element of the success of prose, and, the other way around, the driest prose carries elements of the defeat of poetry. Prose is not entirely capable of expressing what it wants to say as it gets entangled in the obscurities entailed in the physiognomy of the word. As Sartre emphasizes on account of Valéry, one cannot control all the risks attached to a word: "no one can understand a word to its very bottom" (*WL* 37n5). Yet, these signs of mixture do not prevent him from maintaining the distinction. Notwithstanding the impossibility of pure form, Sartre maintains the essential predisposition of genres, with each genre having an unmistakable formal mandate to realize. As he says, "If the prose-writer is too eager to fondle his words, the *eidos* of 'prose' is shattered and we fall into highfalutin nonsense. If the poet relates, explains, or teaches, the poetry becomes *prosaic*; he has lost the game. It is a matter of complex structures, impure, but well-defined" (ibid.; emphasis in original).

18. "Reality and Its Shadow" is certainly a challenging text, not only for its heavy anti-aesthetic agenda but also for its relations to Sartre's work. Sartre's name is *not once* mentioned in the text despite his strong presence in the argumentation. Seán Hand's footnotes in the English translation fill in this void very well. He indicates the presence of Sartrean ideas in the first and the last sections focusing on art and criticism, and revolving around the issues of knowledge through art and the commitment of literature, as well as in the third section targeting Sartrean (and Husserlian) image theory (RS 2, 5). Without a doubt, the path of the essay is seriously prescribed by Sartrean categories. It is as if there were an elephant in the room and we could not pronounce its name. The elephant is nevertheless

called by its name when the editor mentions both Sartre's *Temps Modernes* articles (later on collected in *What Is Literature?*) and *L'imaginaire* (*The Imaginary: A Phenomenological Psychology of Imagination*, trans. Jonathan Webber [London: Routledge, 2004]) in the preface to the essay (*Les Temps Modernes* 38 [1948]: 769–70) and criticizes the lack of reference to these works in—what he takes to be—Levinas's problematic: the disengagement of the artist in a prehuman milieu and his or her reintegration to the world. Merleau-Ponty (who authored the preface) faults Levinas for not examining thoroughly enough Sartre's ideas on engaging literature (769). Whether Levinas wryly did not want to name the target (Sartre) in his critique or did not have direct access to these works is difficult to say; one thing is sure, it was a rather brave move on his part to hand in the article for publication in Sartre's magazine, in the heyday of Sartrean philosophy.

19. "There is no question of considering this disruption [of immanence] as a purely aesthetic event. But the word poetry does not after all name a species whose genus is referred to by the word art. Inseparable from speech (*le verbe*), it overflows with prophetic meanings" (SM 159). See also a few pages above: "And perhaps we are wrong to name art and poetry that exceptional event—that sovereign forgetfulness—which frees language from its servitude towards the structures in which the *said* prevails. Perhaps Hegel was right as far as art is concerned. What matters—call it poetry or whatever—is that a meaning should be utterable beyond the confines of Hegel's completed discourse" (153).

20. Thanks to the advances of the internet, a quick search will provide access to the audio recording of "Tenebrae" recited by Celan himself. Is this really poetry? It is, indeed, very difficult to say (which may be the case whether we take a Levinasian angle or not). A lot more or a lot less than that—this is the impression one gets, hearing these sentences of utmost purity, arousing the listener in a curious way, and expressing an unrelenting *demand*.

21. On this point of closure, being collected into totality in the works of culture, see "Signification and Sense" (*HO* 18); "The Philosophical Determination of the Idea of Culture" (*EN* 154).

22. *Otherwise than Being* picks out an equally mixed, curious position for art, in a somewhat gray zone of the said, not entirely in opposition to the saying. Where do the arts stand in this complicated narrative of the saying—as the author is trying to demonstrate—prevailing in the said? Although Levinas does not discuss this, it seems clear that the arts are taken to function primarily as cultural products and modes of knowledge in which the said reigns. After all, works are the prime place where things and the world get designated; the logos of the work is highly instrumental in exhibiting/thematizing and, as such, effecting a closure in the world. Yet, this is not the final word in the story as Levinas's stress on the two-sided nature of the said proves. Other than designation, he marks out another hidden function of the said in language: next to the nominal, he points to a verbal aspect of the being of the world. The said is home to Being not only as substantial and identical with itself but also as breaking down and exposing the

constant temporalization of things, the "silent resonance of the essence" (*OB* 40). Art then proves to be the field where this clandestine yet decisive side of Being comes to the fore, where things and their qualities resound in their essence, and the verbalness of Being is revealed. This means the temporalization of the world exposed in the *materiality* of the work, with sense impressions standing out rather than blending into the object reference of the work: in painting red reddens, in music sounds reverberate, and in poetry "vocables, material of the said, no longer yield before what they evoke, but sing with their evocative powers and their diverse ways to evoke, their etymologies.... Poetry is productive of song, of resonance and sonority, which are the verbalness of verbs or essence" (40). What is most interesting is that, as Levinas points out a few pages later, this secondary, verbal aspect of the said does not block but, in one way or another, promotes the saying (47). Art is not exclusively about the promotion of the said, but, via the said, something more. As Bokody points out, for Levinas the verbalness, the resonance, of a proposition lays bare a hidden modification without change in the heart of Being and, as a result, occasions a dissolution of the said. (Bokody, *Érdeknélküliség és felelősség*, 39.) In a sense, the *echoes* of the saying are still heard in designation; the resonance of Being is not entirely petrified in nouns. As Levinas argues, "The predicative statement...stands on the frontier of a dethematization of the said, and can be understood as a modality of approach and contact" (*OB* 47). (I thank Péter Bokody for pointing to this section of the text and, as it were, lending me an aid to making sense of these extremely dense pages.)

23. The 1988 interview "De l'oblitération" dedicated to the putative ethical competence of the arts runs along a similar problematic of plasticity. The aim of this discussion is to determine if the obliterations of art manage to pierce the underlying plastic essence of art and — similarly to the face — introduce ethical alterity into the self-sufficiency of Being. Levinas admits that works of this type, such as the obliterated geometrical forms and buildings of Sosno or the equally obliterated reality of Gogol, as seen in the exaggerations and the unnecessary detail of *The Overcoat*, uncover deformations in the silent and radiant order of beauty. In a sense, he admits that the image is allowed to signify as other than image in these erasures of Being (*De l'oblitération*, 30). Such an interruption of the image eliminates what pertains to false humanity in things (22). At the same time, this tendency of art does not apply to all art works and, even in the case of the lucky few, does not surpass a certain ambiguousness. Levinas quite explicitly speaks out against the enchanting domain of the aesthetic that pertains primarily to Being and needs to be surpassed in the direction of the *nonsensuous*, something other than Being, in "mature humanity" (28).

24. Concerning Levinas's insistence on *the unapparent phenomenon* and the origins of the term in Heidegger, see Dominique Janicaud, "The Theological Turn of French Phenomenology," in Dominique Janicaud et al., *Phenomenology and the "Theological Turn": The French Debate* (New York: Fordham University Press, 2001), 28–34. Attila Szigeti discusses these ties connecting Levinas to Heidegger in further detail in *Tárgyiasítható-e a másik és az idő?: Az intencionalitás*

megfordulása Lévinasnál [*Can We Objectify the Other and Time?: Levinas and the Inversion of Intentionality*], *Erdélyi Múzeum* 66, no. 3–4 (2004): 78–89.

25. My decision to return to the early texts and focus on the work of language may be further supported by Levinas's repeated insistence on the use of the word in the 1988 interview: "Ce qui est méditation important, c'est le mot, parce que le mot atteste la relation à quelqu'un.... L'oblitération, je suis d'accord, fait parler. Elle invite à parler. Vous dites: l'oblitération interrompt le silence de l'image. Oui, il y a un appel, du mot, à la socialité, l'être pour l'autre" (*De l'oblitération*, 28).

26. It is true that Levinas starts "Reality and Its Shadow" with the problematic of art versus criticism. The discussion of criticism basically frames the whole meditation. Still, it is not until the final section of the essay that his message on the importance of critical activity over and against the completion of art reaches its prominence (RS 1–3, 12–13).

27. In the wider context of our investigations, the apparently Hegelian flavor of these thoughts cannot be left unnoticed: the introduction of philosophical criticism over and against an essentially immanent aesthetic calls to mind Hegel's treatment of the reflection on the work of art as a primarily philosophical engagement (and not, as was maintained by the Romantics, like Friedrich Schlegel, as part of the aesthetic). Kai Hammermeister, *The German Tradition in Aesthetics* (Cambridge: Cambridge University Press, 2002), 95.

28. Levinas's words describing Blanchot (SM 158n1), cited above at note 15.

29. Kevin Hart touches on these difficulties of placing Levinas between Blanchot and Sartre in Kevin Hart, "Ethics of the Image," in *Levinas Studies,* vol. 1, ed. Jeffrey Bloechl and Jeffrey L. Kosky (Pittsburgh: Duquesne University Press, 2005), 121, 125–26. It is certainly not easy to thematize this fluctuation in Levinas's work and establish if there is any logic in Levinas's siding with either of these two authors at a certain point in the corpus and what consequences such a countenance would have on his ties with the other. What makes these interconnections in this triangle of thinkers so interesting is the complication in locating the exact origins of *the ethics of the image:* doubtless, there are traces of these origins in both authors for Levinas (just like the nontruth of the image is both the source of and a hindrance to philosophical truth in art). My understanding is, nevertheless, that it is his ties with Sartre that provide the lasting features of Levinas's ethical-aesthetic program. In *What Is Literature?*, Sartre understands the work as standing in a fundamental connection with the Other, the reader, to whom the work is offered and whose intentional activity—his or her generosity—will ultimately call the work into being. To a large extent, Levinas follows this program; the fundamentally ethical insight on the *donation* of the work in Sartre (*WL* 53) is developed in new directions in "Reality and Its Shadow" and "The Transcendence of Words." Levinas is more interested in the successful expression of the work than in the defeat inherent to its plasticity that it carries. This means that, much in line with what the editor says in the preface to "Reality and Its Shadow," Levinas wants to recuperate art for the sake of truth, to reengage it, and not set anchor in the "little hell of the eternity of literature" ("Préface à 'La réalité et son ombre,'" *Les Temps Modernes*

38 [1948]: 770). Unlike Blanchot, Levinas and Sartre do not want to mask a fundamental defeat as victory. They are working to see where there is a loophole in the system, a possibility of reintegrating the exteriority of the image into the texture of the world. I take Levinas's interest in the event of the outside and his decision to observe this event in its larger context of its return to the world and ethical signification as proof of this point. And, behind this common track in their thinking lies a significant amount of Hegelianism, an essentially *romantic* concern to develop the closed plastic on a more open stage where the dynamism of thought, the possibility of ethical knowledge, holds sway.

30. Also underlined by Robert Eaglestone. See his *Ethical Criticism: Reading after Levinas* (Edinburgh: Edinburgh University Press, 1997), 118.

31. See, for example, "Is Ontology Fundamental?" from 1951 (*BPW*), "Liberté et commandement" from 1953 (*Liberté et Commandement* [Montpellier: Fata Morgana, 1994]), "Philosophy and the Idea of Infinity" from 1957 (*CPW*).

32. See "Is Ontology Fundamental?," *BPW* 3–5.

33. Emmanuel Levinas, "God and Philosophy," in *Of God Who Comes to Mind*, trans. Bettina Bergo (Stanford, CA: Stanford University Press, 1998), 57–58. It could be argued that the whole of Levinas's philosophy is defined in opposition to this unit of the aesthetic-phenomenological enterprise (and that this antipathy manifests itself in his relationship with Heidegger and, to some extent, Bergson). As Richard Cohen argues, Levinas's project is by no means about uncovering, be it in the ontological or epistemological sense, what is hidden in *Being* or *reality* ("Some Reflections on Levinas and Shakespeare," 156). To the contrary, Levinas denies the equation drawn between intelligibility and the manifestation of Being in the entire course of Western philosophy; the primacy of the source of aesthetically motivated questioning — manifestation as a basic principle of knowledge — gets refuted in his work. As Levinas sees it, if manifestation were the sole foundation of knowledge, the case of being would be about nothing else than a tendency toward *clarity* in the intentional thematization of experience. There would be no validity outside of this framework: "This is a thematization from which derive, or to which are susceptible, all the potentialities of experience, as they press toward it or await thematization" ("God and Philosophy," 57). The adventure of experience would be about the clarification of the obscure, and nothing else. The question of being and truth would be meaningful only in a framework of totality. Of course, Levinas is trying to bring to the fore the disinterestedness of the exteriority looming on the horizons of consciousness, something that cannot be accounted for intentionally and assembled in consciousness yet is constitutive in knowledge. Behind the incessant recovery and ever greater clarity of presence, the apperception of a ceaseless re-representation, there lies the other forgotten by the same (58–60).

34. "In its entirety, sound is a ringing, clanging scandal" (TW 147).

35. The change to the voice is described by Petitdemange, in the case of the work of art, as a change from the seeing of the image to the voice, and it has to be seen primarily as an attempt in which the ethical handicap of art is, to some

extent, corrected (Petitdemange, "L'art, ombre de l'être ou voix vers l'autre?," 90). In a sense, art as plastic will always come off badly in any comparison with the face; its incapacity to compete with the irreversible transcendence of the Other (that he or she is placed unambiguously above me) is beyond a doubt. This insight on the limits of plasticity (even in the field of music) is a massive one; it should heavily influence our relationship and preclude any fully fledged agreement with art. On the other hand, with the introduction of criticism this situation may be reversed: art in speech—as Petitdemange argues on the same page—acquires a par excellence unfinished status.

36. The object always "refers to the project and labor of the knower" (*TI* 65).

37. Once this ethical-metaphysical purport of language is taken on board, it is also understood that meaning does not reside in what is given, as an ideal essence offered to the mind's eye, within the context of visibility. Meaning is not on the level of intuitive data communicated to the interlocutor. As Levinas phrases it, "to signify is not to give" (*TI* 66). To the contrary, meaning is in the face that speaks (even without it actually speaking). Meaning surfaces in one's exposedness to the exteriority of Being; it is, as was seen above, taught, that is to say, expression beyond intuition and the thoughts of the same. As Levinas phrases it somewhat poetically (but all the more adequately), it "comes from the heights, unforeseen, and consequently teaches its very novelty" (66).

38. Despite their uniquely Levinasian ethical character, these thoughts on the performance of the knowing being (especially with respect to the risks of losing something of the known in the very process of knowing it) have a pronounced Hegelian flavor. His interests lie, and the signs of this are visible all around the book, in the separated individual and its inclusion in plain, univocal sense without losing its independence. Levinas does not want the integration of this separated being into the whole via understanding; instead, he wants the emergence of this being in a novel type of rationality, through the "straightforwardness of the face to face" (*TI* 183), that is, exteriority. On these grounds, it is no surprise to see Levinas proceed to action and the placement of action in history, where he discovers the abovementioned violence operating in knowledge again (66–67). And it is surely not too much of a stretch to see a parallel, in terms of the violence exercised, between the agent of history authoring actions and the artist authoring works of art. Levinas's text definitely supports the reading of the work (*oeuvre*) as a work of art. There are numerous hints that the phenomenon in which the interlocutor is judged in absence could be the object of art: "He has been understood like a prehistoric man who has left hatchets and drawings but no words" (181). Or: "Through works alone the I does not come outside; it withdraws from them or congeals in them as though it did not appeal to the Other and did not respond to him, but in its activity sought comfort, privacy, and sleep. The lines of meaning traced in matter by activity are immediately charged with equivocations, as though action, in pursuing its design, were *without regard* for exteriority, without attention" (176; emphasis in original). Most probably, there is a more extensive link in the background, pertaining to the idea of completion, which applies to

any object completed and left unattended. "Yet we might wonder if we should not recognize an element of art in the work of craftsmen, in all human work, commercial and diplomatic.... The artist stops because the work refuses to accept anything more, appears saturated. The work is completed *in spite of* the social or material causes that interrupt it. It does not give itself out as the beginning of a dialogue" (RS 2). Things in their finalized form start to resemble themselves and turn into an image; as Levinas argues, they enter a course extrinsic to themselves and will be situated outside of the world. Accordingly, the disengagement is broken in critical discourse, where the agent, the craftsman, or the artist is — as I cited above — relinked to real history (12).

39. This opening into higher levels of objectivity is quite tangible in discourse, and even in the width and breadth of the words used. From the thesis on teaching that takes the place of givenness, other radical insights follow, such as concerning the alleged referential relationship between objects and language, in which words are taken to signify a certain idea. As Levinas maintains, even the word takes teaching as its essential characteristic rather than being a sign. It is because of this height, this ethical surplus, of the Other, that words can "awaken" ideas (although Levinas would prefer "teach" here), and not the other way around. The themes of objective knowledge look self-sufficient and "ready" to mean; yet, in actual fact, it is teaching that *actualizes* the word. On this view, it is only in discourse (or, in the case of art, in critical discourse) that the word is in its fully blown ethical status, that is, where it is *the word that means*. This surplus is certainly not visible in the dead, written letter. The actuality of speech rips the word from this situation, appearing misleadingly complete. Ideas teach one on account of the discursive activity of the master. "The object is presented when we have welcomed an interlocutor" (*TI* 69). As such, the anarchy of facts is overcome in the contribution of the master: apparently, this is another aspect where *the anarchy of the spectacle* is outplayed by the eminence of the ethical for Levinas.

40. Cf. Staehler, "Images and Shadows," 135.

41. Levinas's negative portrayal of the critical *profession* is very similar in its tone to Sartre's onslaught on the critic in *What Is Literature?* (*WL* 28–30).

42. This line of thought, a sensitivity to threats that the exotic reality of the work holds with respect to the author's singularity, was on Levinas's agenda ever since *Existence and Existents*, where he argues that "an artwork as a whole expresses what we call the world of the artist. There is a world of Delacroix and a world of Victor Hugo. Artistic reality is a mind's means of expression. Through sympathy for this soul of things or of the artist the exoticism of the work is integrated into our world. That will be so inasmuch as the alterity of the other remains an alter ego, accessible through sympathy" (*EE* 49).

43. See *EI* 21–24, 114–18.

44. "In broaching, at the end of this work, the study of relations which we situate beyond the face, we come upon events that cannot be described as noeses aiming at noemata, nor as active interventions realizing projects, nor, of course, as physical forces being discharged into masses. They are conjunctures in being

for which perhaps the term 'drama' would be most suitable, in the sense that Nietzsche would have liked to use it when, at the end of *The Case of Wagner,* he regrets that it has always been wrongly translated by action. But it is because of the resulting equivocation that we forego this term" (TI 28n2).

45. The eminence of Cohen's take on Levinas's aesthetics definitely lies in his understanding of the work as something to be awakened from its slumber in interpretation. Reading *Otherwise than Being,* he sees the work as a "call for exegesis" (*OB* 41, quoted by Cohen in *Levinasian Meditations,* 159). His theory of artistic signification—in which the success of interpretation comes from both exegetical insight and what he calls the "thickness," the affluence, of the artificial world of the artwork—is phenomenologically speaking quite intriguing. Further research could concentrate on the exact place of this critical intervention, determining how and where exegetical development takes effect. At times, Cohen seems to advance the conclusion that the articulation is carried out after the course of reception, in a commentary. He describes hermeneutic activity through the examples of commenting on Shakespeare or a can of Campbell's soup; in any case, the point is that the exegete "bring out [the] potential heat and light" (160) of these works. As he phrases it a couple of pages later in the text, it is wisdom that blows life into the shadow frame and the "very animation of the work comes by philosophical commentary" (164). At other times, however, just like when he stresses the identity of reader and critic, he gives a wholly different view of the unfolding of ethical "experience" in reception. In his words, "To read is to translate. But to translate is...to redeem" (154). This statement suggests that the process of ethicization—translation—already kicks off in the silent course of reception by the reader/redeemer, before the oral critical activity. For a modest attempt to join this discussion and determine the course of ethical development, see Akos Krassoy, *Spectacle and Critique: A Phenomenological Theory of Art in Levinas* (PhD thesis, Katholieke Universiteit Leuven, 2014).

46. Another piece where the work of philosophical criticism is tangible is Levinas's essay "The Other in Proust," from 1947. I would put the author's speaking out theoretically against the artwork's magic, only to discover the mystery of the Other in the thematic of *The Captive,* down to the work of critical discourse. It is a case example of *ambiguity:* whereas in the first part of the text Levinas faults the plastic for its indeterminacy (for "the very structure of appearances which are both what they are and the infinity of what they exclude," *LR* 162), by the end he conveniently forgets about these equivocations and settles on the troubled relationship between ego and the self opening in the solitude of existence. Levinas discovers ethical meaning in the indeterminate realm of the aesthetic. He does precisely what he describes in "Reality and Its Shadow" (see RS 13): by performing philosophical criticism, he puts into movement the immobile plastic and makes it speak.

47. As Robert Eaglestone argues regarding the case of literature, Levinas's drawing of a demarcation between the intimacy of art and the critical act is quite problematic. Could the critic really exile art altogether, depriving him or herself

of *the ground* that feeds his or her work—could he or she basically divest him or herself from his or her profession? This ground is, after all, clearly the motivation for reading, for our concern for literature. Eaglestone refers to Geoffrey Hartman, who in *Criticism in the Wilderness* claims that criticism is, practically, a genre of literature, thereby raising fears that even the critical stage would get implicated into the putative "vicissitudes" of the aesthetic (Eaglestone, *Ethical Criticism,* 109). Further, he quotes George Steiner, who in his *Real Presences* states that all "serious art...is a critical act" in the end (109–10). It is critical communication itself. Eaglestone contends that "to ask for criticism to save art may be like trying to jump higher than one's shadow: asking art to save itself from art" (110).

Tracing a Traumatic Temporality:

Levinas and Derrida on Trauma and Responsibility

Cathrine Bjørnholt Michaelsen

For more than three decades, Jacques Derrida and Emmanuel Levinas develop their conceptions of trauma and responsibility in close, critical, and engaged readings of each other's works.[1] In a text first published in 1973, Levinas explicitly considers different aspects and implications of Derrida's "new style of thought," as well as his own relation to Derrida, describing their recurring crossing of paths as "a contact at the heart of a chiasmus," which is further said to constitute "the very modality of the philosophical encounter" (*PN* 56, 62).

Since the publication of "Force of Law: The 'Mystical Foundation of Authority'" in 1990, in which Derrida makes the somewhat surprising announcement that justice can be considered the undeconstructible condition of deconstruction (*AR* 243), as well as the subsequent publication of *Specters of Marx* in 1993, which is often designated as the work in which Derrida begins to consider ethico-political concerns more explicitly than hitherto, there has been much scholarly discussion about a so-called "ethical turn" of deconstruction.[2] Throughout the 1990s and up until this day a tendency prevails among certain scholars to strive for the establishment and legitimization of a more or less harmonic accordance between Levinas and Derrida with reference to concepts that preoccupy them both (e.g., "justice," "hospitality," "the other," or "responsibility"). However, as Martin Hägglund has convincingly argued, a certain disjoining of Derrida and Levinas is required in order not to conflate what ultimately amount to two very different styles of writing and thinking. Such disjoining is particularly important when it comes to an issue such as responsibility, which is too often and too quickly categorized as an "ethical issue," as if such a categorization were self-explanatory.[3]

The aim of this article is not to carry out a comparative study focusing on the similarities and dissimilarities of the writings of Derrida and Levinas. Instead, the article is an attempt to let a "third" voice arise from the ongoing philosophical conversation between Derrida and Levinas, which is neither entirely accordant nor discordant, in order to emphasize a certain traumatic temporality of responsibility that finds a space in both their works while indicating the subtle nuances of disjuncture separating these spaces. In what follows, I therefore wish to explore some of the most significant displacements to which the notions of trauma and responsibility are subjected throughout the writings of Derrida and Levinas, as a result, to some extent at least, of their repeated chiasmic encounters.

By way of introduction, it should be noted that both Derrida and Levinas transport the notion of trauma away from its most frequent psychopathological, psychoanalytic, or neurological areas of interpretation, just as they transport the notion of responsibility away from its usual autonomist or decisionist connotations toward a more extensive space of signification.[4] Bearing this introductory note in mind, the question concerning what precisely enables this transport of trauma will direct the approach of the article. In other words, the article will question what it is about the structure of "trauma" or "traumatism" that allows the somewhat "fearsome" generalizations—to employ

Derrida's own formulation from "Typewriter Ribbon"[5]—to take place in the writings of both Derrida and Levinas.

The suggestion in what follows will be that it is the peculiar temporality of trauma that allows for the generalizations, openings, and disseminations of trauma in Derrida and Levinas. More specifically, this traumatic temporality inscribes itself through an interruption of what might, with a reference to Heidegger, be called the vulgar understanding of time.[6] Drawing attention to the temporality of trauma as a vehicle of transportation, the article advances in six main sections, each exploring different aspects of the relationship between temporality, trauma, and responsibility displayed in Derrida and Levinas.

Traumatic Temporality

As is well known, at least since Freud, trauma only becomes a trauma belatedly, or *after its own fact,* since a trauma only manifests itself by withdrawing itself in the traces it leaves behind, that is, by its aftermath and its effects of repetition and deferral. Trauma is somehow simultaneously recognized and unrecognized, or recognized as unrecognizable, and therefore cannot be confronted directly. Freud's famous terms for this traumatic condition or this condition of trauma are "belatedness" or "afterwardness" (*Nachträglichkeit*) and "delaying," "deferral," or "retardation" (*Verspätung*).[7] However, this constitutive belatedness is not the only peculiarity concerning the temporality of trauma; the traces left behind by the trauma also have a certain futurity about them, inasmuch as they carry with them a threat so forceful that the traumatic traces seem to come, in fact, from the future. In Freud, this strange future of a pastness manifests itself in a "compulsion to repeat" (*Wiederholungszwang*), which is supposed to provide a form of protection for the one who is traumatized.[8]

What becomes a trauma is therefore not something that has taken place sometime in a past that was once but no longer is present. Instead, as Derrida points out in one of his lectures in *The Beast and the Sovereign,* what makes an experience or an event traumatic is the way in which the concrete effectivity of the experience or the event overflows its own present, toward a past and toward a future that will never have been nor become saturated with presence.[9] In this manner, the "original" experience or event that comes to be traumatic only after the fact cannot be remembered or represented as such, that is, it cannot become reintegrated as a once present member of a narrative whole, but can only be repeated once more as an*other* experience or event. Effectively, the traumatic event strikes a blow at the teleological order of history and exposes successive time as being radically out of joint.[10] The temporal peculiarity making an event or experience traumatic is the circumstance that trauma *remains* traumatizing in such a way that the pastness of trauma continues to proceed as if from the future. As Derrida clarifies in *Rogues: Two Essays on Reason,* trauma "takes place when one is wounded by a wound that has not yet taken place, in an effective fashion, in a way other than by the sign of its announcement. Its temporalization proceeds from the to-come."[11]

With this brief outline of a certain traumatic temporality in view, what does it mean, for instance, when Levinas, in *Otherwise than Being,* designates the very subjectivity of the subject as traumatic in reference to a responsibility that makes the subject unique and irreplaceable?[12] Or when Derrida in several places argues that every event worthy of its name can to a certain extent be characterized as traumatic, and that philosophical discourse and experience, when alive, advances "from traumatism to traumatism"?[13] In the attempt of coming to an understanding of these questions concerning traumatic temporality, I will take my point of departure in Levinas, although my approach will proceed with constant reference to Derrida.

Traumatic Subjectivity

Something appears to have happened in the 13 years separating the publication of Levinas's two major works *Totality and Infinity* (1961) and *Otherwise than Being, or beyond Essence* (1974). Something has happened to the *subject* in this interval of time; a certain displacement of the very subjectivity of the subject appears to have taken place.

In order to clarify this displacement of subjectivity in Levinas, let us take a closer look at two propositions concerning subjectivity to which Derrida draws attention in his speech *Adieu to Emmanuel Levinas*. The first proposition, from *Totality and Infinity*, reads as follows: "The subject is a host" (*TI* 299). The second proposition comes from *Otherwise than Being*, but returns frequently in Levinas's subsequent works: "A subject is a hostage" (*OB* 112). Apparently, the subjective displacement from host to hostage marks an enormous difference. On the one hand, a host is usually associated with initiative, invitation, reception, willingness, and welcome. On the other hand, a hostage usually evokes very different connotations, such as passivity, unwillingness, unpreparedness, and violence. However, taking an etymological approach, one must bear in mind that the French "hôte" is more ambiguous than the English "host," as the French term may designate both a host and a guest, but also a foreigner, or a stranger,[14] thus making the welcome of the subject and the law of hospitality more intricate than they may appear at first glance.[15] In any case, what is at stake in both of these propositions is the subject in relation to the other, and, as such, the propositions concern the question of subjectivity in relation to both responsibility and hospitality.

Now, returning to the question of "trauma," the term trauma appears only once in *Totality and Infinity* and this appearance takes place in relation to "discourse" depicted as "the experience of something absolutely foreign... *a traumatism of astonishment*" (*TI* 73).[16] In *Otherwise than Being*, by contrast, the term "trauma" in all of its inflections appears so frequently it would not even be informative to count the number of instances. This difference in wording does not necessarily signify a disagreement between *Otherwise than Being* and *Totality and Infinity*, even though it certainly does mark a shift of accent. The question of concern in this context is what makes the hostage-subject, as depicted in *Otherwise than Being*, specifically traumatic in light of the temporality of trauma previously outlined.

In contrast to the supposedly hospitable subject of *Totality and Infinity*, which appears to be somehow capable of receiving and "welcoming the Other" (*TI* 27), the subject of *Otherwise than Being* is taken hostage in a "traumatic hold of the other on the same, which does not give time to await the other" (*OB* 141). As Derrida reads it, the reason for this impossibility of awaiting and, therefore, the impossibility of preparing a welcoming reception, is that the other is always and at the same time more ancient and more futural than the subject (*AR* 407). For Levinas, this preoccupation with the other signifies an infinite responsibility without choice overturning all intentionality on the subject's part. Before *I* have the opportunity to either welcome or reject, the other assigns and obsesses *me*. This delayed responsibility of subjectivity is also why the writing of Levinas changes perspective from a nominative "I" to an accusative "me."[17] The hostage subject is always already accused in its being, entailing the necessity of no longer writing *of* the "ego" or "egoity" as a universal or transcendental structure, but rather of writing *in* the first person singular *from* the outset of this "trauma of accusation" (*OB* 15), that is, from a *me* who has already been called before *I* had the opportunity to pay attention: "The temporal continuity of consciousness is *overwhelmed* whenever it is a 'consciousness' of the Other, and 'against all expectation,' counter to all attention and anticipation" (*BPW* 72). Levinas calls this relation to the other, in and by which the subject is first constituted, diachronic or anachronistic in order to emphasize the impossibility of its becoming synchronized. The other comes before me in an anterior passing that both *pre*cedes and *ex*ceeds my being, and the being of ontology in general—albeit an anteriority that comes to pass only *as though* it were posterior.[18] This anteriority of the other is designated as *pre*-original and *an*archical, not because it would be more original than the origin or more grounding than the ground, but precisely because, in the diachronic relationship with the other, the time is out of joint.

Stating that the traumatic hold of the other is pre-originary is simultaneously to erase the myth of a present origin of the subject, which is moreover why "originary" should be read as having been crossed out.[19] The subject is subjected before it has a chance to protest or consent to this subjection always before its time, *avant la lettre,* which is why the subject, like the white rabbit of *Alice's Adventures in Wonderland,* shall always be too late to meet its responsibility in good time.[20] Hence, the subject shall always only arrive at an originary belatedness, an originary deferral in relation to an anarchic trace whose origin remains secret. Accordingly, subjectivity in *Otherwise than Being* is nothing more and nothing less than a primordial delay, a belatedness of the subject, which comes to be only *après coup,* after the blow struck by the anarchy of the other. This diachronic condition situates the subject in a relationship with the other where the subject is torn from its own beginning, torn from its equality with itself, or stolen from itself at its own birth, as Derrida writes echoing Artaud.[21] Moreover, and contrary to Hegel's statement in the *Phenomenology of Spirit* that "the wounds of the Spirit heal, and leave no scars behind,"[22] the wounds of the hostage subject always already subjected to the other never heal but scar endlessly and incessantly.

Accordingly, Levinas designates the subjectivity of the subject as "a malady of identity, both accused and self, the same for the other, the same by the other" (*OB* 69), whose whole existence consists of terms such as *assignation, obsession, persecution,* and *substitution.* Although such determinations of subjectivity reverberate negatively and degradingly, Levinas emphasizes their positive, or, rather, affirmative constitution by regarding them as essential traits of responsibility.

TRAUMATIC RESPONSIBILITY

In *Otherwise than Being*—a work dedicated to the uncountable, ununderstandable, and unmournable victims of National Socialism—Levinas delineates responsibility precisely in relation to trauma. The subject as hostage is always already responsible, answering to, and thereby affirming the appeal of the other before even deciding to do so. The appeal of the other to whom I am subjected is traumatic *because* it is unrepresentable, inappropriable in the present, impossible to interpret, internalize, or digest in any other way. What the subject bears witness to in the confrontation with the other *as* other is the trace of an infinite that has never been present and that therefore may never be recuperated by representation, memory, or any other works of mourning. Nevertheless, this infinite trace traumatically exerts its command from the finite face of the other. As Levinas makes clear in *Of God Who Comes to Mind,* "The unassumable [*inassumable*] trauma is to be stricken by the *in-* of the infinite, devastating presence and awakening subjectivity to the proximity of the other." Furthermore, this traumatic awakening comes to mark "a thinking thinking more than it thinks" (*GCM* 70).

To what, then, does this appellation of the other appeal? What is its command? According to Levinas, the other simply appeals not to be killed. Of course, this commanding appeal *not to be killed* says exactly what it says: do not take the life that is making its appeal to you. However, according to both Derrida and Levinas, the commanding appeal also says something else, namely: do not actuate or precipitate the death always already at work within this very life. The command of the other is also an appeal not to kill, that is, not to make finite, not to put an end to the infinite trace that always makes the other more, always makes the other otherwise than how I might conceive of him or her, by ignoring or denying, by naming or classifying the other to death. Responsibility, strictly speaking, is always a response to the other who remains *wholly* other and who cannot be represented *as such,* since the other is precisely what resists, distances itself from, and threatens the authority of any *as such* in general. Therefore, the trauma of which the subject is an aftereffect not only strikes a blow at the chronological, linear, or teleological order of time, it also interrupts the order of representation as such. The trace of trauma comes to re-mark a certain blindness of subjectivity, a certain blind spot of vision and reflection, as well as a certain bad conscience of consciousness (see *OS* 73 and *GCM* 172–77). Traumatic responsibility interrupts and calls into question the very sovereignty of consciousness and all the concepts traditionally aligned with it, such as autonomy, light, reason, law, and, perhaps most importantly in this context, judgment. As Levinas writes, "the consciousness is affected, then, before forming an image of what is coming to it, affected in spite of itself" (*OB* 102).

Both Levinas and Derrida turn to language and discourse in order to discern some traces of this responsibility toward the future anteriority of the other. As Derrida articulates it in an interview, "When one is born into a language, one inherits it because it is there before us, it is older than us, its law precedes us."[23] Levinas would probably call this ancient law of language the law of the other before which the subject is subjected, and by which the subject is always already taken hostage. In *Otherwise than Being,* subjectivity is exposed precisely as "a bottomless passivity, made out of assignation, like the echo of a sound that would precede the resonance of this sound" (*OB* 111). Pre-originarily assigned to responsibility, the subject—like Echo—is bereft of the possibility of speaking on its own initiative, in its own name, or according to its own law, that is, autonomously. Instead, the subject is called into question prior to any questioning through a heteronomous movement that Levinas calls "a responsibility over and beyond the logos of response" (102). This condition of responsibility entails that even against my will, *despite myself,* and contrary to what I might say or wish to say, my mere saying is always already an opening toward and an affirmation of the approach of the other, and thus already caught up in responding to this other who withdraws from the said in giving me the breath for the very Saying. Moreover, this Saying constitutes the very significance of language in signifying like an open mouth "exposed like a bleeding wound" (151) before language scatters into words.

According to Levinas, the pro-vocation or the calling-forward by the other constitutes the very condition for every human Saying and for the human spirit as such, which is also the reason why Levinas, in

Totality and Infinity, makes the strong statement that "it is not I, it is the other that can say yes" (*TI* 93). In several places, Derrida responds to this statement of Levinas's by redoubling the unheard *yes* of the other before the beginning with another *yes* that must always be subsequent, inasmuch as "there is no *first yes,* the *yes* is already a response. But since everything must begin with some *yes,* the response begins" (*AEL* 24). Once again, we are back at the complexity of hospitality and at the substitution of the host by the guest.

Furthermore, Levinas emphasizes the fact that whenever and whatever I am saying, I am always saying it in obedience to this law of responsivity—knowing not whence my saying comes—thus exposing "the inspiration or prophecy of all language" (*OB* 152). Hence, in-spiration, the giving of breath for saying, is a form of alienation, albeit an alienation constituting the very subjectivity of the subject by awakening it to its unique responsibility for the other. Elsewhere Levinas describes this strange constitution as an *"alteration without alienation"* fissuring the core of the subject's interiority and awakening in it a *"despite myself* that is more me than myself" (*GDT* 187). This constitutional alteration furthermore indicates the paradoxical condition of incondition of human existence, namely that "paradoxically it is qua *alienus*—foreigner and other—that man is not alienated" (*OB* 59).[24] Levinas's insistence that the subject constitutes an alien without being alienated from itself distances him from more traditional renderings of alienation, in underlining that alienation is not a question of successive causality; there is not *first* a constituted identity, which would *then* be lost or betrayed in alienation *all the while* preserving the possibility of returning to itself. Instead of reinstating the process of identification as a movement of return, Levinas designates the selfhood of the subject as a "recurrence to oneself [that] cannot stop at oneself, but goes to the hither side of oneself" (114), because from even before the very beginning the "other is in me and in the midst of my very identification" (125). According to the law of inspiration sketched out above, "a reversal of heteronomy into autonomy"

(*GDT* 200) might occur to allow the subject to speak and write from out of its unique singularity. However, this occurrence always takes place belatedly by responding to an anterior address, thus reaffirming it as an anarchical affirmation *of* the other. The echoing *yes* of the subject thus becomes an affirmation of responsibility toward the unconditional but conditioning *yes* of the other—"yes, yes." Additionally, as Derrida has it, this repetitive *yes* "is even what ties in depth the injunction of memory with the anticipation of the future to come,"[25] situating the subject once more as always in the diachronic temporality of trauma.

Partings at the Crossroads? An Uncertainty of Substitutional Responsibility

Returning to the oscillation of responsibility in Levinas between subjective hosts and hostages, hospitality and persecution, openness and intrusion, Derrida makes the suggestion that it designates "the very test of substitution: to be one at the place of the other, the hostage and the hôte of the other" (*AR* 387). In order to come to a further understanding of traumatic responsibility, we are obliged, then, to enter into the *unthinkable of substitution* (de)centering on the critical notions of *dissymmetry, irreplaceability,* and *irreciprocity* as well as on how these notions operate in the relation of responsibility between the subject and the other, or, rather, how they operate in the subject *of* the other.

Even though Derrida puts forward some reservations and poses some critical questions regarding Levinas's rendering of substitution, it nevertheless remains a continually renewed source of inspiration throughout his writings. Moreover, Derrida's supplementary displacements of substitution always occur in a thinking with and against Levinas that brings out almost undetectable nuances of difference within the very relation of substitution. Furthermore, the development of the notion of substitution in *Otherwise than Being* can be read, in part at least, as Levinas's response to two of Derrida's most critical assertions in "Violence and Metaphysics" regarding *Totality and Infinity*. First, the assertion that according to Levinas's adequation of the ego and the Same, "there would be no interior difference, no fundamental and autochthonous alterity within the ego" (*WD* 109). Second, the assertion that Levinas's critique of Husserlian intersubjectivity, as an assimilatory or analogical relation overlooking the immediate violence of the face-to-face encounter with the Other, itself runs the risk of committing metaphysical violence against the alterity of the other by ignoring "the unsurpassable necessity of (nonobjective) mediation" (124), confirming the separation or distance necessary in order to respect the absolute singularity of the other.[26]

Let us begin to approach the unthinkable, then, by turning to Levinas's rendering of the difficult notion of substitution. As previously mentioned, Levinas recounts a displacement of subjectivity from a nominative host to an accusative hostage experienced in a traumatic recurrence of the subject to itself as another. In *Otherwise than Being* Levinas refers to this displacement, which marks out a passage from the ego-economical time to the time of the other, with the term *substitution*. Something happens to the subject in the encounter with the other *as other* that not only violently interrupts the subject's reductive perception of the other by opening in it the trace of infinite transcendence: the subject is also thrown back upon its abyssal existence. The relation with the otherness of the other called substitution is therefore a double-bound movement related to the irreducible ambiguity of a transcendence "without aiming and without vision, a 'seeing' that does not know that it sees" (*GDT* 139), which Levinas emphasizes by splitting the movement into two "orientations": trans*a*scendence and trans*de*scendence.[27] In brief, transdescendence designates a certain contraction or turning inwards wherein subjectivity is experienced as an anarchical determination by a transcendence preceding and exceeding its immanence as an anterior posteriority, such that the presumed authority of the subject is to be derived from an irreducible heteronomy, that is, from the other in the same. Transascendence designates an experience in the encounter with the other of a trace of infinite withdrawal, which

Levinas names by different unnameables—predominantly "the idea of infinity," "Glory," "the Good beyond Being," "God," or "illeity."[28]

As an intrusion of "the third," which is co-instantaneous with the face-to-face encounter, *illeity* not only designates an alterity of the other, but also an alterity in myself, since it traces an alterity that has always already called upon "me" before "I" had the opportunity either to listen to or ignore it: "This allegiance before any oath is the Other in the Same; that is, it is *time*, the *coming to pass* [*se passer*] of the Infinite" (*GDT* 201). *Illeity* designates the dictation that comes from I know not whence, but that I receive as a trace from an immemorial past and from an unforeseeable future in the proximity of the other who sends me toward the infinite: "The *illeity* in the beyond-being [*l'au-delà-de-l'être*] is the fact that its coming toward me is a departure which lets me accomplish a movement toward a neighbor" (*OB* 13). Thus, substitution refers to the situation of recurrence in which the insignificance of the *there is* (*il y a*) of solitary existence and of the tragicomic concern for the subject's own being turns into a significant modality of being-for-the-other: "The *there is* is all the weight that alterity weighs supported by a subjectivity that does not found it" (164). In this inversion the subject experiences another significance behind the insignificant *there is* of being, which it is unable to make significant by itself, and which does not depend upon any activity of subjectivity but instead upon the radical passivity of the subject elected as the irreplaceable support of everything other: "There is deliverance into itself of an ego awakened from its imperialist dream, its transcendental imperialism, awakened to itself, a patience as a subjection to everything" (164).

Because of the all-encompassing but radically impotent support demanded of the responsible subject, Levinas has often been reproached with propagating an untenable and hyperbolic asymmetry in the substitutional relationship between the subject and the other.[29] For instance, Hägglund comes to the conclusion that Levinasian ethics is not founded on "an intersubjective encounter" since all one has to do is "to place yourself face-to-face with someone else to realize that the asymmetry assumed by Levinas is self-refuting. If you and I are standing in front of each other, who is the other?"[30] I concur with Hägglund about the necessity of posing the last question, "who is the other?" However, the importance of this question attains its prominence only by taking seriously the premises of Levinas's own logic of substitution, that is, dissymmetry, irreciprocity, and irreplaceability. The objection that Levinas fails to "found his ethics on an intersubjective encounter" does not give heed to one of the most important experiences unfolded in *Otherwise than Being*, namely, the experience of the impossibility of writing or speaking *of* the "I" as a universal structure, because of the necessity to speak or write *from out* of a "me" always already accused, placed in the accusative by another. *This* is the fundamental dissymmetry; the fact that I am always limited to my own perspective and cannot escape it, although this perspective is not one that I have chosen.[31] It is precisely this fundamental dissymmetry that does not allow for a symmetrical inversion of the type suggested by Hägglund when he writes that "whoever advocates a Levinasian ethics will be confronted with a merciless irony as soon as he or she comes up to someone else and face-to-face declares, 'You should subject yourself to the Other,' which then literally means, 'You should subject yourself to *Me*, you should obey *My* law.'"[32] Contrary to such a reciprocal inversion, the subject of *Otherwise than Being* emphatically experiences that the law of the other will never be *my* law, because it is a law to which I am subjected *despite* or *without* myself (*malgré soi*). For the same reason, it is not a law that I dispose of or that I can transfer to another "I"—and, for the same reason, Levinasian ethics does not and cannot prescribe normative codes of conduct valid for everyone. As I have attempted to show in the previous sections, the temporality of traumatism and the exposure to substitution are at work in the subject's relation to the other from the very anarchic beginning (before the beginning) and do not impose on or overtake an already constituted subject, simply because they constitute the very subjectivity of the subject. There is not *first* a subject to which the subjection to the other happens and to which the subject can *then* choose to submit itself or not; rather the subject happens to itself in and as subjection to the other, and "this trauma has surprised me completely [*traumatisme qui m'a absolument surprise*]" (*OB* 148).

Turning now to Derrida, some of his most critical reservations are, from my perspective, firstly toward a certain "axiomatic certainty" that seems to prevail in Levinas's rendering of substitution, and, secondly, toward the "criteria of exceptionality, of irreplaceable singularity, of unicity" (*AR* 419) that seem to follow from such axiomatic certainty. The axiomatic certainty that Derrida critically questions concerns Levinas's apparent confidence in the capital *Good,* which, although it transcends being and power, still somehow manages to orientate the relation between the subject and the other. The metaphysical *Good beyond Being* [*Bien au-delà de l'Être*] is what guarantees that the orientation of subjectivity in substitution remains unidirectional and irreversible; the subject is always situated "under," gazing "upwards" toward the infinite elevation of the other, and the other can never substitute for the subject in its responsible subjectivity, since only the irreplaceable subject can substitute for the other responsibly.[33] The "good violence" (*bonne violence*) or the "violence of non-freedom" (*la violence de la non-liberté*) (see *OB* 15, 43, 57, 123) that traumatizes the responsible subject also protects us from the risk of confusing ethics with arithmetic, since if substitution were reversible *no one* would be ultimately responsible. It is precisely the legitimacy of such a stabilized and "hierarchizing dissymmetry" (*AEL* 95) that Derrida (and what by him is called deconstruction) persistently questions, since if the responsibility to substitute for the other is what makes the subject irreplaceable, then what does it make the other if not, precisely, replaceable? If the subject can substitute for any other this makes any other substitutable, except for the subject, who is an exception who remains unsubstitutably unique in substitution. The question is, then, how such a dissymmetry avoids reducing the infinite singularity of the Other to what can ultimately be replaced by any other. But also, inversely, how the uniqueness of the responsible one ultimately avoids becoming substitutable.

We must be careful here since the nuances of Derrida's critique and the differences it offers to Levinas's thinking of substitution are extremely subtle and complex. As I see it, Derrida's main reservation does not concern the irreducible irreciprocity and dissymmetry of substitution, but the certainty of a unidirectional orientation in this relation of irreciprocity and dissymmetry, which perhaps comes too close to the certainty of a good consciousness that Levinas himself continually warns against. As always, Derrida is paying rigorous attention to Levinas's text—to the point of reading Levinas against himself—when he suggests that the "thinking of substitution leads us toward a logic that is hardly thinkable, almost unsayable," namely, "that of the possible-impossible, the iterability and replaceability of the unique in the very experience of unicity as such" (*AEL* 70). Because the anarchic election of the subject that makes its responsibility irreplaceable is to be thought inseparably from the substitution that seemingly contradicts it, substitution precisely leads us to think "the unique as *hostage* responsible for all, and therefore substitutable, precisely there where [*là même où*] he is absolutely irreplaceable" (*AR* 365).

From my perspective, the inseparability of irreplaceability and substitution goes straight to the wound of traumatic responsibility, which expropriates the subject of any place of its own while simultaneously demanding of it to be singularly one in the place of the other (*l'un-pour-l'Autre*). This is indeed one of the most difficult and paradoxical, perhaps even impossible, thoughts to think: the diachronic contemporaneity of substitution and dissymmetry, of replaceability and uniqueness, which in Derrida's terms comes to be rearticulated as iterability and singularity, or eventness, and which designates the subject as an irreplaceable substitution, that is, as an irreplaceable without place.

Even though Levinas insists that the one responsible cannot be substituted in its substitution for all, this one is not to be confused with some autonomous, personal or self-contained core of identity; instead, one becomes oneself only in "breaking up the limits of identity" (*OB* 114). What Levinas designates as the "oneself" (*soi-même*) is "the unqualifiable *one,* the pure *someone*" who becomes unique only through "an exposedness to the other where no slipping away is possible" (50). The one who cannot be substituted is not a personal *I*, but a certain anonymous other within myself who "bears its name as a borrowed name, a pseudonym, a pro-noun...it is first a non-quiddity, no one, clothed with purely borrowed being, which masks its nameless singularity [*singularité sans nom*]" (106).[34]

Thus, it is not *I* who bears a proper name that takes responsibility, but the nameless other in myself who assigns me to an inescapable and irreplaceable responsibility. The Other may demand responsibility from me and no other, but it is demanded from me in the place of the other, which is to say, it is the other in myself and not I who must respond: "It provokes this responsibility against my will, that is, by substituting me for the other as a hostage" (*OB* 11). However, how can one be irreplaceable if one does not have a proper place? Well, precisely in the place of the other, and this place of expropriation is what both Levinas and Derrida call responsibility: "Responsibility is not my property, I cannot reappropriate it, and *that* is the place of justice: the relation to the other."[35]

Yet the alterity of myself does not produce an identification of the one and the other; rather, the relation of the one and the other remains a relation of separation, an unrelated relation of irreducible distance, that puts identity in question to the point of expelling it outside of itself such that it can only recur "in itself as in exile" (*OB* 103). To Levinas, this recurrent exile is synonymous with the incarnation or corporeality that "makes one other without alienating" (109). In *Totality and Infinity,* Levinas refers to this irreducible interval of distance in the relation without relation to the other as a "curvature of space [*courbure de l'espace*]" (*TI* 267), which can also be transferred to the irreciprocity and dissymmetry of substitution as well as to the irreducible ambiguity of transcendence. Moreover, it is precisely the irreciprocal dissymmetry of the substitutional relationship that "keeps me solitary and unmatched [*dépareillé*] in regard to the other" (*GDT* 181).[36]

Again, the unmatched solitude of the responsible one does not refer to some substantive kernel of interiority. Far from such a notion, Levinas refers to the responsible one implied in the intrigue of substitution as "a fissured subject, one without a core who does not have to-be, but rather has to-substitute-itself" (*GDT* 195). *There is* a solitude in Levinas that depends entirely upon the relation with the other. This is not a solitude of solidity, self-certainty, or self-sufficiency. On the contrary, it is the solitude of not being able to exist by oneself—alone. It is a solitude of absolute dependency hollowing out any identity of one's own. Depriving me of any independent sense of self, *I am the other*, not because I would then be identical with the other—which would leave no solitude to remain—but because without the other I can only continue to exist as deprived of myself, leading an anonymous existence in absolute solitude. *There is* a solitude stemming from inevitability of having to survive the existence of a nonexistent in case of abandonment by the other, of having to survive the absence of the other. A solitude stemming from the awareness that without the other only the *there is* remains and that I only become myself as an expenditure of myself without return, that is, as "a passivity without reserve, to the point of substitution" (*OB* 151). We all share the solitude of this unreserved passivity even though we can never have it in common. The subjectivity of the subject does not emerge as the constitutive foundation of meaning but instead as always already subjected to the meaning of being responsible for the (well-)being of the other all the way to death and beyond. In other words, substitution displaces the insignificance of bare solitary existence to an infinite significance as support and subject for the other: "The incessant murmur of the *there is* strikes with absurdity the active transcendental ego, beginning and present. But the absurdity of the *there is*, as a modality of the-one-for-the-other, signifies" (164).

According to Derrida, this radical and traumatic dissymmetry of substitution in Levinas responds to "an experience of the Good that elects me before I welcome it, in other words, of a Goodness, a good violence of the Other that precedes welcoming" (*AR* 364). However, the question of how one welcomes the capital Good that infinitely precedes and exceeds the one responsible for welcoming without a place of its own remains. How can the disappropriated one take responsibility upon itself? How to distinguish between the infinitely other of oneself and the infinitely other of the Other, if the only sense of self one senses is the inescapability of having no propriety over oneself? How can one do what one cannot do but is nevertheless assigned to do? Or, as Derrida succinctly poses the question of the response: "How to do the impossible? Only the other in me can do it, and decide—this would be to let him do it [*le laisser faire*], without the other doing it simply in my place: here is the unthinkable of substitution" (365).[37] At this point of radical questioning, Derrida aligns the aporetic logic of substitution with a series of other "aporias" or "undecidables" that return to haunt his writing, for example, forgiveness, the gift, or hospitality, which brings us to the next section.

Undecidable Responsibility

Despite his apparent confidence in the capital *Good beyond Being*, it is my impression that Levinas is acutely aware of the plenitude of its unavoidable contaminations by being (and all its menaces of power, categorization, representation, war, etc.), and that he does not believe in a pure possibility of overcoming ontology through ethics. Moreover, the assertion of such an overcoming would only be tantamount to the accomplishment of a good conscience, which would no longer fear the possible violence of its own presence. According to Levinas, the bad conscience of the responsible one can never be terminated since the mortal demand of the Other remains infinite. Although I am elected the responsible subject for everything and everyone, as Levinas insists, I can never measure up to this responsibility simply because it is beyond or without measure (*démesuré*): "It is like something that would become increasingly distanced or that would distance itself more and more as one approached, like a distance that is more and more untraversable" (*GDT* 191).

According to Derrida, however, it is not sufficient to affirm the infinity of the other's demand and the excessiveness of responsibility, one also has to confront the unpleasant circumstance that one cannot stop at this unconditioned affirmation; one always has to make the attempt of traversing the untraversable. In other words, confronted by the other's infinite appeal to justice one cannot remain undecided; one always has to make a decision, which will inevitably prove to be finite. In fact, it is because of finitude that one is always forced to negotiate and decide the infinite *now in every instance,* that is, one is always forced to negotiate the unnegotiable and decide the undecidable.

Derrida calls this nonnegotiable unconditionality of negotiation the "congenital perjury of justice" since it designates the unavoidable circumstance that "as soon as there is substitution, and as soon as there is a third [*un troisième*], I am called by justice, by responsibility, but I also betray justice and responsibility" (*AR* 388). My responsibilities are never pure since *I* cannot avoid betraying one as soon as *I* try to exert another.[38] This also means that there is always a risk of the incomparable singularity of the other becoming contaminated with comparisons, the "who" becoming contaminated with the "what," or ethics becoming contaminated with arithmetic ("one would have to write *arithméthique*") (411). However, this possibility of betrayal inherent to responsibility is necessary since, in order that responsibility not be turned into a process of irresponsible calculation, it must "open itself to what always risks being perverted," that is, to "the chance of letting the other come" (*AEL* 35).

The traumatic nonorigin of responsibility is at once a wounding and an opening — a wounding of an immemorial past that opens toward the coming of the other. Levinas describes this wounding opening as an "inside-out domain of the soul" that "does not close from inside" (*HO* 66). However, as Derrida emphasizes, this openness of the future always yet to come (*à venir*) marks an undecidability regarding the difference between promise and threat, or between messianicity and traumatism,[39] because, in order to come *as* other the other must interrupt unexpectedly, surprisingly, even violently. The other as wholly other can only come as an uninvited visitor and as an absolute stranger (*hôte*) for whom no welcoming can be prepared; all the while no host (*hôte*) can be determined in advance, but only ever *after the fact*. Moreover, if the other is to *remain* other, this uninvited coming can never become domesticized. One can never accommodate to the coming of the other; rather, the other will remain infinitely strange, which also entails that the coming of the other will never cease coming, and will never cease interrupting and disturbing the subject in its intimate identity.[40] As previously mentioned, Levinas calls this infinite interruption a "good violence," designating the only resistance against the violence of the Same, or the violence of a supposedly self-conscious freedom, that repeatedly tries to absorb, assimilate, or neutralize any alterity by thematization, objectification, or other protective measures. Precisely because of this unforeseeable and irreducible exteriority for the subject of experience, every event in its very eventfulness may be said to be traumatic, regardless of whether this event will eventually turn out to have been either joyous or painful.

The attempt to attend to the infinite of the other, or to the absolute singularity of the other exceeding all my notions, visions, or thoughts of the other, is concurrently an attempt to attend to all the categorizations, classifications, representations that we constantly and violently subject each other to. Responsibility is an attempt not to forget this forgetting of absolute otherness, and not to let disappear the disappearance of the excess of the other. However, some disappearing of disappearance, just as some forgetting of forgetting, remains unavoidable in a finite attempt to act responsibly, which necessarily always sacrifices another responsibility.

As Levinas emphasizes, there is always already betrayal precisely because "everything shows itself at the price of this betrayal, even the unsayable" (*OB* 7). Nonetheless, Levinas further emphasizes that it is an obligation of philosophical thought to conceive of this original betrayal — which first makes possible not only communication, manifestation, and representation, but also tradition, continuity, and society — since philosophy is also "called upon to conceive ambivalence, to conceive it in several times" (162).[41] Philosophy must incessantly negotiate the ambivalence of its own language — the ambiguity of the saying and the said — by alternating between original betrayal and the delayed attempt to reduce this betrayal, as also between indiscretion and discretion, manifestation and secrecy, speech and speechlessness, and between law and justice. Only in adhering to this ambiguous threshold "where transcendence can only be heard in words that betray it while they endeavor to translate it" (*GDT* 239)[42] may philosophy be designated as "the wisdom of love at the service of love" (*OB* 162). Thus, infidelity may be inevitable but it is the very task of philosophy to remain faithful toward this infidelity.[43]

Therefore, the *Good* in Levinas does not constitute some transcendental signpost according to which the responsible subject can orientate itself toward the other with the certainty of a good conscience. Rather, as previously mentioned, there remains an irreducible ambiguity in Levinas's rendering of transcendence. The question that imposes itself is, then, *how* the two main configurations of alterity in Levinas's writing, the *there is* and *illeity*, relate to one another and, furthermore, to what extent it is possible to differentiate the two "orientations" of transcendence from one another. How might the anonymous experience of the bare *there is* of existence be related to the experience of unique substitution for the Other in the passage toward *illeity*? In the last analysis, these are questions that cannot be answered unequivocally if transcendence is to remain transcendent, but we will nevertheless attempt to draw out some further indications in order to understand better why transcendence, according to Levinas, must remain ambiguous: "To support without compensation, the excessive or disheartening hubbub [*remue-ménage*] and encumberment of the *there is* is needed" (*OB* 164).[44]

Over the course of his writings, Levinas's understanding of transcendence comes to be somewhat altered and nuanced. As Allen points out, Levinas's earlier writings, up until and including *Totality and Infinity*, appear to operate within a more or less clear distinction between transdescendence and transascendence by assigning the movements to the domains of aesthetics and ethics, respectively.[45] However, this distinction within transcendence becomes gradually blurred throughout some texts following 1961.

In "Reality and its Shadow" (1948), Levinas envisages the artwork—especially the image, but also the rhythm of music—as representative of a petrified interval of time that appears "as though death were never dead enough, as though parallel with the duration of the living ran the eternal duration of the interval—the *meanwhile* [*l'entretemps*]" (*LR* 141). Following Kant, Levinas regards the aesthetic transcendence as a form of disinterestedness, though this is not the case in its later ethical emphasis on a kind of disinterestedness where the subject substitutes for the Other in a nonindifference without self-interest. In the 1948 essay, artworks are said to possess their spectators with a fascination so comprehensive that "our consenting to them is inverted into a participation" (132). This is a participation, moreover, in which the fascinated subject is drawn into the shadow realm of art as a distorted reflection of reality, thus becoming a part of his own indifferent representation: "It is so not even despite itself [*pas même malgré lui*], for in rhythm there is no longer a oneself, but rather a sort of passage from oneself to anonymity" (133).

In sharp contrast, *Totality and Infinity* presents its readers with a transcendence that necessarily constitutes a trans*a*scendence, since, as a metaphysical movement, it is instigated by the idea of infinity that designates a height and a nobility inverse to the submerging trans*de*scencence in which Levinas detects a certain irresponsibility, inhumanity, and monstrosity (see *LR* 141). As a corrective to these rather unidirectional readings of transcendence, some of Levinas's later writings introduce a duplicity or ambiguity into transcendence in such a way that the call from on high of *illeity* appears inseparably bound up with the descent into the abyssal depths of the *there is*. The absolute trans*a*scendence toward the infinite alterity of *illeity* necessarily passes in the direction of its own withdrawal into complete indistinction from the abandoned trans*de*scendence of the *there is*: "God is not simply the first other but other than the other, other otherwise [*autre qu'autrui, autre autrement*]... transcendent to the point of absence, to the point of his possible confusion with the agitation of the *there is* [*le remue-ménage de l'il y a*]" (*GDT* 224).

Herewith, Levinas exposes a radical uncertainty in the experience of transcendence, namely, the disheartening experience that one can never with certainty differentiate between the presence of absence and the absence of presence, between the *il* of *il y a* and the *il* of *illéité*. An uncertainty that also entails that one can never be certain about the "goodness" or "badness" of the infinite movement, that is, one can never be certain if the orientation of transcendence is beyond oneself and upward toward the Other or downward toward the abyssal existence of oneself.[46] In this context, the full extent of Jean Wahl's influence becomes evident when Levinas, in a reading of Wahl from 1987, considers a transcendence that remains hierarchically and orientationally indeterminate: "A bursting [*éclatement*] toward the heights or a descent toward the depths of the sensible world; trans-ascendence and trans-descendence are purely, and pure, transcendencies" (*OS* 62). In designating both orientations as pure, Levinas also points to the possible risk irreducible to the trial (*épreuve*) of transcendence, that is, to the "interchangeability of the *beyond* [*l'au-delà*] and the *hither side* [*l'en deçà*]—of the very high [*très haut*] and the very low [*très bas*]" (57), since "everything alternates in the metaphysical experience" (63).

With his emphasis on the irreducible ambiguity of transcendence, Levinas is apparently making space for the unsettling thought that not only does *illeity* come infinitesimally close to the *there is*, but this infinite interval also opens up a whole series of other uncertainties, or undecidables, to use Derrida's term. For example, that love comes infinitely close to the death drive, faith infinitely close to eroticism, nonindifference infinitely close to disinterest, *il* infinitely close to *id*, substitutional responsibility infinitely close to anonymous irresponsibility, and reality infinitely close to the shadow realm of art. The possibility that the transcendence toward the unnamable name "God" or the "Good beyond Being" ends in the divine comedy of God's abandonment, whereby "God" becomes a mere echo of the *there is*, and whereby transcendence is inverted into an incessant recurrence to immanence and to the impossibility of *not* continuing to exist in abandonment.[47]

To Levinas, the relation to the other *as* other must necessarily take place in such a double-bound movement, so that the *interval* of transcendence is not transgressed or surmounted. Both the *there is* and *illeity* signify the irreducibility of "that gap (*décalage*), that break in continuity" (*OS* 57) constituting the condition of both the possibility and the impossibility of a relationship with the other. In order for the relation without relation to leave the alterity ab-solute (both separated and holy), it can only take place in an interval of transcendence that transcends transcendence toward immanence (see *PN* 116), and therefore "transcendence, the beyond essence which is also being-in-the-world, requires [*il faut*] ambiguity" (*OB* 152). The infinite withdrawal of the Go(o)d as time signifies that not even a God can save us now, since, as abandoned actors trapped in a divine comedy taking place in between the theater and the temple,[48] we can only always act responsibly uncertainly, that is, *as if* a "Good beyond Being" makes sense. According to Levinas, this irreducible uncertainty stems from the circumstance that "the Good cannot enter into a present nor be put into a representation. But being Good it redeems [*rachète*] the violence of its alterity, even if the subject has to suffer through the augmentation of this ever more demanding violence" (15). Thus, the transcendent experience signifies an incessant ordeal (*épreuve*) of the oneself always already disappropriated of itself. A oneself whose only path of orientation is formed in a perpetual deferral of an unavoidable betrayal and in an unfaithful fidelity toward the irreducible alterity of the Other. A oneself who attempts to respond to a responsibility infinitely exceeding the finitude of the responsible one: "There is in this transcendent movement an accomplishing of oneself that is at once a destruction of oneself, a failure that is triumph" (*OS* 81).

Throughout all of Levinas's writings, time does not signify a fall, a corruption, or an apostasy from an eternal *Good beyond Being*. Quite the reverse, time signifies a relation to *infinity in finitude* exposed through a good violence. Levinas's conception of an anarchic, diachronic, and traumatic time is an attempt to think without skipping the intervals of time or mending holes in the texture of being. It is a thinking that attempts to think in and with the interruptions of thought that constitute the condition of (im)possibility for a relation to the other as other: "Time signifies this *always* of noncoincidence, but also the *always* of the *relationship*, an aspiration and an awaiting, a thread finer than an ideal line that diachrony does not cut. Diachrony preserves this thread in the paradox" (*TO* 32).

Such diachronic time is a time of trauma and patience and such paradoxical thinking is a patience of impatience that attempts to defer the time of calculation, comprehension, and determination. Such time is a time of hope hoping beyond hope and beyond revelation. Time as a patience of impatience and utopian hope is a prophetical or a messianic time that awaits without expecting the awaited and that clears a space for the coming of the other and for the absolute alterity of the next instant: "Time is deferred, is transcended to the Infinite. And the awaiting without something awaited (time itself) is turned into responsibility for another" (*GDT* 139).

Closing Remarks

The subject awoken to its unique responsibility simultaneously becomes a subject taken hostage by the other in his, her, or its unrepresentability. Responsibility, in one of its most demanding senses, has to do precisely with the unrepresentable, unnamable, and unassumable that traces the infinite *surplus,* or the overflowing of meaning by the other.[49] Perhaps one could make the assumption that in Levinas, as in Derrida, the appeal of the other is not so much an appeal for recognition in a Hegelian sense, or in any other sense, of being seen for what or who one is. Rather, it is an appeal to let the other keep its secret, to care for and to preserve the secrecy of the other. Hence, responsibility in a sense comes to designate an attempt to bear witness to that which cannot be witnessed and to give testimony to that *blinding alterity* of the other both "inside" and "outside," if such distinctions still signify anything determinable when dealing with traumatic substitution.[50]

Again, responsibility is an attempt to become aware of the imperialist tendencies that consciousness continually repeats in order to protect itself against the traumas of otherness, and to become aware of the possible cynicism of a good conscience that would be the ultimate forgetting of forgetting, the ultimate disappearance of disappearance. For Derrida, this ultimate and forgetful disappearance, which entails those absolute misfortunes where all possibility of witnessing has disappeared, must be thought as continually possible, since, as he emphasizes in "Freud and the Scene of Writing," an inerasable trace would not be a trace at all, it would be a full presence.[51]

Furthermore, the attempt to pay attention to the blind spots in relation to the other also entails that traumatized responsibility is delivered over, or abandoned, to the ordeal of the undecidable. Nothing is given in advance for responsibility; no rule, no criteria, no norm may serve as a guarantee of good ethical conduct, which is why ethics as first philosophy must necessarily remain anarchical—without foundation. Nonetheless, it is precisely "the abyss of this non-response" (*AR* 400) that conditions the unconditionality of justice and responsibility. In order to be just, the response must be reinvented each and every time the subject is called into question by the singular appeal of the other.⁵²

Traumatic responsibility in this extra- or pre-moralistic sense denotes an originary exposure to the exposedness of the other. To be violated by the good violence is to be wounded by the other's exposure to evil (the evil done by others of the other, by the other to itself, or by no one — by sickness, hunger, catastrophe, or death) without escape. The eventfulness of trauma strikes the present as *both* the prior coming to pass *and* the future coming to pass [*en revenant*] once more of an unprecedented visitor. As Levinas writes, "The subject is born in the beginninglessness of an anarchy and in the endlessness of obligation" (*OB* 140).

Under this obligation the task of responsibility becomes in(de)terminable because it answers to the infinity in the finitude of the other. Responsibility will never have been responsive enough, attention never attentive enough, the awoken never wakeful enough, since nothing ever authorizes the certainty of a good conscience. One can never be *re*sponsible in advance, but always only *after the fact*. The endeavor of breaking this double bind of an immemorial past, as the indeterminability of origin, and a radical futurity, as the indeterminable principle of determination, in order to achieve the good consciousness of an accomplished responsibility would only result in tragedy, since, as Schürmann elucidates, "tragic denial is necessary for the univocal law to be born."⁵³ However, as previously mentioned, ethics as first philosophy signifies precisely the incessant attempt to negotiate ambiguity and thus a resistance to the birth of univocal laws.

In light of this impossible responsibility, and by way of closure, how are we to read the "Thou shalt not kill" written in the mortal face of the other? Perhaps this interdiction can only say what Blanchot makes it say in his *The Step Not Beyond*, that is, "do not kill he who will die in any case... do not infringe on dying, do not decide the indecisive, do not say: this is done, claiming for yourself a right over this 'not yet'; do not pretend that the last word has been spoken, time completed, the Messiah come at last."⁵⁴

Notes

In addition to the abbreviations at the front of this volume, the following are also used: Jacques Derrida, *Acts of Religion* (*AR*), ed. Gil Anidjar (New York: Routledge, 2002); Jacques Derrida, *Adieu to Emmanuel Levinas* (*AEL*), trans. Pascale-Anne Brault and Michael Naas (Stanford, CA: Stanford University Press, 1999); Jacques Derrida, *Specters of Marx* (*SOM*), trans. Peggy Kamuf (New York: Routledge, 1994); Jacques Derrida, *Writing and Difference* (*WD*), trans. Alan Bass (London: Routledge and Kegan Paul, 1978).

1. Derrida often mentions Levinas and his concerns of thought explicitly, whereas Levinas's dealings with Derrida are mostly of a more implicit and discreet nature. The three most influential texts by Derrida devoted to the writings of Levinas are "Violence and Metaphysics," first published in 1964 and reprinted in *WD*, 79–153; "In This Very Moment in This Work Here I Am," first published in 1980 and reprinted in *Psyche: Interventions of the Other*, vol. 1, trans. Peggy Kamuf et al. (Stanford, CA: Stanford University Press, 2007), 143–90; and Derrida's eulogy "Adieu," delivered at the cemetery of Pantin following the death of Emmanuel Levinas in December 1995, first published in *Libération*, December 28, 1995, and reprinted in *AEL* 1–14.

2. See, for instance, Peter Baker, *Deconstruction and the Ethical Turn* (Gainesville: University of Florida Press, 1995); Simon Critchley, *The Ethics of Deconstruction: Derrida and Levinas* (Edinburgh: Edinburgh University Press, 1999) and *Ethics–Politics–Subjectivity: Essays on Derrida, Levinas, and Contemporary French Thought* (London: Verso, 1999); David Wood, *The Step Back: Ethics and Politics after Deconstruction* (Albany: State University of New York Press, 2005).

3. See Martin Hägglund, *Radical Atheism: Derrida and the Time of Life* (Stanford, CA: Stanford University Press, 2008), 76–106.

4. For an exposition of the possible relevance of Levinas's rendering of trauma to psychotherapeutic practices, see Martin Dornberg, "Trauma und Verwundbarkeit bei E. Levinas und in der Traumatherapie," in *Psycho-logik 3: Jahrbuch für Psychotherapie, Philosophie und Kultur* (Freiburg: Karl Alber, 2008), 195–212.

5. Jacques Derrida, *Without Alibi*, trans. Peggy Kamuf (Stanford, CA: Stanford University Press, 2002), 159.

6. See, for instance, Martin Heidegger, *Sein und Zeit*, vol. 2 of *Gesamtausgabe* (Frankfurt: Klostermann, 1977), 534–77, and *Der Begriff der Zeit*, vol. 64 of *Gesamtausgabe* (Frankfurt: Klostermann, 2004), 77–115.

7. See, for instance, Sigmund Freud, "Project for a Scientific Psychology," vol. 1 of *The Standard Edition of the Complete Psychological Works of Sigmund Freud*, ed. James Strachey (London: Hogarth, 1966), 356; "Further Remarks on the Neuro-Psychoses of Defense (1896)," vol. 3 of *The Standard Edition* (London: Hogarth, 1962), 164–67; "Beyond the Pleasure Principle (1920)," vol. 18 of *The Standard Edition* (London: Hogarth, 1955), 12, 29. Derrida often employs Lacan's translation of *Nachträglichkeit* by *après coup* (see Jacques Lacan, *Écrits* [Paris: Éditions du Seuil, 1966], 256, 839), which is particularly appropriate in the context of trauma since the French *coup* very precisely captures the multiple

meanings of the Greek root of τραῦμα signifying both "a wound," "a hurt," "an injury," as well as "a hard blow." According to Derrida, *Nachträglichkeit* and *Verspätung* are not only key concepts when it comes to Freud's theory of trauma, their significance is far more extensive, so much so that they even come to "govern the whole of Freud's thought and determine all his other concepts" (*WD* 203).

8. See, for example, Freud, "The Uncanny (1919)," vol. 17 of *The Standard Edition* (London: Hogarth Press, 1955), 218, 234–38, and "Beyond the Pleasure Principle," 19ff.

9. See Jacques Derrida, *The Beast and the Sovereign*, vol. 1, trans. Geoffrey Bennington (Chicago: University of Chicago Press, 2009), 38–39.

10. The phrase "the time is out of joint" is from Shakespeare's *Hamlet*, act 1, scene 5, when Hamlet is approached by the ghost of his father who recalls him to his impossible task of rejoining time by avenging an already committed crime, thus exhibiting a certain responsibility to the past which becomes the future of Hamlet. Perhaps the lack of action on Hamlet's part (he never actually gets around to killing the killer of his father) refers to the impossibility of retying the knot of time so as to make past and future join hands. According to Derrida, however, it is not merely in the case of trauma that time is out of joint; rather time is constitutively disjointed *as* time. Concerning the disjointedness of time see Derrida's reading of Heidegger's discussion in "Der Spruch des Anaximander" on the dis-jointure *(Unfug, adikia)* and jointure *(Fug, dike)* of Being (*SOM* 27–32). See also Derrida's discussion of Aristotle's conception of time developed in the fourth book of the *Physics* in "*Ousia* and *Grammē*: Note on a Note from Being and Time," in Jacques Derrida, *Margins of Philosophy*, trans. Alan Bass (Chicago: University of Chicago Press, 1982), 29–68. See also Martin Heidegger, *Holzwege*, vol. 5 of *Gesamtausgabe* (Frankfurt: Klostermann, 1977), 355–73.

11. Jacques Derrida, *Rogues: Two Essays on Reason* (Stanford, CA: Stanford University Press, 2005), 104–05.

12. See *OB* 56, 87–88, 111–22.

13. Jacques Derrida, *Points: Interviews, 1974–1994*, trans. Peggy Kamuf (Stanford, CA: Stanford University Press, 1995), 381. See also Derrida, *Without Alibi*, 159; and Jacques Derrida, "An Interview with Professor Jacques Derrida," interview conducted January 8, 1998, by Michal Ben-Naftali, trans. Moshe Ron, http://www.yadvashem.org/odot_pdf/Microsoft Word-3851.pdf, 2.

14. See Émile Benveniste, *Le vocabulaire des institutions indo-européennes* (Paris: Éditions de Minuit, 1969), 1:87–101.

15. Concerning the aporetic law of hospitality, see the session on "Hostipitality," *AR* 356–420. See also *AEL* 41ff.

16. This traumatism of discourse repeats itself in Levinas's distinction between "the Saying" (*le Dire*) and "the said" (*le dit*) in *Otherwise than Being* and elsewhere, to which we will return further on in this article.

17. Thus Levinas brings to the fore "an irreplaceable oneself [*soi-même*]. Not strictly speaking an ego [*un moi*] set up in the nominative in its identity, but first constrained to.... It is set up as it were in the accusative form, from the first

responsible and not being able to slip away" (*OB* 85, ellipsis in original). We will return to this irreplaceability of the "oneself" in the context of "substitution" in a later section.

18. This "logically absurd" diachrony is unfolded already in *Totality and Infinity* in the context of a discussion concerning Descartes's third *Meditation*. See *TI* 54ff. The third *Meditation* is significant to Levinas because it is where Descartes makes the discovery that the idea of God anachronistically provides the condition for the self-evidence of the cogito, in a similar manner to how the subject called into responsibility becomes aware of the pre-originary infinity of the other always overflowing the very idea of infinity.

19. See *WD* 203. In applying the term "crossed out" (*sous rature*), Derrida is referring to Heidegger's famous movement of reading under erasure developed in "Zur Seinsfrage" (1955). See Martin Heidegger, *Wegmarken*, vol. 9 of *Gesamtausgabe* (Frankfurt: Klostermann, 1976), 385–426.

20. Lewis Carroll, *Alice's Adventures in Wonderland* (Boston: Branden Books, 1948), 10. See also *OB* 150, 162.

21. See Antonin Artaud, *Artaud Anthology*, trans. Jack Hirschman (San Francisco: City Light Books, 1965), 58–59, 226. See also "La parole soufflé," *WD* 169–95.

22. G. W. F. Hegel, *Phenomenology of Spirit*, trans. Arnold V. Miller (Oxford: Oxford University Press, 1977), 407.

23. Jacques Derrida, *Sovereignties in Question*, ed. Thomas Dutoit and Outi Pasanen (New York: Fordham University Press, 2005), 104.

24. See also the essay "No Identity" where Levinas, in reference to the "I am a stranger on earth" of Psalm 119:19, conceives the human condition as follows: "Men seek one another in their incondition of strangers. No one is at home. The memory of that servitude assembles humanity" (*HO* 66).

25. Jacques Derrida, *Archive Fever: A Freudian Impression*, trans. Eric Prenowitz (Chicago: University of Chicago Press, 1998), 79.

26. Derrida designates this structure of mediated intersubjectivity as "the transcendental symmetry of two empirical asymmetries" (*WD* 126).

27. Levinas borrows the terms "transascendence" and "trandescendence" from Jean Wahl's *Existence humaine et transcendance* (Neuchâtel: Éditions de la Baconnière, 1944), 34–56.

28. Levinas introduces the term *illéité* in the transitional time between *Totality and Infinity* in the two successive essays "La trace de l'autre" (1963) and "La signification et le sens" (1964).

29. See, for instance, Paul Ricoeur, *Oneself as Another*, trans. Kathleen Blamey (Chicago: University of Chicago Press, 1992), 337–41; and Michel Haar, "The Obsession of the Other: Ethics as Traumatization," *Philosophy and Social Criticism* 23, no. 6 (1997): 100–06.

30. Hägglund, *Radical Atheism*, 89.

31. Levinas insists on this dissymmetric limitation and its inescapability from his earliest texts, for instance in *On Escape* where he writes of "the fact of being

riveted to oneself, the radical impossibility of fleeing oneself to hide from oneself, the unalterably binding presence of the I to itself" (*OE* 64).

32. Hägglund, *Radical Atheism*, 90.

33. Even if the other is suppressed to the bottom of a social hierarchy, the other is always designated with a certain elevation of height (*hauteur*) and nobility (*noblesse*) (see *TI* 41). However, I do not concur with Hägglund's objection to Levinas's notion of asymmetric substitution, that it can only be upheld if the other is presupposed as being "primordially good," thereby denying or reducing the unpredictable alterity of the other. To my knowledge, Levinas never posits the other as either "good" or "bad." Instead, Levinas posits the primordial *exposure to the other* as a "good violence," which is designated as "good" because it testifies to an impossibility of not responding to the other, whereas other instances of violence stem from the more or less illusory ways of avoiding this unavoidable responsibility, for example by ignoring, reducing, overlooking, or eliminating the other. This originary violent exposure to the other, which is also an exposure to the exposure of the other, certainly does signify a responsibility toward both the high and the low, for example to all the victims of genocides, holocausts, hate crimes, or terrorisms, but its most demanding and perhaps also most traumatizing aspect is that it also signifies a responsibility toward all the perpetrators, offenders, criminals, and terrorists. This is so precisely because responsibility has nothing to do with *choosing* to submit oneself to one or the other or to their particular beliefs or the reasons for their actions. Instead, my responsibility toward the other is unconditional because it exempts no one, no matter under which conditions. I am responsible for everyone despite any normative or axiological judgments I might form about them as being either "good" or "bad" or behaving "well" or "badly."

34. In this regard, Levinas affirms certain aspects of what he calls the "grandeur of modern antihumanism—which is true beyond its own rationale." Accordingly, the "truth" of modern antihumanism "consists in making a clear space for the hostage subjectivity by sweeping away the notion of the person," and by virtue of this clearing antihumanism is right in spite of itself "insofar as humanism is not human enough" (*GDT* 182).

35. Jacques Derrida, "'On Responsibility,' an interview with Jacques Derrida, Jonathan Dronsfield, Nick Midgley and Adrian Wilding, May 1993," *PLI: Warwick Journal of Philosophy* 6 (1997): 27.

36. As Levinas clarifies it in *Otherwise than Being*: "Glory is but the other face of the passivity of the subject.... Inspired by the other, I, the same, am torn up from my beginning in myself, my equality with myself. The glory of the Infinite is glorified in this responsibility. It leaves to the subject no refuge in its secrecy that would protect it from being obsessed by the other, and cover over its evasion" (*OB* 144).

37. In his *The Writing of the Disaster*, Blanchot unfolds this paradoxical structure of substitutional responsibility in Levinas with remarkable clarity: "responsibility, which separates me from myself (from the "me" that is mastery and power,

from the free, speaking subject) and reveals the other *in place* of me, requires that I answer for absence, for passivity. It requires, that is to say, that I answer for the impossibility of being responsible." Maurice Blanchot, *The Writing of the Disaster*, trans. Ann Smock (Lincoln: University of Nebraska Press, 1995), 25.

38. As Derrida further clarifies the impasse of responsibility: "I can respond only to the one (or to the One), that is, to the other, by sacrificing that one to the other. I am responsible to any one (that is to say to any other) only by failing in my responsibilities to all the others, to the ethical or political generality. And I can never justify this sacrifice, I must always hold my peace about it. Whether I want to or not, I can never justify the fact that I prefer or sacrifice any one (any other) to the other." Jacques Derrida, *The Gift of Death*, trans. David Wills (Chicago: University of Chicago Press, 1995), 70.

39. Derrida coins the adjectival term "messianicity" in contrast to any substantive messianism, which latter would wait for some more or less determinable Messiah, in order to account for a radically open-ended awaiting without a horizon of expectation for "the coming of the other, the absolute and unpredictable singularity of the *arrivant as justice*" (*SOM* 33). Likewise, this essentially undetermined and hesitant form of awaiting necessarily opens up to a coming of the unknown that could turn out to have been traumatic. However, as Derrida affirms, this "messianic hesitation does not paralyze any decision, any affirmation, any responsibility. On the contrary, it grants them their elementary condition. It is their very experience" (213).

40. On the subject of this logic of intrusion, see Jean-Luc Nancy, *Corpus*, trans. Richard A. Rand (New York: Fordham University Press, 2008), 161–70.

41. See also the following note of clarification by Levinas in *Humanism of the Other:* "Because, unless one would renounce society and drown in limitless responsibility for others all possibility of answering in fact, one can avoid neither the said, nor letters, nor lofty literature, nor understanding of being, nor philosophy. One cannot do without them if one holds to manifesting to thought—albeit in deforming it—the beyond of being itself. Manifestation at the cost of a betrayal, but necessary to the justice resigned to tradition, continuity, institutions, despite their very infidelity" (*HO* 76n11).

42. As Levinas points out in the context of another work, this statement "refers to the saying that every translation (*traduction*) is a betrayal (*trahison*)" (*OB* 187n3).

43. In calling upon this pious infidelity, I am referring to the ingenious readings of Hölderlin by Philippe Lacoue-Labarthe. In these readings, Lacoue-Labarthe frequently coins the enigmatic thought or structure of a faithful infidelity, which alludes to the "'categorical turning-away' of the divine." See Philippe Lacoue-Labarthe, "Hölderlin's Theatre," in *Philosophy and Tragedy*, ed. Simon Sparks and Miguel de Beistegui (London: Routledge, 2005), 124–30. According to Lacoue-Labarthe, the adherence to the threshold of ambiguity of which Levinas writes becomes possible only by the impossible movement of trying "to be faithful to what tolerates only infidelity." Philippe Lacoue-Labarthe, *The Subject of*

Philosophy, ed. Thomas Trezise, trans. Hugh J. Silverman (Minneapolis: University of Minnesota Press, 1993), 13.

44. For an interesting account of the intricate relationship between the two configurations of transcendent alterity in Levinas, see Kris Sealey, "The 'Face' of the *il y a:* Levinas and Blanchot on Impersonal Existence," *Continental Philosophical Review* 46 (2013): 431–48. See also William S. Allen, "Dead Transcendence: Blanchot, Heidegger, and the Reverse of Language," *Research in Phenomenology* 39, no. 1 (2009): 69–98.

45. Allen, "Dead Transcendence," 77ff.

46. Although I agree with Critchley that the irreducible ambiguity of transcendence is not always in the forefront of Levinas's writing, especially in his early works, I do not think he pays enough attention to Levinas's own hesitations concerning the unidirectionality of transcendence toward the "good." This is the case, for instance, when Critchley writes that "the *il y a* is the shadow or spectre of nonsense that haunts ethical sense *but*—and this is crucial—for Levinas ethical sense cannot, in the final instance, be confused or conflated with an-ethical nonsense. The *il y a* is a threat, but it is a threat that must and can be repelled." Simon Critchley, *Very Little…Almost Nothing* (London: Routledge, 2004), 246n48. As will become clearer in what follows, I am not so certain about Levinas's certainty regarding the avoidance of such confusion.

47. As Blanchot, one of Levinas's most profound readers, emphasizes, "The *there is* is one of Levinas's most fascinating propositions. It is his temptation, too, since as the reverse of transcendence it is thus not distinct from it either." Maurice Blanchot, "Our Clandestine Companion," in *Face to Face with Levinas,* ed. Richard A. Cohen (New York: State University of New York Press, 1986), 49.

48. Levinas explains: "For this formula 'transcendence to the point of absence' not to mean the simple explicitation of an ex-ceptional word, this word itself has to be put back into the significance of the whole plot of the ethical or back into the divine comedy without which it could not have arisen. That comedy is enacted equivocally between temple and theater, but in it the laughter sticks to one's throat when the neighbor approaches—that is, when his face, or his forsakenness, draws near" (*BPW* 141).

49. In this regard, Levinas is paying tribute to Derrida's work when he affirms that "what appears truly in deconstructive analysis as a lacking to self is not *the surplus* (which would be yet another promise of happiness and a residuum of ontology) but the *better* [*le mieux*] of proximity, an excellence, an elevation, the ethics of before being or the Good beyond Being" (*PN* 61).

50. The formulation of a "blinding alterity" is borrowed from Lacoue-Labarthe's text "The Fable," where he writes of "an almost unthinkable movement" that, to some extent, resembles the subject becoming hostage in *Otherwise than Being,* that is, "a kind of turning inside out by which we would move to that outside of ourselves which is already our interiority, by which we would no longer be either 'outside' or 'inside,' but would experience our intimacy as that

blinding alterity forever beyond us and to which nevertheless we are destined." Lacoue-Labarthe, *The Subject of Philosophy*, 12.

51. See *WD* 230.

52. Elsewhere, Derrida calls this unconditional condition of responsibility the "law of finitude," which designates in its turn the "law of decision and responsibility for finite existences, the only living-mortals for whom a decision, a choice, a responsibility has meaning and a meaning that will have to pass through the ordeal of the undecidable" (*SOM* 109).

53. Reiner Schürmann, *Broken Hegemonies*, trans. Reginald Lilly (Bloomington: Indiana University Press, 2003), 27.

54. Maurice Blanchot, *The Step Not Beyond*, trans. Lycette Nelson (Albany: State University of New York Press, 1992), 108.

"Flipping the Deck"

On *Totality and Infinity*'s Transcendental/Empirical Puzzle

Jack Marsh

How does one perceive a transcendental condition?
— Martin Kavka

...if it is legitimate to hold Levinas to the standards that he himself imposes on certain other philosophers.
— Robert Bernasconi

I do not believe that there is a transparency possible in method. Nor that philosophy might be possible as transparency.
— Emmanuel Levinas

The question of the precise methodological status of the face has yet to be satisfactorily resolved. The best evidence for this claim perhaps lies in texts intended to introduce Levinas to a general philosophical audience. If even first-rate philosophers wrestle still with the puzzle *Totality and Infinity* bequeaths us, we seem to still await a full and precise diagnosis. For example, Michael Morgan holds the "face-to-face and the responsible self — they are one thing characterized from two perspectives — are" "the transcendental condition for meaningful human life," yet elsewhere concedes, "it is unavoidable that in some sense or other the face-to-face does occur as an actually lived experience." If Morgan's own nuanced treatment of this question still lands him in equivocation, the problem is certainly *not* Morgan's own.[1] As Atterton notes, Morgan must finally hold that Levinas's method is a "transcendental enterprise *of a certain sort.*"[2] But of what sort? Indeed, this question has been asked or analyzed in one way or another from the beginning of *Totality and Infinity*'s English-language reception.[3] Of course, Derrida was the first to broach the question of *Totality and Infinity*'s general intelligibility, alleging that Levinas ultimately succumbs to a form of empiricism. Of course, de Boer was the first to mount a rigorous Cartesian reading of the text as an (apparently) "ethical transcendental philosophy." Of course, Bernasconi's response to de Boer, and his creative repetition of Derrida's critical point, was the first to give the problem a precise formulation.[4] Derrida, de Boer, and Bernasconi hand us the now canonical problem of what I will call the text's "transcendental/empirico-metaphysical puzzle."[5] The issue boils down to Levinas's dual insistence that the face "cannot... be stated in terms of experience," yet is nevertheless "reflected *within* experience" (*TI* 25, 23, 67, 260). How should we understand Levinas's references to various "formal structure[s]" — "of language," "of interpellation," "of the idea of infinity" — next to talk of "pure" or "concrete moral experience" (195, 79, 64, 53)? Does the Other occur in "pure experience," or is she "deduced" as a condition of possibility for experience in general? In this essay, I will propose an internal *explanation* for *Totality and Infinity*'s longstanding methodological puzzle. By proposing to "explain" this puzzle, I am making at least three distinct claims: to show (1) *that* the text suffers from genuine incoherence, thus confirming the general criticism of Derrida, Bernasconi, and others, (2) precisely *how* this incoherence follows from the details of Levinas's own explicit method, and (3) precisely *why*, philosophically, he may have constructed and performed his method as he did.[6] By proposing to *explain* the book's incoherence, I can also make specific hermeneutic predictions. If *Totality and Infinity*'s transcendental/empirico-metaphysical puzzle is genuinely aporetic, it follows that no resolution to it is possible on the text's own terms.[7] As such, any attempt to resolve the puzzle must either (1) augment the text's own descriptions, (2) utilize other philosophical resources to render its claims coherent, or (3) precisely attempt resolution in either a transcendental or empirico-metaphysical direction. As it turns out, extant scholarship reflects just these hermeneutic strategies.

Over the years many philosophers have contributed to this longstanding debate, variously arguing for or against the general intelligibility of Levinas's account of the face. On the one hand, scholarship that questions the text's intelligibility does so from a variety of methodological perspectives.[8] On the other hand, scholarship that mounts a defense of the text seems to proceed in one of three ways: by (1) apparently repeating *Totality and Infinity*'s methodological problems, (2) anticipating Levinas's later work, read to rectify these problems, or (3) utilizing other philosophical resources in an attempt to render its arguments coherent. I will set the first two aside, since the relevant scholarship is either subject to my impending criticism, or rests on a reading of Levinas's late work. Scholarship that utilizes other resources precisely reflects the above predictions by either augmenting or going outside the text, and tends to resolve in either a transcendental or empirico-metaphysical way. As one might expect, empirico-metaphysical coherence strategies tend to downplay Levinas's appeals to purely formal structures, and invariably utilize one or another type of quasi-realist *logic*. Theodore de Boer and John Drabinski present spirited and rigorous coherence strategies in precisely this form.[9] And as one might expect, transcendental coherence strategies tend to take either Kantian or Husserlian form. In Kantian form, transcendental readings of the face understandably downplay or ignore Levinas's reference to "experience" by stressing the cognitive *meaning* of the face.[10] In Husserlian form, transcendental readings tend to re-outfit talk of "experience" to align with the affective/perceptual dimensions of phenomenological-constitutive processes.[11] Martin Kavka and Steven

Crowell present spirited and rigorous coherence strategies in these general directions. Beyond extant scholarship, Levinas himself seems to circulate between transcendental and empirico-metaphysical readings of his own work. For example, in his interview with Emmanuel Hirsch, Levinas holds, "but I like to insist...on the primordial *intellectual* role of alterity," and "to *think* the other as other, to *think* him or her straightaway before affirming oneself, signifies concretely to have goodness" (*IR* 105, 106; my emphasis). By contrast, in an interview with Florian Rötzer, he holds, "Responsibility for the other is *the experience* of the good, the very meaning of the good, goodness. Only goodness is good." (135; my emphasis). What is ultimately interesting in both Levinas's self-interpretation and the above coherence strategies comes down to this: transcendental strategies must ultimately sacrifice the text's plain empirico-metaphysical claims to either transcendental *Life* (Crowell) or transcendental *Ideas* (Kavka), and either way give up his explicit appeals to *pure bodies* allegedly "exterior" to theory. Likewise, empirico-metaphysical strategies must ultimately sacrifice the text's own transcendental claims to either a theistic (de Boer) or materialist (Drabinski) *logic,* and either way give up Levinas's appeals to *pure meanings* allegedly "exterior" to thought. The *only* way to keep both *pure* "exterior" *bodies* and *pure* "exterior" *meaning* is to "flip the deck."

Fig. 1. "Poker Dealer," by Daniel Chichester, 2015.

By way of introduction, a good metaphor for grasping *Totality and Infinity*'s circularity is something like the "deck-flipping" of a poker dealer. As in the above photo: the "other" remains stable and outside the series of cards (the ace of spades in figure 1). On the one hand, when Levinas or Levinasians are faced with criticism of the text's explicit empirico-metaphysical language, they "flip the deck" to the language of transcendental "condition of possibility," "deduction," "not an experience," etc. (*TI* 27, 28, 25). On the other hand, when Levinas or Levinasians are faced with anti-formalist, anti-transcendental criticism, they "flip the deck" back again, using quasi-realist language of "pure experience," "pure sensation," "pure qualit[ies]," and the critique of "pure thought" (67, 187, 136, 27). Back and forth, either way, the Other remains outside the series, and at either end of the flip always appears as the "first." As Levinas performs this deck-flipping, he is performing something like a gestalt switch: the Other, its structural status, and alleged determinative meaning, remains stable (remains atop the deck and guides the flip either way), while the surrounding logical and justificatory infrastructure is transformed, here utilizing formal-transcendental claims to describe and justify his position, there using empirico-metaphysical claims to do so. On one pole, the Other is construed as *transcendent fact,* on the other pole, the Other is construed as *transcendental idea*. One reason *Totality and Infinity*'s transcendental/empirico-metaphysical question remains a puzzle, and hard to sort out, is that the respective methodological infrastructures he is switching between are each relatively coherent, and the deck-flipping in play is premised in a phenomenological vocabulary that lend his claims *prima facie* plausibility. With notable exceptions, the entire tradition of Levinas scholarship simply circulates within this circle and repeats its game, deploying one or the other descriptive/justificatory discourse depending on the type of criticism being addressed.[12] There is textual support for both transcendental and empirico-metaphysical readings, and this is the entire problem. There are no resources within Levinas's text to resolve the puzzle or adjudicate the question, because it is *built into* his explicit method.¹³ As I will shortly show, *Totality and Infinity*'s explicit account of theory is viciously indeterminate. This indeterminacy empowers his "flipping," making it hard to initially detect, and ultimately renders some of his central claims arbitrary.

Given the history of Levinas scholarship and the prevailing interpretive consensus that seems to dominate the general presentation of Levinas's philosophy, it's not enough for me to simply point to the circularity through purely textual analysis. Indeed, if the general criticisms of Derrida, Bernasconi, and others have failed to provoke a thorough reckoning, my more detailed diagnosis would likely fare no better. If I stop at textual analysis, I might be accused of "misunderstanding" what Levinas is up to, perhaps in such a way that my critic simply repeats the problem I'm treating. I would therefore fail to clarify *Totality and Infinity*'s methodological puzzle, as is my aim. To avoid this, I must render the circularity more fully transparent at the precise level of its structural function, rather than *only* at important, though nevertheless particular, moments of its performance in Levinas's actual descriptions. My "flipping the deck" metaphor, and the logico-justificatory gestalt "switching" it tracks, nicely captures my proposal for how the puzzle might be properly understood, but to fill out this proposal requires at least two further tasks.

First, beyond only confirming *that* the text suffers incoherence, I must show—precisely and in detail—*how* this incoherence is *built into* its own methodological construction(s). Next, if my proposed "deck-flipping" description is accurate, and if this accuracy is fully established by detailed methodological analysis, I must finally propose a textually plausible reason for *why* Levinas constructed and performed his method as he did. Only by confirming *that*, showing *how*, and proposing *why* can my "deck-flipping" metaphor move beyond rough description to a more *precise explanation* of *Totality and Infinity*'s transcendental/empirico-metaphysical puzzle.

FACT OR IDEA?

Why fact or idea? As I will show in more detail, Levinas himself forces this question on us. He everywhere claims that any "third term" or mediating structure does "violence" to the alterity of the other and the singularity of the self.[14] This assertion renders *all* discourse, in general and as such, guilty of "violence." This suggests to me that there is something wrong with the claim that concepts are "violent" per se. But given the serious consideration granted this assumption in extant scholarship, simply rejecting the claim outright is not enough. For this reason, and by the fact that Levinas himself explicitly rejects all mediation, his own logic forces this question on us: is the Other a *transcendent fact* or *transcendental idea?* This guiding question pushes the intrinsic equivocalness of Levinas's method into the open. Levinas is quite clearly using both Kantian and empirico-metaphysical vocabulary within his phenomenological debate with Husserl and Heidegger. This is the entire problem. If I were to tell a long and complicated story about Husserl's categorial intuition, his subsequent embrace of transcendental idealism to fully twist free from the psychologism controversy that haunts his "realist" phase,[15] Heidegger's rejection of this neo-Kantian debate through creative use of categorial intuition in his own transcendental ontology, and Levinas's attempt to outgun Heidegger, no clarification of *Totality and Infinity*'s methodological puzzle will have taken place. Levinas's own explicit method is summoned *against* Husserl and Heidegger, and wielded *against* the entire tradition. His method proceeds as just the "deck-flipping" I'm proposing, and therefore no question-begging comparisons to Husserl or Heidegger's work can ameliorate the problem.[16] In other words, Levinas's method must be evaluated on its own terms.

Levinas between Realism and Idealism

Levinas explicitly claims that his "analyses are guided by a formal structure: the idea of Infinity in us" (*TI* 79). The idea of the infinite is unique, since it implies that "content overflow[s] the container" for finite minds (204). Now, Levinas also insists that "the formal structure of language... announces the ethical inviolability of the Other" (195). How do the formal structure of "the idea of Infinity in us" and "the formal structure of language" relate? The answer to this question constitutes nearly the entire story *Totality and Infinity* has to tell. These two formal structures are related by what Levinas calls "the formal structure of interpellation" (69) or what he'll come to call *discourse* (64–65). As it turns out, interpellation is described as not *only* a formal structure. Levinas's account of discourse is just his description of the face, where the idea of the infinite is allegedly "put into me" (see 26, 86; *EI* 91). The face is presented as "pure experience," or as an event a purely passive and sensible ego *undergoes* (*TI* 67, 260). How are we to interpret these references to "formal structure" and "pure experience"? Let's consider.

Now, if "discourse" is inherent to the "formal structure of language," then my interlocutor is a necessary and irreducible *element* of this structure. Here, *all* Levinas's descriptive rhetoric is precisely what he claims it is *not*: "empirical and contingent data, laid over [a] formal skeleton" (*TI* 38). Here, *all* empirical faces are *instantiations* of the interlocutor pole of the formal structure of discourse, and this discourse structure supplies *norms* that *universally* govern *all* language users. In the order of *fact* (for example, natural history), the discourse structure comes late. In the order of *meaning*, the discourse structure comes first (e.g., we can't do biology without supposing discursive norms, scientific practice refers to them). Interlocutors remain, of course, "other," but only in a relative sense determined by the discourse structure itself, apparently inherent to and constitutive of the "formal structure of language." Adding content to this structure, or any worldly instance of discourse, does not and *cannot* alter it, since this structure and its norms are necessarily presupposed in any conversation. At the absolute minimum, this is what it means to be a transcendental structure. Whenever Levinas or Levinasians talk of "ethical *transcendental* conditions," this is what they are actually summoning, protestations to the contrary notwithstanding. If, on the other hand, "the formal structure of language" is *dependent* on the idea of infinity, and if further the idea of infinity is "*put into me*," then, indeed, talk of the face, "pure experience," "breaking up of [merely] formal [thought] structures," etc. does not merely involve "empirical and contingent data, laid over [a] formal skeleton," but describes or articulates a genuine metaphysical event occurring in remote (biographical or historical) yesteryear, accessible via reconstructive abstraction through some form of "real," as opposed to purely conceptual, relation. In this case, discourse is not *only* a formal concept, but is derived from the "fact" of the Infinite, the "fact" of its idea "being put into" finite minds, and the affective "fact" of the Infinite's "manifestation" in actual faces and speech contexts. On the one hand, if the "formal structure of language" is a counterfactual transcendental discourse structure, then *thought determines being*, that is, discursive norms do not rely on any particular description of how the world stands for their validity. On the other hand, if the "formal structure of language" is *dependent* on specific metaphysical facts and experiences, then *being determines thought*, that is, discursive norms are grounded in a higher-order moral realism (say, natural law, objective virtues, religious ethics, etc.) embedded in higher-order accounts of our empirico-metaphysical nature. Some suitably mediating positions, wherein norms are sensitive to their contexts of application and "facts" are sensitive to competing interpretations, are just that: *mediating*, that is, inevitably involving either deliberative or hermeneutic infrastructures where the relation between fact and norm is explicitly rendered, and where others remain *relative* as either *co*-performers or *co*-determinants of the relevant infrastructure.[17] What must be noticed here is that, in both cases, all selves and others are held subject to universally valid norms, and come to be descriptively/conceptually mediated in a variety of different ways (biologically, culturally, etc.). In both cases, some kind of normatively governed account of *freedom* is in play. Has Levinas given moral realists, Kantian constructivists, or hermeneutic phenomenologists good reasons to adopt his position? Probably not, and precisely because his method appears arbitrary and equivocates on questions central to meta-ethical and philosophical debate. As we are about to see in more detail, Levinas clearly "flips the deck," leaps back and forth between idealist and realist justificatory/descriptive vocabulary throughout the text, and by excluding any mediating structure he leaves himself no means to render his circle virtuous. If we try to adjudicate *Totality and Infinity*'s puzzle in light of what transcendental and realist moral philosophy are, variations of what I roughly describe here are our fundamental choices.

LEVINAS'S METHOD: "OVERFLOWING" CONCEPTS

The key to Levinas's whole method is packed into his notion of "the overflowing of concretization," of "the overflowing of finite thought by...content," of "content overflowing the container," or in short, "[content] overflows the concept" (*TI* 153, 49, 197, 204, 41). Such constitutes the core of his intrinsically equivocal method and renders his "deck-flipping" possible. "Overflowing," "surplus," "exceed" and their cognates occur some 60 times throughout *Totality and Infinity*. As with nearly every other key term in the text, Levinas's use is not always consistent. But, in general, Levinas uses these notions to specify moments where concepts don't or can't do all the semantic work. The paradigmatic instance of "content overflowing the concept" is, of course, the idea of the infinite. But he also uses this notion in his ego analysis. Here is a sample of typical uses:

> This sinking one's teeth into the things which the act of eating involves above all measures the surplus of the reality of the aliment over every represented reality. (129)

> The event of dwelling exceeds the knowing, the thought, and the idea in which, after the event, the subject will want to contain what is incommensurable with a knowing. (153)

> Infinity is transcendence itself, the overflowing of an adequate idea. (80)

> What counts is the idea of the overflowing of objectifying thought by a forgotten experience from which it lives. (28)

Whenever Levinas attacks idealism, he always in some way refers to "overflowing," "surplus," or "exceeds." In each case, it seems intended to distinguish between the *lived immediacy of "real" experience* over against mere reflection on or communication about this experience. If we subtract the "overflowing" from "contents overflowing concepts," for example, by thinking of or talking about our experience, the immediacy is lost. His various talk of overflowing is at the basis of his claim that thought distorts, and that conceptuality is "violent." In its methodological function, "overflowing" fundamentally means *sensible force in the lived moment,* "an ultimate relation with the substantial plenitude of being," or "manifestation…over and beyond form" (*TI* 133, 66).

Unfortunately, this distinction can't do what Levinas wants it to do. No one doubts that thinking of or talking about having fun isn't necessarily *to be having fun*. Levinas's critique of idealism is premised in attributing what amounts to subjective metaphysical idealism to Kant and Husserl, and his critique of ontology is premised in attributing a precritical conceptual determinism to Heidegger. Here, constitution means something like full-fledged *creation,* where an idealist Subject or impersonal Being fully "create" the objects or entities they constitute. In opposition to these straw men, Levinas must and does posit a naked empirical reality populated by all sorts of self-standing entities merely awaiting egoic notice. He uses a general distinction between thought and experience to *posit rules* held to determine logically distinct meaning-domains, such that he can assert, on four separate occasions, in four separate contexts, that *x* "does not belong to the order of" *y* (*TI* 101, 135, 161, 172). Clearly, simply describing an uncontroversial difference between an event of thinking and an event of fun doesn't justify the controversial claim that enjoyment is "transcendentally" prior to thought. While I can certainly enjoy thinking, it is by no means clear that enjoyment structurally and necessarily orients thinking in general. Why do I still engage in thought when I am *not* enjoying it, or when it causes me suffering? If "enjoyment…[truly] does not belong to the order of thought" (135), then Levinas himself could not have written *Totality and Infinity*. Enjoyment would remain simply and wholly inaccessible to thought: *not thinkable or communicable at all*. If "the order of enjoyment," as opposed to thought, only specifies a difference between actual moments of enjoyment and reflection on those moments, then Levinas has failed to constitute a truly distinct meaning domain. He is doing something else, for example, classifying types of experience. Mere classification does not justify his claim that sensibility "is incommensurable with a knowing" (153), nor does it institute a legitimate rule for what can or can't count as knowing.[18] Indeed, a relatively determinate account of knowledge is what *Totality and Infinity* fundamentally *lacks*. Sensibility must rely on either mind or world—or mind *and* world—to ultimately discriminate between types of experience or particular regions of meaning. Levinas wants moral sensibility to do the primary and orienting labor, but clearly such meaning must fundamentally suppose either structures of mind or structures of world to do its semantic work. Some suitably interactionist position, where mind and world are co-constituting or reciprocally determinative, necessarily requires categorial or conceptual mediation, and therefore precludes access to putatively "absolute" singularities or alterities. While Kant distinguishes between theory and practice and grants the latter priority, *both* are *cognitive* in nature, that is, Kant discriminates between different kinds of meaning, but *finite mind* is what ultimately does the discriminating in its original relation to the world. While Heidegger grants priority to practice over theory, he *actually describes* how this priority functions, and lays out the ontic-transcendental structures that render this priority describable. Unlike Kant or Heidegger, Levinas's own construal of meaning in terms of "content overflowing concepts" allows him to equivocate on what does the philosophically determinative work: here pointing to ideas, there pointing to sensible force, as what ultimately constitutes or validates meaning. Levinas's own account of theory never *precisely* specifies *how* meaning is constituted, or *how* pre-theoretical meaning opens upon the theoretical.[19] Content overflowing concepts points to being/experience and thought/concept—structures of *world* and structures of *mind—at once,* couched in a *simultaneous* rejection of all mediation.[20] In the midst of Levinas's anti-concept polemic, his own "contents overflowing concepts" invariably utilizes concepts. Consider: "the idea of Infinity is transcendence itself, the overflowing of an adequate idea" (*TI* 80). This implies that transcendence is *more*, not *less*, than adequate. If "overflowing" simply means the sheer presence of *sensible/affective force,* then adequation, here, is still the determinant of *truth*.[21] For example, tomorrow I intend to go to the pub and have a rollicking good time. I intend to do this because the last three times I went to the pub, I in fact had a rollicking good time. If tomorrow I *fail* to have rollicking good time, my expectations will have been *unfulfilled,* and I'll judge the experience *inadequate*. Clearly, the presence, absence, or intensity of a particular "affective moment" doesn't *ruin* or contest adequation, but precisely supplies the *norm* by which I judge subsequent experiences as more or less adequate. On reflection, I might identify a reason for this failure: say, I was thinking too much about Levinas's description of enjoyment instead of letting myself loose in the moment. In this case, a particular episode of thinking has short-circuited my intention to enjoy, but this clearly in no way challenges the accessibility of enjoyment to thought, or renders thought less necessary because it is not in each case pure enjoyment. The whole episode *supposes* the *memory* and *anticipation* without which I would be constitutively unable to *know* that I ever have, or ever will, enjoy. Levinas's attempt to define the ego as just its immediate enjoyment—as pure instant in the moment—fails to actually exhibit the *transcendental* "priority" of sensibility to thought.

The *same* goes for the "other." When I converse with another human face, I necessarily hold either culturally mediated assumptions or reflectively held commitments that *prestructure* what and who my interlocutor *is*. What can it mean to claim that the "affective force" of my interlocutor's sheer presence *contests* these assumptions or commitments? How might this "overflowing" show my preconceptions to be *inadequate*? If my interlocutor insistently and earnestly *tells me* "I am a god," he would straight away fail to *fulfill* my expectation of, say, rationality. I would judge him to be insane and in need of psychiatric care. If my interlocutor proceeded to demonstrate his divinity claim by, say, flying around the room, bodily dematerializing and rematerializing, recounting to me all my deep, dark secrets, or causing a stack of money to materialize out of thin air, I would initially assume that *I am insane,* either hallucinating or dreaming. But if my life continued on in its otherwise normal rhythm, if a bank validated the magic money he bequeathed me, if I introduced him to my wife, friends, and Daniel Dennett, and they, too, after repeated observation and due consideration, agreed he really is more than human, my preconceptions will have been veritably *contested*. They would be *altered*. I would continue on expecting merely human interlocutors to behave and speak in anticipated ways, while admitting a whole new class of potentially divine interlocutors, and revise my ontology accordingly. The purchase, here, is that "content overflowing concepts"—*all by itself*—does absolutely *nothing* to contest ontology, concept inclusion, or the mediations involved in any particular face-to-face encounter. An interlocutor might behave or talk in unexpected ways, but they nevertheless *act* and *speak*. She or he is a living body, born of a mother, becomes a relationally autonomous actor capable of intentional movement, a language user capable of giving reasons, etc. Her or his experiences and choices are ultimately their own, but this ownness does not solely issue from an indeterminate vortex of pure qualities, nor do I become aware of their ownness by tilting my ear while earnestly squinting at their face. For a face to actually contest either my conventional assumptions or reflectively held commitments, she or he must either *perform* a subversion of them (like our potentially divine magician), or *argue for* and exemplify a better set of commitments. Without performatively or thematically *showing me* that my expectations are wrong, indifferent, unethical, or unreasonable, my expectations are in each case *fulfilled*. I fully endorse Levinas's desire to grant interlocutors their originality, but arbitrarily positing a purely immediate "absolute" alterity does not get the job done. Recognizing the other's originality *supposes* the *memory* and *anticipation* without which I would be constitutively unable to *know* that I ever was, or ever will be, contested. Levinas's attempt to present the other as just its immediate presence fails to actually exhibit the *real* "priority" of sensibility to thought.

Now, I expect my Levinasian friends might chime in here and claim I simply "misunderstand" his claims. For example, they might say something like this: "The question is: what makes your intention to go to the pub possible? What must be presupposed by intentionality as such? The face is an answer to this question. Levinas is ultimately claiming (1) Your enjoyment is who you are, and by this meaning you *utilize* thought to seek and repeat happiness as an end. You can't have fun by sheer will. In just this way, sensibility is prior to thought. In your above example, you intend to go to the pub in order to have fun, not, say, to sell popcorn or perform sociological observation. (2) Your divine magician perfectly exemplifies Levinas's point. He burst the bounds of your expectations. Every interlocutor intimates just this sort of unpredictability, and its sense is primarily moral. Moreover, revising your ontological assumptions does *not* revise your moral presuppositions. If your divine magician used his power to murder and enslave, you would rightly conclude he is evil. The face gives us an unalterable ethical transcendental principle, a necessary presupposition that structures all discourse, even discourse with a putative divinity. The unpredictability and moral sensibility of the face make this, and all intentionality, possible. We can choose to ignore this fact through indifference or exploitation, but it remains a fact. In just this way, ethics is prior to ontology."

To the first point: Selling popcorn and performing sociological observation are available possibilities. Enjoyment *alone* doesn't motivate *all* my acts and is not the totality of what I am. I like enjoying. I like the rare moments of contentment that visit me. Enjoyment and contentment do partly motivate my various activities, but they cannot do all the motivating work. Why do I continue on in whatever activity when I am *not* enjoying it, or when it causes me *dis*contentment? At the end of the day, because I strive to achieve creative and moral excellence, to live a good life. In this light, Levinas's ego analysis is quite inadequate. My intentionality presupposes historically mediated and socially constituted contexts of motivation and the contestable self-conceptions they involve. Sensibility is one aspect, but not the entirety, of these contexts. Levinas's ego analysis seems explicitly intended to set the stage in such a way that "absolute alterity" talk can appear plausible. However salient some of his particular analyses might be, they do not rectify the severe problems I diagnose here. If enjoyment doesn't constitute the totality of my motivation, then Levinas's claims remain unvindicated. Simply setting aside sociality as wholly irrelevant to our sense of identity, only to admit it late on the basis of "absolute alterity," seems artificial and strategic, rather than phenomenologically disinterested and justified.[22]

To the second point: But your rejoinder doesn't touch the central issue. Your own claims imply that the otherness of the other is *not* "absolute." I can judge our divine magician's acts by what are taken to be *universally* valid norms. If our putatively divine entity can be *subject* to normative moral evaluation, then unlike a cat, a rose, or the Grand Canyon, s/he is the sort of entity susceptible to such evaluation, that is, an *intentional being*. Levinas's talk of "asymmetry" is an exotic way of saying that the binding force of norms is not contingent on whether others treat me in kind, or according to the same normative light. I happily grant this point, without granting the arbitrary claim that norms spring whole from our affects, or that they are purely and unilaterally imposed. Your "unpredictability" claim brings my own point into relief: I *expect* others to act variously, and this expectation is not purely normative but mediated by various natural, cultural, and ontological notions on *who* human beings are. The best descriptions grant relational, normatively governed autonomy to human beings and individual language users, and the capacity for (relatively) creative self-determination this involves. But even this is always in some way embedded in larger assumptions or reflectively held commitments on how the world stands. Norms don't depend on these descriptions for their validity, but neither is it possible to simply abstain from description. Since Levinas himself cannot and does not avoid it, why suppose that conceptual mediation is violent? In *Totality and Infinity,* Levinas tries to *thematize* the difference between self and other as purely and sublimely moral, and this seems a transparent attempt to a priori exclude all competing ontologies. It works like this: concepts are violent, therefore ontology is violent, and therefore any descriptive attribution of *common* properties or capacities is violent. Levinas can label any interlocutor he might debate as "immoral" by reference to his or her own brute and passive individuality, rather than listening to what they say, and arguing with them, or watching what they do, and revising his picture of the human in its light.[23] What is sold as "respect for the other" in fact gives a basis for simply ignoring others, or worse: accusing them before they even speak. Of course, Levinas himself must assume common properties or capacities; for example, language use. On his own terms, if it were not for the communicative dimension, all mammals would be faces. Of course, positing "absolute alterity" and using it to build a concept of humanity has the following, quite convenient, implications: he can charge all comers (everyone but skeptics and Levinasians) with "violence," while at the same time using "alterity" to *define* an identity ("humanity"). This is contradictory and arbitrary. He can always claim that what humans share is merely contingent to what we truly are as individuals: "absolutely other." Positing "absolute alterity" as both a critical and constructive notion places him in a bind: if we take his critical use seriously, he is not entitled to use alterity to positively construct concepts, even a concept of humanity. If he is entitled to mediate alterity in positive concept construction, then it cannot be the case that *pure* alterity is a useful critical concept. Levinas's "deck-flipping" is precisely an attempt to skirt this issue. It necessarily involves performative contradiction on his own terms. As Derrida noted, Levinas forces us to choose between respecting "absolute alterity" and performing "violence" by mere speech. I reject that choice. The very nature of the choice tells me the problem lies in Levinas's claims, not in concept use *per se*. Simply setting aside our conceptual capacities as wholly irrelevant to our sense of being obligated, only to admit them later on the basis of "absolute alterity," seems artificial and strategic, rather than phenomenologically disinterested and justified.

Levinas's Method: "Reversing" Constitution

Levinas's "deck-flipping" comes to light in this question: is the face a transcendent *fact* or a transcendental *idea*? Since he principally excludes all mediation, he simply switches back and forth throughout the text, here suggesting moral-metaphysical realism, there suggesting transcendental formalism. The methodological hinge of this switch is "the process of constitution...is reversed" (*TI* 128), or what he sometimes calls "deformalization."[24] In order to get the gist of what "reversing constitution" might mean, I must briefly say something about constitution. To brutally oversimplify, constitution is a complex act in which the objects I intend can be recognized and re-identified. As I look at the teacup beside me, I only see a profile. Were I to continually rotate it, I would only ever see profiles. What allows me to grasp the teacup as a *whole* and not merely a succession of profiles? What allows me to recognize any future teacup I might encounter *as* a teacup? What allows me to spontaneously *know* that my teacup and this glass of water "fit" together in a way my teacup and computer don't? Constitution, or the mind's activity of rounding out, organizing, and relating perceptual content. For our purposes here, it's sufficient to know that constitution empowers the re-identifiability of anything I might encounter in the world, that is, that the relations in play are ultimately *minded achievements, not* necessarily sewn into the fabric of the world. When Levinas talks of "reversing" constitution or "deformalizing" various objects, he means something like this: *this* apple is "reversed" from "fuel-object" to something yummily enjoyed, "reversed" from an instance of a kind to "sweet nectar I devour," etc. Of course, this presents no fundamental challenge to Husserl or Kant. It rather creates intractable problems for Levinas's position. His term for what we find at the other end of this "deformalizing reversal" is *substance*. Presumably, he's making use (in phenomenological translation?) of Aristotle's "substance," that is, "real" individuals.

> [Affective contents are] distinct from my substance but constitut[e] it. (112)

> The sensible quality already clings to a substance. (137)[25]

On Levinas's view, all the things and elements I enjoy "constitute" my lived sense of wholeness and identity, that is, my "substance." And when I move from immediate enjoyment to dwelling and labor, the "*pure* qualities" I enjoy are attributed "substance," or that which makes them recognizable and re-identifiable as what they *are* (TI 188–89; my emphasis). The problem is clear. He is presenting what we might call a *seesaw* theory of constitution: reversing constitution and deformalizing concepts terminates in an "overflowing" sensible/affective force shot from "real" bodies through allegedly "pure" qualities. Are wholes sewn into the fabric of the world, such that we grasp them by inference or by "discovery" of "real" relations? Or are wholes rather the constituted achievement of minded activity? Levinas asserts the former *and* the latter *simultaneously*, couched in a concurrent rejection of all mediation. On his own descriptions, deformalization (1) *starts with* concepts, (2) "reverses" to "real" bodies and qualities interposing a temporal gap between affection and thought, yet nevertheless (3) retains "the possibility of a representation that is constitutive" (169). Clearly, he is dancing in a question-begging circle. On his own terms, faces *must* initially be posited as wholes in order for "overflowing containers" to work. In just this way, ethics *depends* on either mind or world—or mind *and* world—to supply a form to "exceed." Clearly, he is "flipping the deck": in reversing the process of constitution, the constitut*ing* becomes the constitut*ed*. "Thinking constitutes objects" becomes "experienced objects constitute thinkers."

> [The ego's] needs...affirm "exteriority" as non-constituted, prior to all affirmation. (127)

> The epiphany that is produced as a face is not constituted. (207)

In both of these cases, "overflowing" as the real presence of sensible/affective force is at the basis of his claims for nonconstitution. Whenever an *x* the ego experiences or encounters is "non-constituted," it becomes what does the constituting and is given a different label ("enjoyment," "ethics"). Whenever Levinas summons "overflowing," "surplus," or "exceeds," he is summoning empirical bodies, fully accessible "real" individuals, and some unspecified "real" relation, while nevertheless couching his meaning claims in phenomenological terms. When this point apparently occurs to him, Levinas then arbitrarily leaps to idealism: sensibility "conditions every empiricism and the very structure of the fact imposed on contemplation" (*TI* 157). He must commit to either the realist, psychologistic account of the genesis of the ego he actually performs, and specify the relations involved, or simply accept that for sensibility to signify it must rely on and pass through either determining acts of consciousness or determinative ontological structures. What he can't do is what he does: simultaneously entitle himself to plainly realist claims utilized against phenomenological constitution, while also utilizing phenomenological constitution against the realism he actually performs. To sheerly assert the ego's indifference to questions of "theory," or merely summon the standpoint under description, is to beg the question. Either transcendental constitution is working behind the naive ego's back, or there is some form of "real" determination going on (as his own descriptions imply).[26] Some of the most nearly nonsensical passages of *Totality and Infinity* are precisely those that try to tackle this problem head on. For example, "the possibility of a representation that is constitutive but already rests on the enjoyment of a real completely constituted" (169). If constitution means one thing here (conferring re-identifiability), then this sentence is plainly nonsensical. If he intends constitution in different senses, he should tell us what they are. Levinas's entire method is premised in a systematic failure to distinguish between *real* and *transcendental* conditionality, *real* and *transcendental* genesis. When attacking Husserl or Kant, real conditionality is summoned against the transcendental. When attacking Heidegger or Aristotle, transcendental conditionality is summoned against the real. When he's responding to critics, the face is presented either as a transcendent *fact* or transcendental *idea* depending on the question being posed.

Levinas's Method: "Theory"

Beyond "overflowing" and "reversal," Levinas's explicit account(s) of theory exhibit just the sort of equivocity one would expect if my reading of *Totality and Infinity* were right:

> Knowledge or theory designates first a relation with being such that the knowing being lets the known being manifest itself while respecting its alterity and *without marking it* in any way whatever by this cognitive relation. (42; my emphasis)

> To know is not simply to record, but always to comprehend (82)

His first statement implies just the kind of innocent recording his second statement denies. This contradiction fits perfectly within my "deck-flipping" explanation of *Totality and Infinity*'s methodological puzzle. The highly polemical account of "comprehension" Levinas performs throughout the text is ultimately driven by his untreated assumption that concepts are inherently "violent." By positing unmediated empirical reality populated by "real" bodies and "pure" qualities, he gives himself apparently virginal "others" the concept is alleged to oppress.[27] For his critique of the concept to hold water, he needs something like the innocent "recording" notion of theory above. Yet for his own phenomenology to do determinative work, he can't renounce comprehension altogether. For the empirico-metaphysical side of the flip, sensible/affective force, "substance," "[seesaw] constitution," (TI 128, 169) real condition, and the *purely* accessible empirical bodies they involve, theory just passively and innocently jots them down on its tabula rasa. Once sensibility registers the human other's empirical body (face), the idea of the infinite is apparently "put into me," and, in a stroke, comprehension apparently becomes fair game. Indeed, "comprehension of this destitution and this hunger establishes the very proximity of the other" (*TI* 200).

Beyond Levinas's explicit methodological concepts, his "deck-flipping" is explicitly performed in transition terms between different stages of description. His ego analysis is ultimately *progressive*. It tells a story of the birth of the ego in enjoyment, its transformation into dwelling, its vigorous laboring activity, its climactic encounter with the Other. Throughout this story, Levinas deploys "overflowing" and "deformalization" in the way I describe above. Each stage is described as an "a posteriori event," as "opening up new possibilities," as "discover[ing] a world," or, in short, "add[ing]" something new (*TI* 152–54, 157, 139). He doesn't want the ego's journey to be purely explicative. Above all, the idea of the Infinite must be "put into me," and he therefore posits "real" others "exterior" to the blind ego in its progressive journey of becoming aware. The ego is made to interact with a wide cast of characters: things consumed, environing elements, welcoming feminines, pagan gods destroyed, and materials exploited. After having apparently won its "separation," the ego finally happens to notice another human face, and the divine word arrives: *Pure Alterity*. Once a specific empirical face has performed its divine postal service, everything changes. What has been to this point a *progressive* story of discovery becomes a *regressive* story of origins. The idea of infinity "put into me" becomes "the common source of activity and theory," that is, *always already there* (203, 27).[28] *Totality and Infinity* perpetually circulates within the following fundamental claims:

> The alleged scandal of [ethical] alterity presupposes the tranquil identity of the same. (203)

And,

> The idea of infinity, revealed in the face, does not only require a separated being, the light of the face is necessary for separation. (150)[29]

"Separation" is presented as both the *ground* and the *result* of the Other's appearance. Moreover,

> Like a shunt every social relation leads back to the presentation of the other to the same without the intermediary of any image or sign, solely by the expression of the face. (210)

And,

> Because my position as an I is effectuated already in fraternity, the face can present itself to me as a face. The relation with the face in fraternity,... the *reference of every dialogue to the third party*... encompasses the face to face opposition. (280; my emphasis)

The face is presented as both the *ground* and *result* of divinely "effectuated" fraternity. Paternity "encloses a [plurality] of the Identical," that is, envelops "the whole of humanity," where *all* selves and others are "at the same time unique and non-unique" (247, 268, 213, 279). Finally, at the level of his explicit methodological statements:

> The method practiced here does indeed consist in seeking the condition of empirical situations, but it leaves to the developments called empirical, in which the conditioning possibility is accomplished—it leaves to the *concretization*—an ontological role that specifies the meaning of the fundamental possibility, a meaning invisible in that condition. (173)

Since "reversing constitution" *starts with* a purely formal idea, and "reverses" to its putatively empirical contexts of origination, the "ontological role" of concretization remains fundamentally indeterminate. Do human bodies *incarnate* the formal idea? Or does the idea of the infinite *originate in* these empirical contexts? Does the *Infinite itself* create these empirical contexts and "reveal itself" in them? Or is the *Infinite itself* "created" in them? What "accomplishes" what? And *how*?

> The production of the infinite entity is inseparable from the idea of infinity, for it is precisely in the disproportion between the idea of infinity and the infinity of which it is the idea that this exceeding of limits is produced. The idea of infinity is the mode of being, the *infinition*, of infinity. Infinity does not first exist, and *then* reveal itself. Its infinition is produced as revelation, as a positing of its idea in *me*. (*TI* 26)

The "production of the infinite entity" implies that *we* "produce" the "reality" of God. Yet "positing... its idea in me" implies that God "produces" *its* "idea" in us. Since content overflowing concept is *nothing other* than the "disproportion between the idea of infinity and the infinity of which it is the idea," his account is viciously circular. The "infinite entity" *must first exist* to "posit its idea in me," yet we must *always already have this idea* to "[produce] the infinite entity." Since the "*idea* of infinity" is cast as a "mode of *being*," Levinas's use of "production" remains indeterminate. Finally,

> The break-up of the formal structure of thought (the noema of a noesis) into events which this structure dissimulates, but which sustain it and restore its concrete significance, constitutes a *deduction*—necessary and yet non-analytical. In our exposition it is indicated by expressions such as "that is," or "precisely," or "this accomplishes that," or "this is produced as that." (28)

Since the first sentence describes *nothing other* than reversing constitution, the very meaning of "produced" and "accomplishes"—the very meaning of "is" throughout *Totality and Infinity as a whole*—remains indeterminate. God remains both an "infinite entity" and the "idea of infinity," and this so-called "deduction" never specifies what precisely is being deduced: the Reality of the Infinite, or its Idea? A "necessary and yet non-analytical" deduction implies a *Real ontological "necessity,"* yet "infinity does not first exist" implies *Ideal transcendental "necessity."* As should be clear, Levinas really does "flip the deck" between *transcendent fact* and a *transcendental idea*. As "the common source of activity and theory," the Other is simultaneously cast as both a "real" metaphysico-Paternal origin and as a "transcendental" "origin of all signification," or, put simply, a *pure idea* necessary for the *general intelligibility* of moral meaning, and a *pure reality* necessary for the *actual existence* of moral human relationships (27, 28, 98).[30]

Conclusion: Why?

Constitution or "effectuation"? Ideal or real relation? Transcendental or psycho-metaphysical genesis? Positing the "relation" between self and other as a "relation without relation"—as between an "absolute" singularity and an "absolute" alterity—bars Levinas from, with Husserl, utilizing the world to mediate the "relation"; bars him from, with

Heidegger, Gadamer, or Ricoeur, utilizing hermeneutic infrastructures that could render his circle virtuous; bars him from utilizing the counterfactuality of purely formal transcendental discourse structures; and keeps him from owning up to the quite conventional metaphysics he performs. All he can do is "flip the deck," or perpetually spin in a vicious and tragic circle. While I have amply indicated the text's circularity, in what sense is this circularity tragic? Levinas writes, "There does indeed exist a human race as a biological genus, and the common function men [*sic*] may exercise in the world" (*TI* 213). On the text's own terms, if my interlocutor is veritably "*absolutely* other" and pure of all mediation, then she is necessarily *also* "absolutely *other*" than her own *bodily form*. This would annul the bodily reference of her demand (her "help *me*!"). The face that suffers and demands is *not* the face that suffers and demands. If we instead hold that her alterity manifests *just in* her singular *Leib*, then inclusion in "there does indeed exist…" is apparently *validated*, rather than *contested*, by ethics, and hence her self-reference is never *pure*. In this case, categorial mediation or concept inclusion is not a "violence" per se. If we finally say that her body isn't *all* that she is, we perform a *mediate* identification, and have simply given up on all talk of her "absolute alterity." Levinas can keep a *pure body* or a *pure meaning*, but he can't keep both *at once*. Since "revelation" was precisely cast as the face's *kath' auto* expression, and since his own descriptions include explicit references to *both* (1) the ego's own experience of suffering *and* (2) existential-categorial "creaturehood," he has *failed* to present a purely self-referring entity.[31] By failing to present a self-standing entity or meaning, Levinas has failed to show that *ethics is "first philosophy."*[32] The descriptions he actually performs rather *show* that the meaning ascribed to the face is *dependent* on (1) human sentience *in general* (empiricist Levinas), (2) human intentionality *in general* (idealist Levinas), or (3) human being-with or creaturehood *in general* (ontological Levinas). Whether the relevant meaning or entity is achieved through empirical generalizations (conventionalism), cognitive performances (Kant), phenomenological-constitutive processes (Husserl), or original and *relatively* open ontological categories

(Heideggerian or theistic ontology), in all cases there is no such thing as *pure* "separation" or *pure* alterity, and hence no "violence" per se by concepts or categories.

Finally, why? This is the big question. As valid and interesting as the question of Levinas's potential psychological motivations might be, I will here restrict myself to the text alone. Why did Levinas construct and perform his method as he did? For my "deck-flipping" description to do *explanatory* work, I must finally propose an answer to this question. As the attuned reader will have already recognized, the reason is not hard to surmise. In the opening sentence of section two, Levinas writes: "In describing the metaphysical relation as disinterested, *as disengaged from all participation*" (*TI* 109; my emphasis). "Participation," it must be said, is the fundamental "enemy" that orients the logic of the text *as a whole*. Participation names the alleged "violence" wrought on the hapless inhabitants of "totality."[33] Levinas's fervent desire to avoid "participation" is ultimately *why* he posits the ego as a "conceptless individual," *why* he asserts sensibility is "the mode in which the break-up of totality...is...accomplished," *why* he posits an "absolute other" as a "void that breaks the totality," and finally *why* he casts "relation" as a "relation without relation" (120, 118, 40, 198, 80). "To break with participation," he assures us, is "to maintain contact" (61), but of what can this contact consist? On Levinas's own terms, the ego can only "breach totality" by *becoming a totality*: the element that "envelops or contains without being able to be contained or enveloped" is "not convertible into exteriority" (131, 132), that is, *completely enveloped by the ego "immersed" in them*, all while *simultaneously* "maintain[ing] contact" with *real* bodies, "*pure* qualities," in "an ultimate relation with the *substantial* plenitude of being," held "distinct from my substance but *constituting* it" (61, 188–89, 133, 112; my emphasis). Likewise, the other can only "breach totality" by *creating a totality*: as "the common source of activity and theory," divine effectuation "encloses a [plurality] of the Identical"—"the whole of humanity"—where *all* selves and others are "at the same time unique and non-unique" (27, 251, 247, 268, 213, 279), all while *simultaneously* maintaining "absolute distance" between *real* bodies ("multiple singularities"), through a *pure* "call from the Other," revealed "over and beyond form" as "the ultimate relation in Being" (36, 251, 67, 66, 48). The sensible ego can only "breach" totalizing concepts through *reference* to *real* "exterior" bodies by *real* external "effectuation." The sensible other can only "breach" totalizing categories by having a *sense* always already "put into her." By enforcing a ban on all mediation, Levinas can only "breach totalities" by alternate and circular appeals to original *sense* and original *reference*, to originary *meaning* and originary *reality*, to transcendental *idea* and transcendent *fact:* "Discourse is thus...a *pure* 'knowledge' or [*pure*] 'experience,' a *traumatism of astonishment*" (26, 73). Astonishing indeed. And why? *Because he arbitrarily declares concepts a sin.*

At the outset, I claimed that *Totality and Infinity*'s circularity is somewhat difficult to detect. But is it really so difficult? My detailed argumentation and excessive use of quotations were motivated by a desire to *show*, once and for all, *that* the text's incoherence is both plain and irresolvable. My analysis of his method endeavored to show *how* this incoherence issues from an intrinsically equivocal account of theory. My proposal for *why* he constructed his method as he did—to avoid the alleged "violence" of concepts or categories—quite plausibly explains the philosophical motive for his aporetic methodological construction and performances. If the criticisms of Derrida, Bernasconi, and others have yet to finally settle the question of the tenability of *Totality and Infinity*'s claims, I hope this focused demonstration might finally get the job done. By incoherently performing both realist and idealist accounts of necessary conditions ("content overflowing concept," "[seesaw] constitution," simultaneous "pure recording" and "comprehension" accounts of theory, etc.), his general claims remain fundamentally *arbitrary*. When a skeptic questions whether the Other is really a transcendent "fact," Levinas will point to the *concept* in "content overflowing concept," or to a *transcendental Idea*. When a realist questions the purely formal character of the idea, Levinas will point to the "content" in "content overflowing concept," or to *a transcendent*

Fact. And, quite interestingly, if a poststructuralist questions the way I've framed this problem, what might he or she do? Point to the "contents" and the "overflowing" in "contents overflowing concepts," or to individual bodies, affectivity, and performativity in asserting the allegedly contingent character of all concepts. *Totality and Infinity* has something for everyone. Its intrinsically equivocal logic and method, and the highly relevant nature of its subject matter, means we can find almost whatever we want in its pages, so long as we embrace the idea that ethics is primary. If the explanation I've proposed is cogent, we can no longer assume such primacy while reading *Totality and Infinity*. Perhaps there *really* is an "absolute other," or perhaps the idea of infinity is a genuine condition for moral intelligibility in general. But if there is and if it is, some other form of description or argumentation will have to reveal it to us.

To conclude, Levinas declares: "I do not believe that there is a transparency possible in method. Nor that philosophy might be possible as transparency" (*GCM* 89). Are transparency in method and royal rationalism the same things? One might insist that for a philosophy that embraces the limits of reason (and, hence, of transparency), *methodological* transparency—of what counts as condition and consequent, what form of relation gets us from the former to the latter, what counts as evidence?, etc.—is even *more necessary*. Without telling readers the explicit methodological norms in play, they have no way to directly assess a claim. In my view, this is to *fail to take responsibility for one's claims*, that is, to "accept...the rules of the [methodological] game, [while] cheating" (*TI* 173). There is no evidence that Levinas cheated on purpose. Indeed, since he reformulated his methodological approach in his late work, he seems to have acceded to Derrida's judgment that *Totality and Infinity*'s problems are irresolvable. Perhaps we should too.

Notes

I owe a special debt of gratitude to the staff and management of Circles Café, Ramada Plaza, Pudong, China, especially Zhang Zi Feng, Wen Long Wang, Luo Dan, and Guo Man Si; and to the gang at Big Bamboo, Pudong, especially Li Jiao Jiao, Shen Fang, Ke Hai Feng, Li Song Jian, Su Lei Lei, and Li Zhen Ni. Without their hospitality, and their generous tolerance for my marathon-research-sessions in their establishments, this essay might never have been composed. Also, I offer big thanks to Steven Galt Crowell and Martin Kavka for their superlative generosity in reading and debating my work by personal correspondence. Finally, I am deeply grateful to Richard A. Cohen and Randy Friedman for their indispensible aid in this essay's development. Without their critical eye, collegial generosity, and personal kindness over the years, this essay would not have been possible.

The epigraphs to this essay are drawn from the following sources: Martin Kavka, "Humanizing Philosophy of Religion: On Language in Levinas and Sellars," *Journal for Culture and Religious Theory* 14, no. 2 (2015): 230; Robert Bernasconi, "Levinas and the Struggle for Existence," in *Addressing Levinas*, ed. Eric Sean Nelson, Antje Kapust, and Kent Still (Evanston, IL: Northwestern University Press, 2005), 180; Emmanuel Levinas, GCM 89.

1. Michael L. Morgan, *The Cambridge Introduction to Emmanuel Levinas* (Cambridge: Cambridge University Press, 2011), 130, 43n23. For Morgan's own nuanced treatment, see Michael L. Morgan, *Discovering Levinas* (Cambridge: Cambridge University Press, 2007), 39–56.

2. Morgan, *Cambridge Introduction*, 53; my emphasis. I'm fully indebted to Atterton here. Peter Atterton, review of *The Cambridge Introduction to Emmanuel Levinas*, by Michael L. Morgan, *Notre Dame Philosophical Reviews,* July 18, 2011, https://ndpr.nd.edu/news/24763-the-cambridge-introduction-to-emmanuel-levinas.

3. See John Wild, "Introduction," *TI* 19.

4. Jacques Derrida, "Violence and Metaphysics: An Essay on the Thought of Emmanuel Levinas," in *Writing and Difference,* trans. A. Bass (Chicago: University of Chicago Press, 1978); Theodore de Boer, "An Ethical Transcendental Philosophy," in *Face to Face with Levinas,* ed. Richard A. Cohen (Albany: SUNY Press, 1988), 83–116; Robert Bernasconi, "Re-reading Totality and Infinity," in *The Question of the Other,* ed. Arleen B. Dallery and Charles E. Scott (Albany: State University of New York Press, 1989), 23–34.

5. For the purposes of this essay, when I use the term "metaphysical" I mean it in the conventional sense. The special sense Levinas tries to attribute the term suffers from precisely the incoherence I will analyze here.

6. I am deeply indebted to the long tradition of critical *Totality and Infinity* scholarship in my own proposed explanation (note 11 below). The "how" and "why" of my proposed explanation are my own original contribution, since, next to Derrida's "Violence and Metaphysics," I have been unable to find a single detailed and focused treatment of *Totality and Infinity*'s explicit method in the scholarship. I am nevertheless also deeply indebted to both Steven Galt Crowell

and Martin Kavka for my proposal herein. Without their superlative generosity in reading and debating my work through personal correspondence, this essay would have likely taken different form. In my view, Crowell is one of the most rigorous phenomenologists of our day. His Heideggerian-normative project is quite fascinating and genuinely original. He has had a transformative influence on my own thinking in ways I'm still sorting through. See Steven Galt Crowell, *Phenomenology and Normativity* (Cambridge: Cambridge University Press, 2013).

7. Moran notices precisely this: "The sum total of these entirely unsupported, not to say downright contradictory, claims about the nature of this so-called nondisclosive encounter with the face is not going to add up to a coherent picture." Dermot Moran, *Introduction to Phenomenology* (London: Routledge, 2000), 352.

8. Beyond Derrida and Bernasconi, other critical treatments include Randy Friedman, "Alterity and Asymmetry in Levinas's Ethical Phenomenology," *Journal of Scriptural Reasoning* 13, no. 1 (2014), http://jsr.shanti.virginia.edu/vol-13-no-1-june-2014-phenomenology-and-scripture/alterity-and-asymmetry-in-levinass-ethical-phenomenology/; Moran, *Introduction to Phenomenology*, 351–52; Jean-Luc Marion, "From the Other to the Individual," in *Levinas Studies*, vol. 1, ed. Jeffrey Bloechl and Jeffrey L. Kosky, 99–117 (Pittsburgh: Duquesne University Press, 2005); Max Pensky, "The Limits of Solidarity: Habermas, Levinas, and the Moral Point of View," in *A Matter of Discourse: Community and Communication in Contemporary Philosophies*, ed. Amos Nascimento, 129–50 (London: Avebury Press, 1998); Paul Ricoeur, "What Ontology in View?," in *Oneself as Another*, trans. Kathleen Blamey, 329–56 (Chicago: Chicago University Press, 1992); David Wood, "Some Questions for My Levinasian Friends," in *Addressing Levinas*, ed. Eric Sean Nelson, Antje Kapust, and Kent Still, 152–69 (Evanston, IL: Northwestern University Press, 2005); and Wild, "Introduction," *TI* 11–20.

9. De Boer, "An Ethical Transcendental Philosophy." John Drabinski, "Difference and Sense: The Problem of Relation in the Work of Emmanuel Levinas" (PhD diss., University of Memphis, 1996). As Bernasconi already diagnosed, de Boer repeats Levinas's equivocal use of the term "transcendental," and his reading ultimately turns on reading Levinas to perform something like the "ontological argument" (De Boer, "An Ethical Transcendental Philosophy," 94). De Boer hence performs something like a theistic (onto-)*logic*, pointing to a "real," as opposed to the mere idea of, the infinite. Drabinski's reading also turns on positing various *logics* to shore up Levinas's account: a "logic of sensibility" (Drabinski, "Difference and Sense," 112), "logic of sense" (123), "logic of exteriority" (115), and a "general logic of materiality" (128–29). Drabinski attributes a *kath' auto* character to both natural entities *and* the face, such that they become two species of a more general "otherness." Correlatively, Drabinski also posits "a general logic of Desire" (111), where need is cast as an alternate mode of desire. In *Totality and Infinity*, desire and need are not presented as signifying two modes of a general logic of sense, these motivations are not presented as correlating to two different instantiations of a general otherness (natural entities, the face), and these alterities are not presented as sharing a single mode of disclosure (expression

kath' auto). Such would render the face *derivative,* in fact, an *expression of a more general logic,* and no longer of solely itself. While Drabinski succeeds in suggesting a way in which "sense-bestowal from the outside" might coherently be construed, his treatment of *Totality and Infinity* is ultimately creative or not what Levinas actually seeks to do. In the final analysis, the logics Drabinski posits are held to relate singularities "unmediated by form" (92). Of what can logics without *form* consist? Purely *formal* relations between abstract marks? Or "real" relations between "real" singular bodies? If the latter, *what,* precisely, is being related, and *how?* De Boer and Drabinski both perform empirico-metaphysical coherence strategies, but in contrasting theistic and quasi-materialist forms. Either way, empirico-metaphysical strategies necessarily *fail* on *Totality and Infinity*'s own descriptive terms.

10. Martin Kavka, "Humanizing Philosophy of Religion"; Martin Kavka, review of *Addressing Levinas,* ed. Eric Sean Nelson, Antje Kapust, and Kent Still, in *Notre Dame Philosophical Reviews,* November 14, 2005, https://ndpr.nd.edu/news/24904-addressing-levinas. I risk doing Kavka an injustice here. He is quite of aware of the fraught character of *Totality and Infinity*'s account of the face, and explicitly presents his readings as hypotheses intended to propose the text's best case. He further admits that on "further examination," his own interpretive strategy might fall "into insurmountable problems" (Kavka, review of *Addressing Levinas*). Kavka seeks to rebut both Wood's Heideggerian critique of the alleged priority of the face and Gallagher's empirical realist skepticism of the face as "transcendent experience." In both cases, Kavka appeals to the essendi/cognoscendi distinction Kant utilizes in the second *Critique* to provide reciprocal justification for freedom and moral law. Setting aside the well-known internal problems Kant's own account must contend with, however we might interpret Kant, Kavka's strategy cannot work for *Totality and Infinity*. Kant is fundamentally dealing in *cognitive performances,* and clearly does *not* hold that we "receive" ideas from *pure* sensible qualities, *pure* experiences, *pure* human bodies, or *pure* divine "effectuators." Kavka is certainly right that "as soon as one turns to science to defend Levinasian ethics, one must turn away from Levinas's specific arguments" (Kavka, "Humanizing Philosophy of Religion," 227). But is it *also* true that Gallagher "has gone wrong" in his claim that Levinas's ethics "'is based on an experience of transcendence encountered in the other's face'" (226)? It *also* seems true that as soon as one turns to [Kant] to defend Levinasian ethics, one must turn away from Levinas's specific arguments. Kavka is well aware that *TI Totality and Infinity* is beset by problems, and acknowledges that these problems may be "insurmountable" (Kavka, review of *Addressing Levinas*). He seems to recognize that the criticism performed by Derrida, Bernasconi, and Wood, while formally sound, perhaps suffers from a certain generality. To acquire sufficient force, "Wood's critique of Levinas must be extended to the sphere of Levinas's method" (ibid.). I will perform precisely this extension herein. In the last analysis, Kantian transcendental strategies must necessarily *fail* on *Totality and Infinity*'s own descriptive terms.

11. Steven Galt Crowell, "Why Is Ethics First Philosophy? Levinas in Phenomenological Context," *European Journal of Philosophy* 23, no. 3 (2015): 564–88,

doi:10.1111/j.1468-0378.2012.00550.x (2012). I risk doing an injustice to Crowell here, since his analysis in this essay alone is ultimately ambiguous. His central claim is that Levinas's ethics contributes to a description of "the conditions necessary for the possession of intentional content" (1). Yet Crowell's positive reading only works by reference to "our experience of the other subject *as* another subject" (ibid.) As *other subject,* not "pure other." Crowell must suppose either analogy-perception in the constitution of the alter ego and the transcendental life this ultimately involves, or existential-categorial *Mitsein.* Either way, "experience" is no longer construed in a *purely* empirical way. Given his "takes place in the recognition of the normative force of a command" (1), Crowell is unhinging obligation from its allegedly *pure origination* in the face. Moreover, he explicitly rejects "the way Levinas begins the systematic part of *Totality and Infinity* with an analysis of 'separation as life' " (7). Crowell must assume either Husserl's *transzendentale Leben* or Heidegger's *Sein* for his own defense of Levinas. The "face," here, becomes either a modification of *being-with,* but nevertheless subject to the *same Seinsfrage* that confronts *all* Daseins, or an *alter ego* subject to the *same* phenomenological-teleological reason that orients *all* transcendental subjects. On either view, claims for "absolute" alterity, "absolute" singularity, and the alleged "violence" of participatory "totality" are simply abandoned on his reading. In just this way, Crowell indirectly exemplifies what I call the Husserlian transcendental coherence strategy for reading *Totality and Infinity.* Crowell is ultimately reading Levinas quite generously, and from the perspective of his own philosophical project. In the last analysis, Husserlian transcendental strategies necessarily *fail* on *Totality and Infinity*'s own descriptive terms.

12. For exceptions, see note 8 above.

13. As Moran rightly notes, "However, [*Totality and Infinity*'s] opaque, metaphorical, inexact style of writing inevitably means that there can never be an authoritative interpretation of his philosophy.... It is pointless piling up quote after quote from Levinas on the nature of the face." Moran, *Introduction to Phenomenology,* 351–52.

14. *TI* 42. Friedman diagnoses precisely this problem, demonstrating how Levinas forces "the acceptance of a moral obligation to an Other predicated on the rejection of the very possibility of relation. For Levinas, *every* subject is a solipsist standing in need of overcoming by moral command" (my emphasis). Randy Friedman, "Alterity and Asymmetry in Levinas's Ethical Phenomenology."

15. See Theodore de Boer, *The Development of Husserl's Thought,* trans. Theodore Plantinga (New York: Springer, 1978), 299–302.

16. There are numerous attempts in the scholarship to justify Levinas's claims through comparison to Husserl's work. For good examples, see Leslie MacAvoy, "The Other Side of Intentionality," in *Addressing Levinas,* ed. Eric Sean Nelson, Antje Kapust, and Kent Still, 109–18 (Evanston, IL: Northwestern University Press, 2005), and Drabinski, "Difference and Sense." As interesting as these attempts stand on their own merits, they necessarily *fail* to justify Levinas's approach, at least on *Totality and Infinity*'s own posited and explicit terms. This is just to say

that if we uproot Husserl's ur-impression, primal association, passive synthesis, etc. from their supportive role in active position-taking and active constitution, we annul the phenomenological character of the passive dimension, and, concomitantly, the necessary status of phenomenological meaning. On Husserlian terms, if the face is going to phenomenologically signify, it must necessarily pass through "the a priori form-system" or transcendental consciousness. Given Levinas's own claim that constitution functions at a temporal remove from sensible experience (see *TI* 127, 169), the temporal gap in play can only be bridged by probabilistic empirical reconstructions or necessary ontological determinations. Levinas's appeal to "actual perception" (127) and "life in reality" (169) over against constitution clearly demarcates the problem. If we instead opt for the Heideggerian comparison, if the face is going to phenomenologically signify, it must necessarily pass through the "the a priori form-system" Heidegger labels "existentials." Levinas's appeals to "as-sociation" [*sic*] (100) over against projective disclosure clearly demarcate the problem. In both cases he is summoning psychologistic, empirically realist terms to twist free from Husserl and Heidegger, while simultaneously laying claim to "phenomenology" couched in Kantian language. Levinas presents the ego as *pre-worlded* (156, 161) yet nevertheless in "contact" (135, 165) with all sorts of "exterior" things. The problem is clear. See Suzanne Bachelard, *A Study of Husserl's Formal and Transcendental Logic* (Evanston, IL: Northwestern University Press, 1990), 191; Derrida, "Violence and Metaphysics," 133, 141. For an interesting treatment of Husserl on passivity and position-taking, see Alejandro Arango, "Husserl's Concept of Position-Taking and Second Nature," *Phenomenology and Mind* 6 (2014): 224–35.

17. On Levinas's own strict methodological terms, we are not licensed to describe his method as a "hermeneutics of lived experience," as Bergo does, for example. See Bettina Bergo, "Emmanuel Levinas," *Stanford Encyclopedia of Philosophy*, July 23, 2006, last modified August 3, 2011, http://plato.stanford.edu/entries/levinas. Since Levinas describes sensibility as yielding both a singular "conceptless individual" and a singular "absolute alterity," and specifies their "relation" as a "relation without relation," he denies himself the right to a hermeneutic relationality and the mediation it inherently involves. This is why Levinas himself never claims title to hermeneutic phenomenology to describe his own method. See *TI* 120, 96, 80.

18. In response to questions on whether animals have a "face," Levinas responds, "The human face is completely different and only afterwards do we discover the face of an animal.... It is because we, as human, know what suffering is that we can have this obligation." When forced to deal with nonhuman alterity, the *epistemic function* or "knowing" dimension of his account of alterity becomes explicit. See Emmanuel Levinas, "The Paradox of Morality: An Interview with Emmanuel Levinas," in *The Provocation of Levinas: Rethinking the Other*, ed. Robert Bernasconi and David Wood (London: Routledge, 1988), 168–80. I'm gratefully indebted to Aaron Bell for aiding me in this insight. Aaron Bell, "The Animal without a Face," unpublished manuscript, 13–14.

19. His account of the third fails precisely from the problems I analyze: "every social relation leads back to" the face, yet only because "my position as an I is already effectuated in fraternity [can] the face...present itself to me as face" (*TI* 213, 280). In the first context, the face is a *transcendental condition* of intelligibility, in the second context, a "revealed" or *real condition*. Theory is left indeterminate, as I show more thoroughly below.

20. Content overflowing concept is an *inherently mediated construction*. Content is *never absent* from its concept, while "overflowing" serves to merely add *immediate sensible force*, or to *individuate* particular concepts. He is switching between psycho-metaphysical and transcendental genesis.

21. To say that obligation is "non-adequation" (*TI* 27, 34) is just to say, tautologically, that it's something like a *norm*, and leaves completely untouched the *nonmoral* presuppositions necessarily in play in the ascription of moral meaning in general.

22. See Friedman, "Alterity and Asymmetry in Levinas's Ethical Phenomenology."

23. Levinas defines the face by coincidence of the expressed and s/he who expresses, formally separating *talking to* and *talking about*. Hence, the alleged ethical meaning of the former licenses simply ignoring the latter. Since conceptual mediation can't be avoided, Levinas wins all debates or defeats all philosophically competing positions a priori.

24. See also *TI* 129, 153, 169; for deformalization, see 50. Notice: the very notion of "deformalization" entails *starting with* pure concepts, and working back to their alleged (transcendental or "real"?) contexts of origination.

25. These two statements show up the problem. Levinas is deploying Aristotle's "primary substances" in his description of the ego's own affective constitution by "exterior" content, while positing "secondary substances" by "miraculous grasp" (163) of an essentially *blind*, "pre-theoretical" ego.

26. De Boer repeats Levinas's question begging by simply asserting that "It is not a condition operative behind our backs, like transcendental apperception in Kant or the clearing (*Lichtung*) of being in Heidegger." De Boer, "An Ethical Transcendental Philosophy," 100. In contrast, Derrida holds that "Levinas's metaphysics...presupposes...the transcendental phenomenology that it seeks to put into question," and that "Just as he implicitly had to appeal to phenomenological self-evidences against phenomenology, Levinas must ceaselessly suppose and practice the thought of precomprehension of Being in his discourse, even when he directs it against 'ontology.'" Derrida, "Violence and Metaphysics," 133, 141. If my own analysis is sound, it amounts to an internal demonstration of Derrida's point within Levinas's own methodological self-description.

27. Derrida makes this same point. "Violence and Metaphysics," 82–83.

28. Levinas is very clearly tracking Heidegger here, but is working with a different account of time. Ego, Face, and Eros can perhaps be read as filling in different content and attributing different meaning to Heidegger's threefold ecstases of unified temporality. But Levinas's use of pure empirical reality and purely accessible empirical bodies (1) renders his realist pole a theistic, rather than a Heideggerian,

ontology, and (2) performs an attribution of original and unmodifiable wholeness to the ego inconsistent with Heidegger's approach. To read *Totality and Infinity* in a phenomenological vein, Levinas must presuppose either Heidegger's historicity or what Rodemeyer calls Husserl's primordial "intersubjective temporality." See Lanei M. Rodemeyer, *Intersubjective Temporality: It's About Time* (Dordrecht: Springer, 2006).

29. Bernasconi first identified this particular circle. See "Re-reading Totality and Infinity," 32.

30. Despite his reference to creation ex nihilo, it's not certain that Levinas's ontological God fully creates human *bodies*, since he seems to be re-outfitting a nonmaterialist reading of biblical creation. In other words, his creative God doesn't necessarily create the material universe, but S/He does create *human consciousness*. Nevertheless, Levinas's own descriptions entail that this involves nonmoral dimensions (reflected in human creativity, for example), and does not occur as *only* sheer moral command.

31. Levinas: "The comprehension of this destitution and this hunger establishes the very proximity of the other" (*TI* 200). "What is essential to created existence is not the limited character of its being" (105).

32. I want to stress: *Totality and Infinity*'s failures do not necessarily belong to Pseudo-Dionysius or Maimonides. For those inclined to theology, my critique of this text doesn't decide more general questions in religious hermeneutics or theological semantics.

33. See *TI* 48. I will stress: the alleged "violence" in question is not merely that of *closed* "totalities," or of strictly deterministic ontology, but of *all totalities*, including ones that involve the *horizonal openness* of "the idea in the Kantian sense." See de Boer, "An Ethical Transcendental Philosophy," 90; Jacques Derrida, *The Problem of Genesis in Husserl's Philosophy,* trans. Marian Hobson (Chicago: University of Chicago Press, 2003), 94–99.

The Recurrence of Acoustics in Levinas

Roberto Wu

Despite Levinas's emphasis on the oral dimension of the encounter with the other, notions such as hearing and listening are far from receiving univocal accounts in his reflections. Yet, Jacques Derrida seems to find clear evidence of their relevance, affirming that "Levinas places sound above light,"[1] which is interpreted as the affirmation of "the transcendence of hearing (*l'entendre*) in relation to seeing (*voir*)."[2] Nevertheless, the second movement of this interpretation inevitably evokes some confusion, for the priority of the sound over light/seeing does not necessarily imply the priority of hearing. Levinas's accounts of hearing (*entendre/audition*),[3] listening, and/or hearkening (*écouter*) fluctuate throughout his philosophical production, and, despite some occasional discussion, they remain secondary compared with speech (*parole*), as in *Totality and Infinity*,[4] on which Derrida bases most of his analysis.[5] It is only in *Otherwise than Being* that they will be more systematically employed, which does not imply, however, a weakening of the priority of speech.

Without contesting the primordiality of speech over hearing, listening, and audition, we aim, however, to investigate the purview of these last concepts by linking Levinas's early account of acoustics with the description available in *Otherwise than Being*. This involves: (1) examining how hearing, listening, and audition relate to sound (and silence) in his discussion of the *there is* (*il y a*), and (2) discussing the integration between these concepts with the acoustic account of *Otherwise than Being*, in which terms like resonance and echo are decisive. By means of this, we make visible some important moments related to acoustics: (1) the resonance of essence, (2) the echo of the otherwise, (3) the resonance of the "mute murmuring" of the *il y a*, and (4) the "forgotten voices" of a tradition apart from ontology.

CREATION OF SILENCE AND THE OVERFLOWING SOUND

In the little essay, "The Transcendence of Words: On Michel Leiris's *Biffures*," published in 1949 and thus contemporaneous to *Existence and Existents* (1947), "Reality and Its Shadow" (1948), and "Is Ontology Fundamental?" (1951), Levinas takes Leiris's work as the motif upon which the themes of hearing and living-world are developed. The reference to these other texts is not arbitrary and scrutinizes that which Gerald L. Bruns calls "aesthetics of materiality."[6] Leiris's surrealism seems to evoke a kinship with Levinas's analysis of the *there is* (*il y a*) in *Existence and Existents*. In opposition to Husserl's and Heidegger's versions of phenomenology, which conceive of being from the angle of givenness (*Sinngebung*), Levinas insists that the materiality of being remains impenetrable despite the attempts of rendering meaning by means of understanding. Therefore, the *il y a* expressly counteracts the intelligibility provided by understanding, which articulates meaning, horizon, and light: "Behind the luminosity of forms, by which beings already relate to our 'inside,' matter [*matière*] is the very fact of the *there is*. . . ." (*EE* 57; ellipsis in original, translation modified / *DEE* 92). Refractory to the advances of light, the *il y a* bespeaks the anonymity that depersonalizes and makes indeterminate human existence, as, for example, in the experience of insomnia: "Wakefulness is anonymous. It is not that there is *my* vigilance in the night; in insomnia it is the night itself that watches. It watches. In this anonymous nightwatch where I am completely exposed to being all the thoughts which occupy my insomnia are suspended on *nothing*" (66/111). The night adumbrates the impersonality of the *il y a*, the fact that there is "an absolutely unavoidable presence" (58/94), which is not an object, but a verb that renders an event in its impersonal form ("It watches"—*Ça veille*). Then, Levinas introduces a description that is important not just for the economy of *Existence and Existents*, but also for his ulterior philosophy, for it anticipates fundamental characteristics of *Otherwise than Being*: "There is no discourse [*discours*]. Nothing responds to us, but this silence; the voice of this silence is heard [*entendue*] and frightens like the silence of those infinite spaces Pascal speaks of" (58; translation modified/95).

It is precisely the voice of the silence that comes from this presence of absence that Levinas refers to, although implicitly, in his essay on Michel Leiris. First of all, there is a form of art based on the primacy of vision, in which a being appears as world, and which "makes beauty in nature, calming it, appeasing it" (*OS 147* / LTM 1093). Nevertheless, Levinas warns, "All the arts, even the sonorous ones, create silence," and silence can be, "at times of the bad conscience, oppressive or frightening" (147/1093). This description can hardly be dissociated from the above quotation of *Existence and Existents*,[7] but Levinas also proposes the necessity of relating with this silence, a "need for critique," that is, the kind of relation that perceives the uneasiness that underlies the "peace of the beautiful" (147/1093) and is aware of the fact that silence is not mere absence, but the announcement of the *il y a*.[8] The silence that even sonorous arts create anticipates the subject matter of the "resonance of silence" in *Otherwise than Being*. Particularly significant is that Levinas extends the scope of silence to all forms of art, for all of them are capable of reflecting the primordial experience that insomnia and horror inflict.

Next, Levinas shifts from the discussion of silence to a consideration of the sound as such, through the perspective of its disjunction with vision, by means of a correlation between sound and excess. He writes, "There is in fact in sound—and in consciousness understood as hearing [*audition*]—a shattering of the always complete world of vision and art. Sound is all repercussion, outburst, scandal. While in vision a form espouses a content and soothes it, sound is like the sensible quality overflowing [*débordement*] its limits, the incapacity of form to hold its content—a true rent in the fabric of the world—that by which the world that is *here* prolongs a dimension inconvertible into vision" (*OS* 147–48/ LTM 1093).

Likewise, a few years after this essay, Levinas will warn us of the limitations of vision and light, as in "Is Ontology Fundamental?" and, with a more detailed account, in *Totality and Infinity,* by taking them as the key components of the dynamic of sameness. Nevertheless, even in this article of 1949 it is already possible to see how the horizon of vision is "shattered," whether in its character of containment and limitation or in its feature of calming and making nature peaceful, because sound "overflows" and exceeds a "form," being therefore "repercussion, outburst, scandal." Levinas describes the surpassing feature of sound in terms of symbol: "the sound is symbol *par excellence*—a reaching beyond the given" (*OS* 148/LTM 1093). In "Meaning and Sense," Levinas explains that "A symbol is not the abridgement of a real presence that would preexist it; it would give more than any receptivity for the world could ever receive" (*CPP* 83/SS 133). A symbol entails an insurmountable gap between orders separated by an excess; therefore, it does not belong to the economy of collateral relations that encompasses the given. Music incarnates the essential feature that underlies every form of art, namely, the movement of going beyond what is given. Levinas performs in "Reality and Its Shadow" the recurrent gesture of identifying understanding and knowledge with the given, a horizon that art attempts to surpass and disrupt: "Does not the function of art lie in not understanding?... Art does not know a particular type of reality; it contrasts with knowledge. It is the very event of obscuring, a descent of the night, an invasion of shadow" (*CPP* 3/RO 773).

At least in one important aspect, the analysis of art in "Reality and Its Shadow" has more affinity with *Existence and Existents* than with "The Transcendence of Words": the former presents the impersonality that art, but especially music, sets forth, while the latter explicitly attaches music with the word (*mot*) and the verb (*verbe*). In "Reality and Its Shadow," the concept of image appears from the outset as opposed to "concept," because conceptuality, to Levinas, implies grasping, understanding, and power over the object. Thenceforth, he conducts his interpretation of art based on a reversal, in choosing image over concept, passivity over power: "An image marks a hold over us rather than our initiative, a fundamental passivity" (*CPP* 3/RO 774). Taking into consideration the above analysis of sound, it is not surprising thus that he affirms that "an image is musical" (3/774), whereas neither image is strictly conceived as optics, as far as Levinas dismantles and reverses what this implies, nor are music and sound restricted to usual theories of acoustics. Assuredly this statement anticipates much of the "listening eye," which will appear more than 30 years later in *Otherwise than Being*.

While deepening the passivity implicated by the experience of art, Levinas asserts the uniqueness of the rhythm. He refuses its definition as "an inner law of the poetic order," stating rather that experiencing it implies some kind of mutual participation: "our consenting to them is inverted into a participation. Their entry into us is one with our entry into them" (*CPP* 4/RO 774). By means of the analysis of rhythm, Levinas takes up again in another domain the issue of the depersonalization of the subject that he has undertaken in *Existence and Existents*. In his analysis of insomnia, Levinas portrays the *il y a* as the unavoidable presence of absence, in the face of which no one is sure if one is the watcher or the one who is watched, and vigilance turns out to be an impersonal event without subject. Something similar occurs with rhythm, for "consent, assumption, initiative or freedom" are terms that reveal themselves to be inadequate to a situation in which someone is "caught up and carried away by it" (4/775). The subject is thus depersonalized: "It is so not even despite itself, for in rhythm there is no longer a oneself, but rather a sort of passage from oneself to anonymity" (4/775). In this anonymity, consciousness and unconsciousness compose a phantasmagorical landscape, as in a "waking dream," even if it is more adequate to characterize it as "a sphere situated outside of the conscious and the unconscious" (4/775).[9] Levinas concludes this moment of his argument by underscoring the uniqueness of his conceptions of rhythm and music, as well as anticipating the theme of the resonance that will play a key role in *Otherwise than Being*:

> Then we must detach them from the arts of sound where they are ordinarily envisioned exclusively, and draw them out into a general aesthetic category. Rhythm certainly does have its privileged locus in music, for the musician's element realizes the pure deconceptualization of reality. Sound is the quality most detached from an object. Its relation with the substance from which it emanates is not inscribed in its quality. It resounds impersonally. [*Il résonne impersonnellement*] Even its timbre, a trace of its belonging to an object, is submerged in its quality, and does not retain the structure of a relation. Hence in listening [*en écoutant*] we do not apprehend a "something," but are without concepts: musicality belongs to sound naturally. (*CPP* 4–5/RO 776)

Deconceptualization refers to the capacity of sound to engender a disruption of subjectivity. Levinas suggests that its overflowing capacity precludes it from being integrated within the horizon of conceptual meaning articulated by vision and understanding. The excess that belongs to the sound finds a parallel with the surplus of non-sense over sense that the *il y a* delivers; in this sense, to listen means to be "exposed" to that which resounds impersonally. This conception of sound returns in Levinas's later works, as in *Otherwise than Being*, although with some important modifications that cannot be easily harmonized with the account we have just presented.

Conversely, in "The Transcendence of Words," the indeterminateness that is characteristic of his descriptions of the *il y a*, and related to the impersonal and to anonymity, is put aside in favor of the verbal sound: "If, however, sound can appear as a phenomenon, as *here*, it is because its function of transcendence only asserts itself in the verbal sound. The sounds and noises of nature are words [*mots*] that disappoint us. To really hear [*entendre*] a sound is to hear a word [*mot*]. Pure sound is verb [*verbe*]" (*OS* 148; translation modified / LTM 1093). This passage is categorical: verb is the grounding of sound; even noises are conceived in terms of words. According to Levinas, there is a decay of speaking in contemporary philosophy and sociology, in which occurs "a disdain for the word" (148/1093). In face of this, he emphasizes how important is the speaking word and gives us the example of Robinson Crusoe's meeting with Man Friday, which is more expressive than his other ties with civilization, such as his artificial utensils or the preservation of "his morality" (148/1093). Levinas describes this event as that "in which a man who speaks replaces the ineffable sadness of echoes [*la tristesse inexprimable de l'écho*]" (148/1093). This observation makes room for his claim that "social relation—the real presence of the other [*l'autre*]—matters" (148/1093–94), a presence that "is fulfilled in hearing [*l'audition*]" inasmuch as the word uttered by the other plays a "transcendent role" in which "verb refuses to become flesh" (148/1094). The "privilege of the living word [*mot vivant*], destined to be heard [*l'audition*]" (149/1094), opposes to the conception of language based on signs, for the latter fails to give an account of speaking as an event; rather, language as a system of signs privileges the writing as being its substance, which, according to Levinas, produces "disfigured words, 'frozen words'" (149/1094). In contrast to frozen words of documents and vestiges (*vestiges*), Levinas conceives the speaking from the perspective of an encounter with the other, in the sense of an interruption: "To speak is to interrupt my existence as a subject, a master, but to interrupt it without offering myself as spectacle, leaving me simultaneously object and subject. My voice brings the element in which that dialectical situation is accomplished concretely" (149/1094).

The Echo of Saying

The ubiquity of themes related to acoustics in *Otherwise than Being* suggests some sort of retrieval of matters that we have just addressed, especially the overflowing character of sound, the link between image and sound, silence, and the *il y a*. Unlike *Totality and Infinity*, *Otherwise than Being* is deliberately expressed through acoustic concepts: resonance, echo, voice, inaudible, listening eye, hearing, silence, and so on.

The priority of speaking over hearing, already enacted in *Totality and Infinity*, is maintained in *Otherwise than Being*, but the latter unfolds the discussion on language stressing the distinction between saying and said. This priority appears in *Otherwise than Being* on different occasions, as, for example, in the formulation "obedience precedes any listening [*écoute*] to the command" (*OB* 148; translation modified/ *AQE* 232), which instead of subordinating obedience to listening, or even establishing an equivalence between them, affirms the primacy and independence of the former from the latter. As in *Totality and Infinity*, in which the speech of the other determines a command to which I must respond, Levinas maintains in *Otherwise than Being* the dignity and the absolute priority of this speech from any acoustical apprehension. This can be developed at least into two directions. First, Levinas explains this priority by means of the theme of creation, in which the creature has already received a command even before he or she begins to understand: "But in creation, what is called to being answers to a call that could not have reached it since, brought out of nothingness, it obeyed before hearing [*d'entendre*] the order" (113/179), for in a sense being is already a response to creation. Second, this priority corresponds to the constitutive anachronism of the fractured encounter with the other: "'Before they call, I will answer,' the formula is to be understood literally. In approaching the other I am always late for the meeting" (150/235). These statements express the idiosyncrasy of Levinas's ethics, in which obedience precedes understanding, as responsibility comes before commitment—a gesture that he calls "the *passing itself* of the Infinite" (150/235). This idea also appears in the following assertion: "The neighbor strikes me before striking me, as though [*comme si*] I had heard [*entendu*] before he spoke" (88/141). The expression "*comme si*" should not be overlooked, for it indicates an analogical treatment of the term *entendre* that prevents a contradiction with the above formulation of the pre-original anachronism. The obedience to the command precedes any uttering of sounds and consequently any hearing in this sense. The anachronism between obedience and hearing elicits the theme of the immemorial past, which comes to us not as presence, but as trace and echo. With regard to the issue of the neighbor, Levinas writes, "In proximity is heard [*s'entend*] a command come as though from an immemorial past [*comme d'un passé immémorial*], which was never present, began in no freedom. This *way* of the neighbor is a face" (88/141). To hear a command, as is asserted here, does not represent an inconsistency with the thesis of the anachronism above presented, for Levinas is not advocating in this last sentence a dependency of the command on hearing, but rather remarking that if and when one hears the command, one attends something that cannot be described as a presence, for the pre-original whence of this command refers to an immemorial past, and, because of this, this particular hearing is described in the mode of *as though*.[10] As with the proximity of the neighbor, also the relation with the third party, the illeity (*illéité*) consists in an order that has already addressed me before any hearing, "It is the coming of the order to which I am subjected before hearing it [*l'entendre*], or which I hear [*j'entends*] in my own saying" (150/234–35). This sentence thus presents the very core of the idea of "the other in the same" (105/167), which means, on the one hand, that "the saying that comes to me is my own word" (150/235), and, on the other hand, that one's subjectivity is based on "an anarchic plot" (105/167). In the dynamic of substitution I am the one who is responsible for the other, but obeying this command differs from responding to orders given in the present; rather, it means that this saying is anarchically inscribed in me: "It is the pure trace of a 'wandering cause,' inscribed in me" (150/235).[11]

A whole acoustic terminology stems from the pre-original anachronism. Inasmuch as saying refuses contemporaneity with the said, the unheard (*inouï*) indicates the priority of the command situated on the level of saying, to which one has been already addressed, and the impossibility of coincidence between the ethical and the ontological: "Then, the trace of saying, which has never been present, obliges me; the responsibility for the other, never assumed, binds me; a command never heard [*jamais entendu*] is obeyed" (*OB* 168/AQE 261). The expression "ambiguity of inspiration" designates the anarchic obedience for-the-other (*pour-l'autre*) and simultaneously the authorship of having receiving and assumed this command inscribed in me, "this unheard-of obligation [*inouïe obligation*]" (148–49/232). Anachronism and ambiguity are not to be suppressed in this case, for they attest "a diachronic ambivalence which ethics makes possible" (149/232). In refusing a primordial role to any apprehension, the unheard reveals the very heart of the Levinasian account of ethics, inasmuch as it radicalizes the disjunction between ethics and ontology. "The unheard-of saying [*le dire inouï*] is enigmatically in the anarchic response, in my responsibility for the other" (149/232).

Far from indicating that concepts such as hearing and listening are excluded from the internal logic of *Otherwise than Being,* the anachronism itself ascribes distinctive roles to them, for what is at stake here is not the perception of some present sound, but the retention of the echo of a saying that resounds in one's ears. The said receives, therefore, a more robust account in this book; instead of being merely a negative demarcation of the apophantic discourse, the said also evokes the saying that resonates in it. "The said, contesting the abdication of the saying that everywhere occurs in this said, thus maintains the diachrony in which, holding its breath, the spirit hears the echo [*entend l'écho*] of the otherwise" (*OB* 44/*AQE* 76). The "unsayable saying [*le Dire indicible*]" exceeds the said and is irreducible to predicative relations, although in a manner in which it "lends itself to the said" (44/76) without being absorbed for or diluted in the latter, whereas "the saying is both an affirmation and a retraction of the said." (44/75). While keeping itself in face of the said and simultaneously in the said, the unsayable saying lets itself be reduced,[12] a reduction that is energized by "the ethical interruption of essence," and which exceeds mere presence or manifestation, for "the breathless spirit retains a fading echo [*écho*]" in "the ambiguity or the enigma of the transcendent" (44/76).

In and through the said, essence encompasses two different possibilities: either it assumes the verbal character resounding in the said, or it becomes petrified in the noun: "in the said, the essence that resounds [*résonne*] is on the verge of becoming a noun" (*OB* 41/*AQE* 71). Essence, in the verbal sense, "resounds [*résonne*] in the prose of predicative propositions" (41/71). To say that essence resounds in the said is to say that it vibrates within the said or temporalizes. Conversely, there is the latent risk of apophansis itself muffling the resonance, and consequently forcing the verb to become mere noun: "This resonance [*Résonance*] is always ready to congeal into nouns, where being will be congealed into a copula and the *Sachverhalt* 'nominalized'" (47/79). The resonance of the verb "is collected into an entity by the noun," and, accordingly, "to be thenceforth *designates* instead of *resounding*" (42/73). More accurately, the double direction of the essence engenders an internal amphibology in which predicative propositions transition from one extreme possibility to another; therefore, an "amphibology of the logos" (*amphibologie du logos*), which corresponds to an "amphibology of being and entities" (*de l'être et de l'étant*) (43/74), takes place. "The said as a verb is *essence* or temporalization. Or, more exactly, the logos enters into the amphibology in which being and entities can be understood and identified, in which a noun can resound as a verb and a verb of an apophansis can be nominalized" (42/72). At first sight, this amphibology leads us to an identification of the essence with the appearance and manifestation of the said, but, more than "making being understood," temporalization likewise makes "its essence vibrate [*vibrer*]" (35/61); in so doing, the saying places itself on the hither side of being (*l'en deçà de l'être*), as the possibility of ethical interruption of the essence.

The term *echo* reveals itself as being fitted perfectly to Levinas's purposes. On the one hand, it refers to the anarchic saying that is always prior to understanding and hearing, and, on the other hand, it bespeaks the passivity of being accused: "The metaphor of a sound that would be audible only in its echo meant to approach this way of presenting one's passivity as an underside without a right side" (*OB* 106/*AQE* 167). Only from the perspective of "a passivity more passive than all passivity" (15/30), that is, from the ethical standpoint of vulnerability and exposure, in which one is addressed in the accusative, may a comparison with echo in terms of recurrence of one's responsibility for others become intelligible. The recurrence of persecution is "prior to all reflection, prior to every positing, an indebtedness before any loan, not assumed, anarchical, subjectivity of a bottomless passivity, made out of assignation, like the echo of a sound [*l'écho d'un son*] that would precede the resonance [*résonance*] of this sound" (111/175). The immemorial past implies a surplus that refuses its identification as a theme in the said, which does not only imply the impossibility of the saying to be completely absorbed by the said, but also demands a redirection of one's attention toward the echo of an anarchic bygone. When referring to the amphibology of being and entities, Levinas points out the disjunction between the possibility of "assembling the dispersion of duration into nouns and propositions," which consequently "lets being and entities be heard [*laisse entendre*]" through the resonance of essence, and the possibility of surprising "the echo [*l'écho*] of the saying [in the said], whose signification cannot be assembled" (27/48).

The impact of the diachrony of transcendence into synchronic time resembles the movement of breathing, which is conceived as "transcendence in the form of opening up [*dé-claustration*]" to the other (*OB* 181/*AQE* 278). The diachrony of breathing, "a diachrony without synthesis" that resembles the very dynamic of the "truth" (183/281), refers to the "movement from here to yonder" (180/276), an "exile in oneself" (182/279) that encompasses an inspiration that is "without a stopping point" and an expiration that is "without return" (182/279). Levinas goes on to say, "In human breathing, in its everyday equality, perhaps we have to already hear [*entendre*] the breathlessness of an inspiration that paralyzes essence, that transpierces it with an inspiration by the other, an inspiration that is already expiration, that 'rends the soul'! It is the longest breath there is, spirit" (181–82/278). Levinas tarries alongside the subject matter of "restlessness of respiration" (182/279) to draw attention to the instant that separates inspiration and expiration, in which the spirit holds its breath and by so doing hears the echo of the otherwise. What is then heard in this contraction of the natural movement of breathing? Levinas explicitly affirms the ethical relevance of this hearing for the diachrony of the-one-for-the-other (*l'un-pour-l'autre elle-même*), a hearing of the resonance of silence.[13] The temporalization of the said in which essence vibrates "lets the pre-original saying be heard [*laisse entendre*], answers to transcendence, to a dia-chrony, to the irreducible divergency that opens here between the non-present and every representable divergency, which in its own way…makes a sign to the responsible one" (10–11/24–25).

IL Y A AND THE RESONANCE OF SILENCE

Levinas's description of the "rustling" of the *il y a* as being a necessary condition for the possibility of substitution has never been so clear as in this passage of *Otherwise than Being:* "*To support* [emphasis in French edition] without compensation, the excessive or disheartening hubbub [*l'écoeurant remue-ménage*] and encumberment [*encombrement*] of the *there is* [*il y a*] is needed" (*OB* 164/*AQE* 255), whereas it awakens the ego "from its imperialist dream" (164/256). Nonetheless, this necessary condition is plainly insufficient to perform by itself the entire movement toward the beyond being, for it is only the encounter with the other that evidences the complete powerlessness of one's self-assurance within the scope of the same.[14]

Levinas has already conceived art as that which creates silence, and stressed the oppressive and frightening character of this silence, in "The Transcendence of Words." One learns from *Existence and Existents* that silence refers to the *il y a*, to the voice of silence that impersonally accompanies every instant of one's existence, as the silence of the infinite spaces described by Pascal. Some important displacements, however, are to be considered, regarding the relation between the *il y a* and silence in *Otherwise than Being*. In this later work, silence refers most of the time to the resonance of essence. The "resonance of silence," of which the "listening eye" is aware, cannot be identified anymore with the silence of the *il y a* of *Existence and Existents*, although there are some undeniable affinities. In *Otherwise than Being*, it corresponds to the amphibology of being and entities and therefore to the amphibology of language in its double reference to verbs and nouns: "Here language does not double up the being of entities, but exposes the silent resonance of the essence" (*OB* 40/*AQE* 70).

In "The Question of Subjectivity," among other texts, Levinas addresses the sense in which the resonance of silence connects with Heidegger: "In its reign of being, being is language—and it is a silent language or the voice of silence, *Läute der Stille*. (In this way, without realizing it, Heidegger would have 'Judaized' the Greeks!) This voice of silence is that which is heard by the poet, who transposes it into human language" (*GDT* 151/*DMT* 173).[15] Levinas clarifies that the expression "resonance of silence" refers to Heidegger's *Läute/ Geläut der Stille*.[16] To employ Levinas's terminology, this expression means the precedence of the said over communication, a said that can be brought to manifestation and intelligibility by the hearing of the poet. Nevertheless, Levinas warns, in so doing it also excludes any possibility of diachrony that resonates in this silence. In what sense could this emphasis on the "voice"[17] of silence have "Judaized" the

Greeks, as Levinas claims? The contrast that Martin Jay offers between these two traditions is helpful: "If the Jews could begin their most heartfelt prayer, 'Hear, O Israel,' the Greek philosophers were in effect urging, 'See, O Hellas.'"[18]

In *Otherwise than Being*, the resonance of silence does not refer anymore, in an exclusive way, to the presence of absence in the middle of the night that oppresses the insomniac, but to the fact that essence vibrates in the said. The "eye that listens" (*oeil qui écoute*) does not capture an object in the light; instead, this expression adumbrates the exposure of the eye to the unbearable silence that resounds, to the "saying that does not say a word" (*OB* 151/*AQE* 236).

Time and the *essence* it unfolds by manifesting *entities*, identified in the themes of statements or narratives, resound as a silence [*résonnent comme un silence*] without becoming themes themselves. They can, to be sure, be named in a theme, but this naming does not reduce to definitive silence the mute resonance [*la résonance sourde*], the murmur of silence [*le bourdonnement du silence*], in which essence is identified as an entity. Once again for the "listening eye" a silence resounds [*un silence résonne*] about what had been muffled, the silence of the parceling out of being, by which entities in their identities are illuminated and show themselves (*OB* 38/*AQE* 67).

Brian Schroeder interprets the listening eye as follows: "For Levinas, the metaphor of the listening eye indicates the approach to move beyond the hegemonic image, paradoxically dehierarchizing the relation between the terms visual/aural, sight/sound, seeing/hearing, while maintaining the ethical superiority of the Other."[19] In a sense, this procedure of "dehierarchizing" extends itself to other concepts of Levinas's philosophy in order to compose a language of the transcendence. This procedure is necessary to disrupt the system of references that we are familiar with, while twisting meanings in order to free new possibilities of addressing alterity. Therefore, the primary role of presenting the awkward expression "eye that listens" has less to do with vision or audition than with our expectations of these concepts;

in other words, Levinas is undoubtedly less concerned with a theory of vision or audition than with a displacing of these terms in order to achieve a space of transcendence, because to him it is not a matter of how a subject can apprehend words and sounds, but rather of how a radical displacement of one's existence is implicated by the encounter with the other. This can be explored in at least two ways. Firstly, the "eye that listens" has paradoxically the same function as Plato's judge presented in the *Gorgias*, the one "divested 'of eyes and ears'" (*OB* 190/*AQE* 250),[20] for both criticize the limitation of the sameness provided by the senses in ethical demands. Secondly, seeing and hearing/listening are disconnected from their usual role in theories of perception to deliver instead a function similar to that of the caress, for the latter, as a fulfillment of proximity, opposes the perceiving mode of touch. When Levinas states, "In every vision contact is announced: sight and hearing caress the visible and the audible. Contact is not an openness upon being, but an exposure of being" (80/128), he is enabling the possibility of thinking the listening eye as performing something entirely different from the traditional functions ascribed to seeing and hearing in ontology. In which way does the listening eye expose itself if not in the sense of allowing one to be stroked by the echo of the saying? As well as caress, the listening eye engenders proximity as proximity,[21] as exposedness to the other, in which "grasping" becomes "being grasped" (75/121).

If the resonance of silence is thus attached to the vibration of the essence within the said, how is the *il y a* described in *Otherwise than Being*? Although there is some coherence with his previous works, where Levinas has engaged it as rustling (*frôlement*) or as "the muffled rustling of the nothingness" (*le sourd bruissement du néant*) (*TI* 146/ *TeI* 156),[22] the *il y a* is rather addressed in *Otherwise than Being* as a modification of the essence, insofar as the "imperturbable essence" turns "as in insomnia, from this neutrality and equality into monotony, anonymity, insignificance, into an incessant buzzing [*bourdonne-*

ment] that nothing can now stop and which absorbs all signification" (*OB* 163/*AQE* 253–54). "Essence stretching on indefinitely (...) is the horrifying *there is*," affirms Levinas, punctuating simultaneously the detachment or "subtraction" of the subject from the essence (163/254): "It is the incessant buzzing [*l'incessant bourdonnement*] that fills each silence, where the subject detaches itself from essence and posits itself as a subject in face of its objectivity" (163/254). This "incessant buzzing," or "intolerable rumble" (*bourdonnement intolérable*) (163/254), fills the silence that resounds in the essence with a "surplus of non-sense over sense" (164/255): "The rumbling of the *there is* [*bourdonnement de l'il y a*] is the nonsense in which essence turns, and in which thus turns the justice issued out of signification" (163/254). Thenceforth, "to find itself again in essence" (163/254) requires from the subject something other than a reversal of non-sense into sense again, whereas every sense is continually dissolved into nullity for the *il y a*—only the diachronic substitution for the other completely achieves that which *il y a* partially performs: in the diachrony, the subject awakened to passivity fulfills the radical passivity of the for-the-other.

These elements should also be considered in Levinas's account of art. He underscores the borderline position of art as follows: "Through art essence and temporality begin to resound with poetry or song. And the search for new forms, from which all art lives, keeps awake everywhere the verbs that are on the verge of lapsing into substantives" (*OB* 40/ *AQE* 70). Art resounds in a way that prevents verbs from becoming nouns, by keeping them *awake*. It is thus the resonance of silence that resounds in art, the silence that art itself creates, which involves two ideas that can be conjoined: in *Existence and Existents,* silence is linked to the very experience of depersonalization, and in "The Reality and Its Shadow" Levinas explains how one is impelled toward anonymity and impersonality by means of art.[23] In a sense, art keeps awake the verb in creating the conditions by which one may experience impersonality, and this always means to bring silence to the fore: "As an impersonal going on, an incessant splashing [*incessant clapotis*], a mute murmuring [*sourd bruissement*], as *there is,* does not essence swallow up the signification that will give light to it? Is not the insistence of this impersonal noise [*bruit impersonnel*] the threat of an end of the world felt in our days?" (140/219). The silence does not draw attention to itself unless something befalls, as when one is overwhelmed by insomnia, or when the work of art ostensibly imposes the "mute murmuring" upon the spectator or listener. It is appropriate to speak of this silence, then, in terms of deafness, as inattentiveness to the resonance of essence: "But it does so in isolation: every work of art is in this sense exotic, without a world, essence in dissemination. To fail to recognize the said *properly so-called* (relative as it may be) in the predicative propositions which every artwork—plastic, sonorous or poetic—awakens and makes resound [*résonner*] in the form of *exegesis* is to show oneself to be as profoundly deaf [*surdité aussi profonde*] as in the deafness of hearing [*n'entendre*] only nouns in language" (41/71).

This deafness may likewise be described as the incapability of hearing the resonance of silence, or the lack of awareness of the amphibology that leads to the pure identification of the saying with nouns. Nevertheless, Levinas also refers to another dimension of deafness, which concerns other traditions besides ontology,[24] as when he criticizes the ontological approach "if one is deaf [*sourd*] to the petition that sounds [*résonne*] in questioning and even under the apparent silence of the thought that questions itself, everything in a question will be oriented to truth, and will come from the essence of being" (*OB* 26/*AQE* 48). Levinas evokes the voices that do not coincide with those of ontology, "inflexions of forgotten voices [*inflexions de voix oubliées*]" (26/48) that resound in the essence. He asks if "there is not heard a voice [*ne s'entend pas une voix*] coming from horizons at least as vast as those in which ontology is situated" in the "mute murmuring" of the *il y a* (140/219). Finally, the moments of "forgotten voices" and the "voice of silence" conjoin with the "voice of the infinite," as in this passage where Levinas relates the infinite with "the beginninglessness of an anarchy and...the endlessness of obligation," which allows him to conclude, "In the absolute assignation of the subject the Infinite is enigmatically heard [*s'entend*]: before and beyond. The extent and accent of the voice in which the Infinite is thus heard [*la portée et l'accent de la voix où l'Infini ainsi s'entend*] will have to be made clear" (140/219).

FINAL REMARKS

Although some of the acoustic motifs that appear in *Otherwise than Being* had been employed in previous works, it is noteworthy that only when Levinas brings to the fore subjects such as the amphibology of saying and said, the immemorial past, and the diachrony of the interruption, among others, are they able to play a more relevant role in his philosophy. Levinas gives new directions to concepts that have appeared before, such as the silence that, besides its well-known connection with the arousal of the *il y a,* is also systematically employed to designate the amphibology of being and entities. On the other hand, there is an expansion of the subjects of his thought by means of acoustics, and terms like hearing and listening are not just occasionally mentioned, as often happened in previous writings, but become crucial to the argumentation. This is unmistakable in the presentation of the main themes: the eye that listens to the resonance of essence, and the hearing that is aware of the echo of the otherwise, the breathlessness of an inspiration, the pre-original saying, the forgotten voices, the infinite, and so on. In this sense, the ubiquity of acoustic terms does not only express a radicalization of his critique of the visible, but takes on and expands his early insight on the capacity of sound and audition to overflow the limits of the sensible and the given, as sketched in his aesthetics of materiality.

Notes

Funding for this research was provided by CAPES-Brazil as a scholarship for postdoctoral studies. The author thanks Chiara Pavan and Stephanie Rumpza for their probing and helpful comments. In addition to the abbreviations at the front of this volume, the following are also used: Emmanuel Levinas, "La realité et son ombre" (RO), *Les temps modernes* 38 (1948): 769–89; Emmanuel Levinas, "La signification et le sens" (SS), *Revue de Métaphysique et de Morale* 69, no. 2 (1964): 125–56; Emmanuel Levinas, "La transcendance des mots: À propos des *Biffures* de Michel Leiris" (LTM), *Les temps modernes* 44 (1949): 1090–95.

1. Derrida writes, "Respect, beyond grasp and contact, beyond touch, smell and taste, can be only as desire, and metaphysical desire does not seek to consume, as do Hegelian desire or need. This is why Levinas places sound above light." Jacques Derrida, "Violence and Metaphysics: An Essay on the Thought of Emmanuel Levinas," in *Writing and Difference,* trans. Alan Bass (London: Routledge, 2005), 123–24.

2. Ibid., 124.

3. According to the circumstances, *entendre* may be translated as hearing or understanding. Unless stated otherwise, the passages discussed here are always related to hearing.

4. For the sake of brevity, we skip the analysis of *entendre, écouter,* and *audition* in *Totality and Infinity,* since it involves an entirely different approach. We will indicate, however, some related aspects throughout this article.

5. In this sense, Ricoeur's interpretation of Levinas in *Oneself as Another* can also give rise to misunderstandings: "the 'appearing' of the Other in the *face* of the Other eludes vision, seeing forms, and even eludes listening voices [*l'écoute des voix*]. In truth, the face does not appear; it is not a phenomenon; it is an epiphany" *Oneself as Another* (Chicago: University of Chicago Press, 1994), 189, translation modified; original at Paul Ricoeur, *Soi-même comme un autre* (Paris: Éditions du Seuil, 1990), 221. It is true that the face-to-face eludes listening to the voice of the other, inasmuch as the obedience of command is prior to listening/hearing. Nevertheless, Levinas also places relevance in "the voice in which the Infinite is thus heard" (*OB* 140), or in the "eye that listens" (30) to the voice and the resonance of silence, or in the hearing of "forgotten voices" (26), as we will develop further.

6. Gerard L. Bruns, "The Concepts of Art and Poetry in Emmanuel Levinas's Writings," in *The Cambridge Companion to Levinas,* ed. Simon Critchley and Robert Bernasconi (Cambridge: Cambridge University Press, 2004), 207.

7. Or from this other passage of *Existence and Existents:* "For the insecurity does not come from the things of the day world which the night conceals; it is due just to the fact that nothing approaches, nothing comes, nothing threatens; this silence, this tranquility, this void of sensations constitutes a mute, absolutely indeterminate menace" (*EE* 59/*DEE* 96).

8. Similarly, horror also denotes a sonorous account: "The rustling [*frôlement*] of the *there is* ... is horror" (*EE* 60; emphasis and ellipses in original/*DEE* 98).

9. "The particular automatic character of a walk or a dance to music is a mode of being where nothing is unconscious, but where consciousness, paralyzed in its freedom, plays, totally absorbed in this playing" (*CPP* 4/*RO* 775).

10. By the same token, in "The Proximity of the Other" one finds again the "as though/as if" relating listening and obedience: "The *for-the-other* arises in the I like a commandment heard by him, as if obedience were a state of listening for the prescription" (*IR* 213).

11. The accusative form is prior to the appearance in the said, insofar as passivity exposes the fact that oneself is not the cause of oneself, but a creature. "The hypostasis is exposed as oneself in the accusative form, before appearing in the said proper to knowing as the bearer of a name" (*OB* 106/*AQE* 167). Moreover, according to Levinas, "The oneself cannot form itself; it is already formed with absolute passivity" (104/165). These passages enable the interpretation of the idea that "The ego is in itself like a sound that would resound in its own echo [*comme un son qui résonnerait dans son propre écho*], the node of a wave which is not once again consciousness" (103/162). Once again, it is important to underline the word "like" (*comme*), because the vocabulary of resonance and echo does not fit with the perspective of the consciousness that Levinas rejects in these passages. The analogy that would result in a dismissal of the unity of consciousness in this last passage will be strongly reiterated some lines afterwards: "Nothing here resembles self-consciousness" (103/163). Of interest to us here is that Levinas rejects subjectivity as consciousness and enacts it as passivity; in so doing, he posits the subject as the one who echoes a pre-original inscription within him/her as the one assigned with responsibility: "The response which is responsibility, responsibility for the neighbor that is incumbent, resounds in this passivity, this disinterestedness of subjectivity, this sensibility" (14–15/30–31).

12. Reduction has the precise meaning of "going back to the hither side of being" or "to the hither side of the said" (*OB* 45/*AQE* 76).

13. Levinas writes, "Transcendence owes it to itself to interrupt its own demonstration. Its voice has to be silent as soon as one listens for its message" (*OB* 152/*AQE* 238).

14. The encounter with the other involves a double character: on the one hand, the other is the one whom I can wish to kill, but any attempt to carry out this task is unfruitful—the face eludes and shows the limits of my powers; on the other hand, it is the other who interrupts the unceasing cycle of having my enterprises undone by the *il y a*, whereas he or she offers an alternative that remains outside the dynamic of power that underlies the contending with the *il y a*. Levinas writes, "Everything that claims to come from elsewhere, even the marvels of which *essence* [emphasis in French edition] itself is capable, even the surprising possibilities of renewal by technology and magic, even the perfections of gods peopling the heights of this world, and their immortality and the immortality they promise mortals—all this does not deaden the heartrending bustling of the *there is* recommencing behind every negation. There is not a break in the business carried on by essence, not a distraction. Only the meaning of the other is irrecusable, and forbids the reclusion

and reentry into the shell of the self. A voice comes from the other shore. A voice interrupts the saying of the already said" (*OB* 182–83/280).

15. A similar explanation is found in *Otherwise than Being*: "The said can indeed be understood to be prior to communication and the intersubjective representation of being. Being would have a signification, that is, would manifest itself as already invoked in silent and nonhuman language, by the voices of silence [*voix du silence*], in the *Geläut der Stille,* the language that speaks before men and harbors the *esse ipsum,* the language which poetry puts into human words" (*OB* 135/*AQE* 211).

16. It is not possible to discuss here what this expression means to Heidegger and in which sense Levinas's reading is appropriate or not. See Martin Heidegger, "Language," in *Poetry, Language, Thought,* trans. Albert Hofstadter (New York: Harper and Row, 1975).

17. *Geläut der Stille* is translated as "the peal of stillness" by Albert Hofstadter. Although Heidegger refers to command (*Geheiß*) and call (*Ruf*) in this text, the term "voice" that Levinas frequently employs does not appear in "Language."

18. Martin Jay, *Downcast Eyes: The Denigration of Vision in Twentieth-Century French Thought* (Berkeley: University of California Press, 1993), 33. The difference between Christian and Jewish tradition is also relevant: "The word made flesh in the Christian tradition was thus a falling away from the Jewish stress on the voice and the ear" (556).

19. Brian Schroeder, "The Listening Eye: Nietzsche and Levinas," in *Emmanuel Levinas: Critical Assessments of Leading Philosophers,* vol. 2, ed. Claire Katz and Lisa Trout (London: Routledge, 2005), 279.

20. See Plato, *Gorgias* 523c–d.

21. "In this caress proximity signifies as proximity, and not as an experience of proximity" (*OB* 80/*AQE* 128).

22. *Sourd bruissement* is also translated as "mute murmuring" in *Otherwise than Being,* as we will see afterwards.

23. The silence of resonance presented in *Otherwise than Being* does not coincide with Levinas's early account of silence in *Existence and Existents*. Among the many discordances, it is noteworthy that the "voice of silence" with which one is confronted while facing the *il y a* appears as "frightening" and "oppressive," as an unbearable silence that reproaches every attempt of the subject to render meaning only by himself/herself. Conversely, this expression is defined in *Otherwise than Being* as the very temporalization and vibration of the essence.

24. "Behind being and its monstration, there is now already heard the resonance [*s'entend la résonance*] of other significations forgotten in ontology, which now solicit our inquiry" (*OB* 38/*AQE* 67).

Bearing the Other and Bearing Sexuality:
Women and Gender in Levinas's "And God Created Woman"

Deborah Achtenberg

Much ink has been spilled on the question of the role of women for Levinas's ethics in accounts containing a gamut of claims, from Stella Sandford's that woman is aligned with sexual difference in such a way that Levinas's attempts to install her within the human fail,[1] to Diane Perpich's that one reason *Otherwise than Being* is preferable to *Totality and Infinity* is that the ethics in the former does not rest on a failed narrative of family life and woman's role in it as ethics does in the latter,[2] to Claire Katz's that there is a rich, positive ethical component to women's role for Levinas since he uses maternity as an example of being-for-the-other.[3]

This essay complements those accounts by giving a detailed analysis of the discussion of women in Levinas's talmudic commentary, "And God Created Woman."[4] Specifically, I ask whether Levinas is right, in his commentary, that, according to Talmud Berakhot 61a, women are not ultimately inferior to men because both men and women are human and their humanity precedes the division of humanity into male and female. I pursue the question by reading the talmudic passage the way Levinas, in his commentary, tells us that we should read Talmud, namely, by situating texts quoted in it in their broader textual context in Torah rather than treating them as proof texts.

When I put quotations cited in Berakhot 61a in their textual context, I find that the male figures treated in the texts from Torah are dismayingly dismissive of women in distress, suggesting that women are treated as inferior, but then learn their mistake and treat the women as equal or even superior, suggesting that Talmud does see them as having a humanity that precedes sexual difference. Nonetheless, I go on to argue, though the talmudic passage does not see women as ultimately inferior to men, it nonetheless treats them as inferior on the day-to-day level and such treatment belies the attempt to treat them as human.

I go on to ask about Levinas's stance toward this problem in the talmudic text, Does he accept the treatment of women as inferior? I argue, to the contrary, that Levinas sees the problem and attempts to overcome it by criticizing two ways the talmudic passage treats women as inferior on the day-to-day level: he rejects the passages' prohibitions on certain types of male contact with women—such as looking at them!—and he reinterprets its association of women with makeup and deception. His stance is more complicated, though, because he goes on to find a kernel of truth to preserve in each of the problematic talmudic positions: in the first, the fundamental ethical ambiguity of sexuality, since sexuality points toward the other as other but also toward one's own satisfaction; in the second, what we might anachronistically call women's ways of knowing that, for Levinas, have a certain ethical superiority over the ways men know. The two resolutions have their own problems, I maintain, since if Levinas is to avoid gender norming and gender hierarchy, he needs to make it clear that both the problematic ethical ambiguity of sexuality and also the ways of knowing he thinks are ethically superior are not essentially associated more with women than with men.

1

Reading Levinas's way, I search out the context of quotations, taking them not as proof texts, but as invitations to interpret. In "And God Created Woman," he says, "each time a biblical verse is brought in as proof it is not likely that the sages of the Talmud are looking in these texts, squeezed every which way in spite of grammar, for a direct proof of the thesis they are upholding. It is always an invitation to search out the context of the quotation" (*NT* 166/*DSS* 130–31). As a feminist, when I search out the context of the quotations Levinas refers to in his reading of Berakhot 61a, I am dismayed. Sad stories, about distressed women and men who do not pay attention to them: do not listen to them (in the case of Manoah's wife), speak to them (in the case of the Shunamite woman), comprehend them (in the case of Hannah). Overall, men who do not recognize women's distress and their humanity.

Eli, the priest, in a well-known Rosh Hashanah haftarah portion, thinks Hannah is drunk when she in fact is wordlessly praying to God for a son: "As she kept on praying before the LORD, Eli watched her mouth. Now Hannah was praying in her heart; only her lips moved, but her voice could not be heard. So Eli thought she was drunk" (1 Sam. 1:12–13).

Elisha, follower of Elijah, would send his servant, not go himself, to save the sick or dying son of the formerly barren Shunamite woman, a woman whom, when she was barren, Elisha had promised would have a child. When the son she bore becomes sick or dying, she says to Elisha, "Did I ask my lord for a son? Didn't I say: 'Don't mislead me'?" Then Elisha says to his servant, Gehazi, "Tie up your skirts, take my staff in your hand, and go" and "place my staff on the face of the boy" (2 Kings 4:28–29). It is striking that he only sends his servant to save the son of this woman who had previously gone out of her way to have a living unit added to her house for him to stay in when he was passing through.

Manoah, father of Samson, does not hear his barren wife when she says a visitor, who announced that she will bear a son, looked like an angel of God: "A man of God came to me," she says, and "he looked like an angel of God, very frightening" (Judg. 13:6). But, the text goes on to say that Manoah offered the man bread and asked his name, for "Manoah did not know that he was an angel of the Lord" (Judg. 13:16).

I want to scream at each of the three men, Who do you think you are? A God in relation to a woman? It's idolatrous. Eli says to Hannah, "How long will you make a drunken spectacle of yourself? Sober up!" assuming her difference is inferiority (1 Sam. 1:14).

Elisha speaks about the Shunamite woman to his servant, Gehazi, in the third person, not facing her. When she would clasp Elisha's feet in supplication, Gehazi, the servant, tries to push her away: "when she came up to the man of God on the mountain, she clasped his feet. Gehazi stepped forward to push her away" (2 Kings 4:27).

Manoah distrusts his wife's ability to discern and follow the instructions of an angel, and asks for personal testimony to reaffirm what she has already said to him. The angel says to Manoah's wife, "You are going to conceive and bear a son. Drink no wine or other intoxicant, and eat nothing unclean, for the boy is to be a nazirite to God from the womb to the day of his death!" (Judg. 13:7). Manoah later on speaks to the same angel, whom he thinks is a man, when he comes on a second visit, and asks him, "What rules shall be observed for the boy?" and the angel says, not surprisingly, the same things he previously said to Manoah's wife: "The woman must abstain from all the things against which I warned her. She must not eat anything that comes from the grapevine, or drink wine or other intoxicant, or eat anything unclean. She must observe all that I commanded her" (13:12–14).

But, as Levinas points out, each of the men learns. When the angel comes on the second visit and goes to see Manoah's wife rather than him, "Manoah promptly followed his wife" (Judg. 13:11) (though even then, as we just saw, he re-asks a question for which his wife already had gotten the answer, and, in addition, nearly gets them killed when he offers a burnt offering to, and asks the name of, an angel).

Elisha, when the Shunamite woman tells him about her sick son, responds, distantly, as we saw, by sending the servant with instructions on how to heal the boy. But, once she refuses to leave Elisha, saying, "As the LORD lives and as you live, I will not leave you!" he finally pays attention to her—"he arose and followed her"—and heals the boy himself, using his whole body to revive him: "he mounted [the bed] and placed himself over the child. He put his mouth on its mouth, his eyes on its eyes, and his hands on its hands, as he bent over it. And the body of the child became warm. He stepped down, walked once up and down the room, then mounted and bent over him. Thereupon, the boy sneezed seven times, and the boy opened his eyes" (2 Kings 4:30–35).

When Hannah explains to Eli her distress, saying, "Oh no, my lord! I am a very unhappy woman. I have drunk no wine or other strong drink, but I have been pouring out my heart to the LORD.... I have only been speaking all this time out of my great anguish and distress" (1 Sam. 1:15), Eli says, "Then go in peace...and may the God of Israel grant you what you have asked of Him" (1:17).

2

I am reading Berakhot 61a the way Levinas himself reads it, by searching out the context of the quotations—though he seems, in fact, to run out of time: "it is getting late," he says, and he must "pass over the text quickly" (*NT* 174/*DSS* 144). His quick *drash* on (interpretation of) the passage is: "Question: Manoah, the father of Samson, is called an ignoramus and uncivilized because it is said in scripture: 'And Manoah walked behind his wife.' But didn't the prophet Elisha follow the Shunamite woman? Answer: to follow can mean to take advice. Essential point: in the interhuman order, the perfect equality and even superiority of woman, who is capable of giving advice" (175/145).

Of course, for Levinas, knowledge and civilization are not always a good thing, and he means to imply that, with some irony, here. Preferable to them is a different kind of virtue, a simplicity, a directness, a responsiveness, that at certain points he calls *droiture* (in French) or *temimut* (in Hebrew): "This uprightness is called *Temimut*, the essence of Jacob." (According to Genesis 25:27, Jacob was an *ish tam*, a simple man, who lived in tents.) *Temimut* is "an innocence without naïveté, an uprightness without stupidity, an absolute uprightness that is also absolute self-criticism, read in the eyes of the one who is the goal of my uprightness and whose look calls me into question." It "is a movement toward the other which does not come back to its point of origin" ("Temptation of Temptation," 48/105). A simple man, an *ish tam*, is a man who goes beyond cultural categories—who goes beyond all categories (here, it's the category of "woman")—to the singular other person him- or herself (here, it's herself), as Eli does when, with his smug assumption called into question, he gives up his stereotype and imperiousness and tells anguished, distressed Hannah to go in peace.

And we should not overlook Hannah's distress, nor that of the two other women. Each is distressed and anguished about what, given their woman's role, is most important to them. Hannah is anguished because she is barren, and "In her wretchedness, she prayed to the LORD, weeping all the while" (1 Sam. 1:10). The Shunamite woman's son is sick or dead and, Elisha says, "she is in bitter distress" (2 Kings 4:27) at the possible loss of her only son. Manoah's wife is frightened at the presence of an angel who announces an end to her barrenness.

And so the talmudic passage (*NT* 163) does not claim that the women, because they are different (for example, because children play such a role in their lives), are inferior. The women are not uncultured and inferior, but, each in her own specific way, in distress. In other respects, they are superior: Manoah's wife can recognize and inspire the presence of an angel where Manoah cannot; the Shunamite woman knows when she needs Elisha's (not, as Elisha thinks, his servant's) help;

Hannah knows how to mourn. The men learn the women's humanity, distress, and, in some respects, superiority, and they move from stereotypic categorization to real concern, real being-for-the-other (in this case, being-for-the-woman).

And this, of course, is what most preoccupies Levinas in ethics: our way of being for another. It is this way of being two, not a more stereotypical way based on sexual difference, that Levinas sees, in "And God Created Woman," as central in the creation story. Berakhot 61a begins with the question why, in "The Lord God made man" (Gen. 2:7), "made" (*vayitzer*), usually written with one *yod*, is instead written there with two *yod*s (*vayyitzer*). What do the two *yod*s mean according to Levinas? That where there seems to be one, there in fact are two. The Lord God, according to Levinas, created not two inclinations, the *yetzer tov* (good inclination) and the *yetzer ra* (bad inclination), as Rav Nahman, son of Rav Hisda, claims, but two creatures. Where you think you have one, you actually have two. Two creatures in one: me, and the person I bear. I bear the other. I respond to her distress. Levinas says, "to create a man was to create in one creature two." (*NT* 165/*DSS* 127). Even more: "What is the human being? The fact that a being is *two* while remaining *one*" (165/128).

One meaning of the doubleness is that the two mean conscience and choice, responsibility and freedom. Another sense is given by Levinas's proof text, which, because it is a proof text, we are invited to search out or spell out: Isaiah 29:16. Levinas cites it to prove that *vayyitzer* implies not two inclinations (*yetzer*) but two creatures. The part that he quotes is "the creature (*yetzer*) said to the Creator he understood nothing" (*NT* 165). But the rest of the passage, which Levinas does not quote, suggests we cannot stay within our own subjectivity, but that we bear an other: "Ha! Those who would hide their plans deep from the LORD! Who do their work in dark places and say, 'Who sees us, who takes note of us?'" (Isa. 29:15). We cannot hide. We cannot be a self by staying within the self. The passage goes on: "How perverse of you! Should the potter be accounted as the clay? Should what is made say of its Maker, 'He did not make me,' and what is formed say of Him who formed it, 'He did not understand'? (Isa. 29:15).

I am not one. I bear God, despite how different God is from me (see *NT* 168/*DSS* 133). Similarly, if I am a man, I am not one, in my maleness, but I bear woman, despite how different woman is from me. The unity of one subject is "unity without synthesis or synchronicity," "duality of the non-interchangeable" (168/133), phrases that nicely summarize the heart of Levinas's ethics.

3

But, wait, despite all this ethical talk, am I right that the talmudic passage does not treat woman as inferior to man? *Woman is to obey man:* According to Rav Abbahu, God wanted to, but could not, produce equality because two equal beings would have meant war. "This initial independence of two equal beings would no doubt have meant war," Levinas says, interpreting the passage. "Real humanity," he also says, "does not allow for an abstract equality, without some subordination of terms," and so woman came after man, metaphorically speaking: "she came after him: the very femininity of woman is in this initial 'after the event'" (*NT* 173/*DSS* 142).

Woman is associated with makeup and deception: In the section called "Appearance," Levinas quotes Rabbi Simeon ben Menasia, who taught that in the passage, "And the LORD God fashioned the rib that He had taken from the man into a woman" (Gen. 2:22), "He fashioned the rib into woman" has to be understood to mean that "the Holy One, Blessed be He, plaited Eve's hair into braids and took her to Adam, for in other countries plaiting is called *binyatha* (building)." "God was the first hairdresser," Levinas says. "He created...the first make-up." "*To build* a feminine being," he adds, "is from the outset to make room for appearance. 'Her hair had to be done'" (*NT* 174/ *DSS* 143). To this talmudic passage, I here add a similar interpretation in a midrashic interpretation of the same passage: "R. Aibu—others state the following in R. Bannayah's name, and it was also taught in the name of R. Simeon b. Yoḥai—said: He [God] adorned her like a bride and brought her to Him, for there are places where coiffure is called building."⁵ The suggestion in the midrash is to translate the passage as "The Lord God made the rib into a woman coiffed or adorned."

Woman bears sexuality within: As a result, a man must not look at her and she must walk behind him: "A man must not walk behind a woman, for his ideas may become clouded," Levinas interprets Talmud as saying, with the reason being the fact "that a woman bears the erotic within herself as a matter of course," plus the supposed realities of masculine psychology (*NT* 174–75/*DSS* 144). The prohibitions are severe and the list is a horrifying one: it is forbidden for a man to walk behind a woman even on a narrow bridge; to cross a river behind a woman (lest he see something of her underthings); to give money to a woman directly (lest he use the occasion to look at her); or to look at a woman. Levinas very quickly moves from this discussion in the talmudic text of, as he calls it, "the priority of the masculine," to the passages quoted at the beginning of this essay on Manoah and his wife, Elisha and the Shunamite woman, and Eli and Hannah (175/145), stories in which the man *did* follow the woman, in the sense of taking her advice, suggesting the humanity of both man and woman. Levinas's point about the male-female inequalities expressed in the talmudic passage is that, in the order of Torah and of Berakhot 61a, humanity precedes these differences: first is humanity; then the differences.

He makes this point in a number of different ways throughout the reading: Regarding the interpretation of the two *yod*s that mentions a head with two faces, he speaks of "unity without synthesis or synchronicity" and the "strange duality of the non-interchangeable," and he goes on to conclude, "Thus woman appears within the human. The social governs the erotic," his point being that the human and social come first and only then gender and sexuality (*NT* 168/*DSS* 133). Regarding the interpretations according to which the "rib" was actually a side or a tail, he says "The fact that a woman is not merely the female of man, that she belongs to the human, is an assumption shared by both disputants: woman is, from the first, created from that which is human" (169/134). The one who believes "rib" actually means face believes in perfect equality, but the one who thinks it means tail — that is, a little, inconsequential thing — thinks therefore that she, like the man, results from a real act of creation (woman almost from nothing since from a tiny bone) (169/135). For the latter interpreter, he says, "It is not woman who is secondary; it is the relationship with woman which is secondary," by which he means the relationship to a woman as a woman rather than as a human being (in other words, the relationship to a woman as a human being is more important than the gendered or sexualized relationship to her as woman) (169/135). Regarding God, Levinas says He "wanted that from the beginning there should be equality in the creature, no woman issuing from man, no woman who came after man. From the beginning he wanted two separate and equal beings" (173/141–42). The point of each of these passages — a point Levinas emphasizes because he agrees with it — is that the woman's humanity precedes and is more important than any inequality. But that means I was not quite right. The talmudic passage does not treat woman ultimately as inferior to man — but it does treat woman on a more day-to-day basis as inferior to man. The inequality, Levinas says, is according to custom, for (awful) example, "According to custom, it is the man who must nevertheless, regardless of the goal, indicate the direction in which to walk" (*NT* 175/*DSS* 145).

4

What is Levinas's stance on the problem of day-to-day inequality, however? Does his thinking suffer from the same problem? Levinas, I believe, is aware of the problem and does, to an extent, mitigate it. He does so in two ways: by rejecting the severe prohibitions mentioned above, and by reinterpreting the makeup and deception charge. *Rejection of prohibitions:* Levinas criticizes but tries to see the best in the list of prohibitions: "The principle," he says, "is healthier than this outmoded rigorism. Relations between equal beings should not become pretexts for ambiguity" (*NT* 175/*DSS* 144–45). He rejects the over-rigorous prohibitions but suggests there are problems intrinsic to equal relations between the sexes. He discusses such problems later in the text: "The feminine has been much defended today as if the relationship with the feminine were only the meeting of the other par excellence, with all the excellences of such a meeting" (175–76/146).

Relationship with the feminine is not simply a meeting with the other as other with its characteristic excellence, namely, the ethical. Why? Because woman is also an erotic object. Levinas goes on: "What of evasions, of all the ambiguity of the famed love life (even when it claims to rise above pleasure)?" (*NT* 176/*DSS* 146). The ambiguity referred to here evidently is the same one discussed in *Totality and Infinity*, namely, that love aims both at pleasure for oneself, and so at satisfaction of one's own needs, and also at the other as other, and so is for the other or transcendent: "this simultaneity of need and desire, of concupiscence and transcendence, tangency of the avowable and the unavowable, constitutes the originality of the erotic which, in this sense, is *the equivocal* par excellence" (*TI* 255 / *TeI* 233). Levinas rejects the outmoded specific prohibitions for men, such as the prohibition against walking behind a woman or looking at her, but wants us to recognize one element of truth alluded to by the prohibitions, namely, the ambiguity of the erotic.

Reinterpretation of the makeup and deception charge: Levinas reinterprets them in the last paragraph of "And God Created Woman," if I understand it correctly. It is worth quoting the whole paragraph: "But who is the man who finds himself behind the synagogue where there is no other door, the man more lost than an idol worshipper? I am asking myself whether it is not the one who, outside the rituals and the laws, which are only the *letter,* believes himself to be 'in spirit and in truth' in the most intimate intimacy of Being. Here he is thrown into the shoreless abysses of interiority. It has never given back those it succeeded in seducing" (*NT* 177/*DSS* 148). The question he asks is who is it that stands apart from the synagogue and from community life even though they are not looking for a better way of entering than is currently provided? Who simply thinks he or she does not need to enter?

The section of Berakhot 61a referred to in this final paragraph of Levinas's commentary is about being behind or following. Rabbi Johanan provides a list of things it is dangerous to be behind and gives a certain order to them. We can presume "being behind" refers back to the discussion we looked at above, of men who follow or walk behind their wives. Whom should we walk behind? More broadly, whom should we follow? (Or, must we say, who should *a man* walk behind or follow? Or, even more must we say, who should *a straight man* walk behind or follow?) In a typical talmudic fashion, Johanan is widening the discussion of a certain danger in following by asking what we (or, what a man) should be more generally wary of following, and, in the process, engaging in a philosophical extension of the meaning of "following" beyond its literal sense, so that, I maintain, it encompasses everything from literal *following* to *being involved in* to *being influenced by* and to *listening to*—and, extending it even further, to consideration of *not following something*, for example, the case of "being behind" meaning "being outside" a synagogue, that is, *not* following or being influenced by a synagogue and those in it. Rabbi Johanan's order of things it is dangerous to be behind, in accord with something like ethical preference (if we may use the term "ethical" in a broad sense, not a narrower Kantian or Levinasian one) is: a lion, a woman, an idol worshipper, a synagogue (when people are inside praying). It is better to follow a lion than a woman. Levinas glosses this to mean that "living life, struggle and ambition" is better than "choos[ing] the sweetness of intimacy, perhaps the dove coos removed from the great upheavals and the great shocks which scan the Real" (*NT* 175/*DSS* 146). It is better to follow a woman, in a life of (heterosexual) intimacy, than to follow an idolater. Levinas thinks Johanan refers to the state, adored as an idol, or, thinking of the state at the time, the Greek gods and Hellenism (176/146). Finally, it is better to be behind an idolater than to be behind a synagogue, on the side opposite the entrance, when those inside are praying. Levinas understands this last ranking to refer to isolation within Judaism: "a *no* uttered to the community" (176/147). This, for Johanan, is the worst of all the dangers.

Presumably what is at issue in the discussion is what can keep one from being a good person or a good Jew. A life of ambition can do that due to the lion-like emotional attitudes it involves. One's intimate life can do that even more due to the erotic passions it involves. Activity in the Hellenized state or within Hellenic religion can keep one even more from being good because of the even more direct temptations to violate perhaps the most important prohibition in Jewish law, the prohibition on idolatry. But staying outside the synagogue can do it the most, perhaps because it is through prayer and ritual more broadly that we build up the strength to resist all the mentioned temptations.

Of course, it is a problem from a Levinasian standpoint—always a problem from a Levinasian standpoint—to think you know truth directly without point of view, standpoint, or framework. Thinking you have truth pure is a type of idolatry. It is the assumption to oneself of a God's-eye view. Even more, regarding Levinas's last paragraph, quoted above, it is thinking you can find what you are looking for—Being, truth, or God—without utilizing text, without hazarding interpretation, and without being given aid by others in community. Without these, you may think you have found Being or truth or God, but you really only have yourself. In other words, idolatry—thinking something is God that is not God—is bad enough, but what is worse than idolatry is thinking you know God without any helper or mediator. It is, we might say, the supreme form of idolatry, since it is idolatry of self.

If such a problem is a common one for Levinas, however, one could ask why he mentions it here specifically? Why does he mention it in relation to woman, the topic of this talmudic reading, and at the end, where it has the most emphatic position? I believe it is due to his desire to put a positive slant on the deception charge made against woman in Berakhot 61a. I conclude this from the fact that when, earlier in the passage, Levinas talks about the plaiting-the-hair interpretation, he not only refers to appearance and the lie, but also puts a positive spin on the (supposed) female connection to appearance, noting that even God gets involved in the deception: "He," God, "created the first illusions, the first make-up" (*NT* 174/*DSS* 143). Even more, Levinas says, "There is in the feminine face and in the relation between the sexes this beckoning to the lie" (his negative point), "or to an arrangement beyond the savage straightforwardness of a face-to-face encounter" (his positive point) (174/143). Woman is to man as Derrida to Levinas, pointing out the limits of empiricism, demonstrating the necessity of "arrangement" rather than pure truth, at least for human beings, born as they are not whole but out of a division and a "wound" (173/142).

Shading, hiding, and cautious framing, then, for Levinas in this passage are not deception but, we might say, taking a cue from feminist theory, "women's ways of knowing." We may, as I do, disagree with the gender norming that asserts that such an adorned, arranged approach to knowing and being comes into the world only with woman's entry—we may even, if we follow gender studies (and he arose and followed gender studies), think it is inadequate and incorrect to see the genders simply as two—but we can appreciate Levinas's effort to exonerate woman not only ultimately but also in the day to day. If he had not exonerated her/we/them in that way, we could have charged not only the Talmud but also him with too great a separation between the ethical (recognition of woman's humanity) and the political (prescribed obedience for a fundamentally sexual and deceptive being).

We can, however, make that charge against Berakhot 61a. If prescribed roles were as different for man and woman as some aspects of it suggest they should be—even if different only by custom—there would be an over-separation of the ethical from the political. How could we not treat woman as essentially inferior if we thought she must always walk behind a man? Or that she by nature must obey?

Or that he must always determine their literal and metaphorical direction? Or that she is fundamentally deceptive? The political, in these cases, would cloud and prevent the ethical.

5

We can still ask, however, whether Levinas's mitigation of the problems that are found in the talmudic text goes far enough. Let us return to and address the issues raised by the three interpreters I mentioned at the beginning of this essay. Similar to what Katz says regarding maternity, we now see that Levinas gives woman an important role in ethics in his talmudic reading, since the shading and framing that he here associates with women are central to Levinas's ethics. That they are central is clear throughout Levinas's writing, for example in the section on the reduction in *Otherwise than Being* where he makes central to philosophy and ethics the reduction of the said back to the saying (*OB* 43–45/*AQE* 56–58). Never think you have comprehended something pure or without standpoint, the passage exhorts us. Recognize that we achieve a said only through a particular saying that could be accompanied by another saying, and another, and another. "A philosopher's effort," Levinas says, is the activity of "reducing the eon which triumphs in the said." Similarly for him, it is "necessary that the saying call for philosophy" so that "the hypostasis of an eon not be set up as an idol" (44/56). The reduction calls on us to be aware of our standpoint. Doing so is central to any attempt to relate to the other as other. Moreover, the passage makes it clear that thinking *a* set of opinions is *the* truth is idolatry. It is hypostasizing an eon, that is, treating a transient set of opinions as though they were fixed, treating a standpoint is if it were the God's-eye view. In "And God Created Woman," Levinas attributes the awareness of standpoint to women, thus giving them a central ethical role.

At the same time, we can question the gender norming involved in attributing such ways of knowing specifically to women. Like Perpich, we can reject resting ethics specifically on a specific normative picture of family life and woman's role in it. "And God Created Woman" is too abbreviated for us to know with really complete certitude whether that is exactly what Levinas is doing in the passage, rather than simply pointing to typical pictures that have been drawn in the past. We can say, though, that if his ethics does rest on fixed gender roles in which "woman" sees standpoint and is tasked with introducing "man" to it, then his mitigation of the problem of day-to-day inequality making ultimate equality impossible is not completely successful.

Similarly, if Levinas accepted the idea that sexuality or a type of sexual bearing is in some way specific to women—the talmudic passage according to him suggests they "bear sexuality within"—his mitigation of the problem regarding day-to-day inequality again would be incomplete. We cannot attribute that position to him here—again due to the brevity of the talmudic reading—but his mitigation of the problems in "And God Created Woman" is not complete without specifically rejecting that idea. Following Sandford, we can say that such identification of woman with sexuality would align woman with sexual difference in such a way as to make the assumption of her humanity impossible. There would be man who, say, is endeavoring to become ethical, and woman, the fundamentally sexual other, who appears in the text when sexual difference is important and whose attractiveness makes achievement of ethical life difficult (for men? for straight men?). We need a different picture, in which both man and woman—both men and women—endeavor to become ethical, variably aid one another to see their standpoints as partial, not complete, and suffer from the ethical ambiguities that sexuality brings.

We need, even more, a much broader picture, in which both straight and nonstraight men and women, both transgendered and non-transgendered people, both transgressive and normative people, do these things. And this goes quite a bit beyond any picture Levinas provides us. Sexual ethics goes way beyond the problem of how we manage our selfish responses to the attractiveness to us (that is, to straight men) of women. It goes to selfish responses to the attractiveness to us of a wide variety of others, given the variety of ways in which our genders are constructed and the wide variety of ways in which we find ourselves attracted to others.

Levinas, then, goes some distance, but not far enough, in correcting the problems in the talmudic text. He gives "woman" an important role in the ethical, but he does not clearly correct some of the talmudic text's harmful stereotyping. What is most beautiful in Levinas's "And God Created Woman"—namely, the discussion of men overcoming stereotyping to see the humanity of a female other, and, in general, the discussion of being-for-the-other in sexual relations—is set in a gender-stereotypical context that would make achievement of such ethical relations impossible.

Opposition to such gender norming and gender hierarchy is important philosophically in evaluating Levinas's ethics. We need to ask how we can preserve what is best in Levinasian ethics without bringing in such stereotyping. Perpich's solution is to accept the superiority in the Levinasian corpus of *Otherwise than Being* over *Totality and Infinity*, since the former does not rest on such stereotyping. I am not convinced of this superiority, as I have stated and argued elsewhere, so I will briefly here suggest another route, namely, that we maintain that the learning from intimacy that Levinas ascribes to man from woman instead is given to people from other people variably in their lives, sometimes to a woman from a man, to a man from a woman, to a transgendered male from a transgendered or nontransgendered female, and so on.

Opposition to such gender norming and gender hierarchy is not just important philosophically but is crucial within contemporary Jewish life and practice, a significant point since Levinas's talmudic reading in part is directed to (then) contemporary Jewish communities. Global Judaism, as is widely noted, is becoming more "orthodox"—for demographic reasons in some cases and in the pursuit of deeper religious substance in others. Given this reality, it is important not to encourage the reinstitution of the marginalization within it of those who are non-normative. Important gains have been made in inclusion of women, lesbians, gays, and transgendered people within contemporary Jewish life and practice. Global Judaism, however, is focusing more than in the past on Talmud study—study that once was de-emphasized in liberal Judaism. This return to the rich source of Jewish ethics found in the Talmud is not unambiguously good, since though the Talmud includes important ethical substance—such as the ethical substance Levinas's talmudic readings are intended to point out—it includes important puritanical and gender-biased components as well. Though Berakhot 61a absolves anyone who remains outside a synagogue if they do so because they seek a different door to get in, members of Jewish textual and liturgical communities are not absolved if, in pursuit of more richly textured religious life, they are responsible for the closing of only recently opened doors—doors to full participation by women and homosexuals, for example.

One final comment. Is Hannah sitting outside the synagogue when she prays her wordless prayer? Who today is sitting outside the synagogue, misunderstood, praying in his/her/their own way?

Notes

In addition to the abbreviations at the front of this volume, the following is also used: Jewish Publication Society, *Tanakh: A New Translation of the Holy Scriptures according to the Traditional Hebrew Text* (*TNT*) (Philadelphia: Jewish Publication Society, 1985), and is the source for all scriptural references in this essay.

1. Stella Sandford, *The Metaphysics of Love: Gender and Transcendence in Levinas* (London: Athlone, 2000), 56.
2. Diane Perpich, *The Ethics of Emmanuel Levinas* (Stanford, CA: Stanford University Press, 2008), 103.
3. Claire Elise Katz, *Levinas, Judaism, and the Feminine: The Silent Footsteps of Rebecca* (Bloomington: Indiana University Press, 2003), 142.
4. *NT* 161–77, originally "Et Dieu créa la femme," *DSS* 122–48.
5. Midrash Rabbah 18.1, in H. Freedman and Maurice Simon, eds. and trans., *Midrash Rabbah: Genesis* (London: Soncino Press, 1983), 1:140.

Interpreting from the Interstices
The Role of Justice in a Liberal Democracy — Lessons from Michael Walzer and Emmanuel Levinas

Nicholas R. Brown

1

As anyone who is familiar with more recent theological debate can attest, the appraisal of the liberal democratic tradition has undergone a radical reevaluation in the wake of Stanley Hauerwas's and Alasdair MacIntyre's scathing critiques. As a result of their blistering assault, religious ethicists and philosophers now find themselves operating within a discursive milieu that is almost the photo negative of the one they previously inhabited. For what has followed *After Virtue* and *After Christendom* is a situation in which compliance with liberal democratic norms is now perceived as actively inveighing against justice rather than as an integral prerequisite to its pursuit.

There are cracks, however, beginning to emerge in the MacIntyre/Hauerwas edifice. For what is becoming disputed and increasingly so among a growing chorus of religious ethicists and philosophers is whether their critical reading of liberal democracy offers the most helpful or even the most biblical way to think through its own moral dimensions as well as those undergirding its relationship with justice.

It is the emergence of these criticisms that forms the basis for this essay. For the thesis that I wish to advance below is that liberal democracy offers religious ethicists and philosophers alike a moral framework and vocabulary from which it is possible to comprehend and enact the normative precepts encapsulated within a biblical understanding of justice. Accordingly, some aspects of my argument will build upon the rhetorical trajectories that have been already charted by the ethicists and philosophers I mention above.

What distinguishes my approach, however, is that I will proceed from a more focused examination of some of the ethical and political undercurrents found within contemporary Jewish thought. More specifically, I want to probe the ethical philosophy of Emmanuel Levinas and the political philosophy of Michael Walzer, for I believe the juxtapositional methodology of interpretation which informs each of their perspectives is illustrative of an interstitial hermeneutic that helps further illuminate the moral compatibility between biblical and democratic accounts of justice.

2

By now, MacIntyre's and Hauerwas's critiques of the liberal democratic tradition have been so thoroughly documented, discussed, and dissected that a review of their perspectives cannot help but have a certain pleonastic quality.

Probably the most significant and disturbing problem that MacIntyre and Hauerwas see belying the liberal democratic tradition stems from its conception of time and space, or more precisely, its lack thereof. For what they discover upon a more careful probing of its moral and epistemological underpinnings is a pursuit of transcendence not dissimilar to Gnostic metaphysics. In the case of liberalism, however, the existential encumbrances to be excised are not corporeal and carnal in nature, but historical and social.

Such conditionalities, surmise liberal theorists, are so shot through with conceptual prejudices that they comprise an interpretative straightjacket that vitiates against the kind of objectivity necessary to engage in a nonparochial process of moral and political discernment. For it is precisely this ability "to be able to stand back from any and every situation in which one is involved, from any and every characteristic that one may possess, and to pass judgment on it from a purely universal and abstract point of view that is totally detached from all social particularity" which MacIntyre sees as constituting "the essence of moral agency" of modern liberalism (*AV* 31–32). Therefore, "liberalism is successful," maintains Hauerwas, "exactly because...[it] provide[s] that philosophical account of society designed to deal with" the moral and political implications such a social and historical denuding portends, namely "a system of rules that will constitute procedures for resolving disputes as they pursue their various interests."[1]

However, what liberalism defines as success MacIntyre and Hauerwas see as anything but. Instead, both judge its "system of rules" to be an insidious prescription for a particularly virulent form of moral nihilism and political bankruptcy. For by stripping moral and political discourse of their historical and social referents, liberalism, ironically and tragically, eviscerates itself of the very heuristic and discursive practices necessary to make those discourses intelligible. As MacIntyre observes in comparing the character of moral judgments conducted within contexts of "classic theism" with those of liberal extraction, the former, he states, "were at once hypothetical and categorical in form...insofar as they expressed a judgment as to what conduct would be teleologically appropriate for a human being" and "as they reported the contents of the universal law commanded by God" (*AV* 60).

"But take away from them that in virtue of which they were hypothetical *and* that in virtue of which they were categorical," he asks rhetorically in referring to the latter, "and what are they?" The answer, in MacIntyre's estimation, is as ineluctable as it is foreboding: "Moral judgments lose any clear status and the sentences which express them in a parallel way lose any undebatable meaning," which means that "such sentences become available as forms of expression for an emotivist self which lacking the guidance of the context in which they were originally at home has lost its linguistic as well as its practical way in the world" (*AV* 60).

Thus, bereft of these necessary linguistic and practical skills as well as the arteries of moral meaning by which they are nourished, liberal theory is forced to engage in a hastily devised form of epistemic bricolage in which it tries to use the mortar of "rationality" to cobble and hold together the detritus of preexisting moral and political traditions in order to fill the moral and political vacuum. Yet, if scrutinized more closely, the patina of "rationality" which suffuses this amalgamation proves to be illusory and ersatz. For what liberal theory actually possesses, claims MacIntyre, is not a coherent moral and political philosophy but the "simulacra of morality" which "now lack those contexts from which their significance derives" (*AV* 2).

Therefore, moral discourse within a liberal milieu is always destined to devolve into a cacophonous mélange of incommensurable moral claims where, according to MacIntyre, "there is no rational way of deciding which type of claim is to be given priority or how one is to be weighed against the other" (*AV* 70). And if there is finally no "rational" way to definitively arbitrate between conflicting moral claims in a manner that is wholly persuasive, then what one is left with is a chaotic moral universe where rationality is but a contrived invention used to "conceal behind the masks of morality what are in fact the preferences of arbitrary will and desire" (71).

Paradoxically, then, what liberalism has ultimately achieved, contend MacIntyre and Hauerwas, has not been an enlightened "system of [moral and political] rules" liberated from the "tyranny of tradition." Instead, it has merely replaced other moral and political traditions with another, and one that proves to be, in more ways than one, just as tyrannous and oppressive as those supposedly more archaic traditions it was intended to supplant. For, by virtue of its cultural ascent and dominance, liberalism has created an impoverishment of interpretative imagination whereby it is now virtually impossible, asserts Hauerwas, to conceive of moral and political life apart from the "story of freedom," which maintains that "people...should have no story except the story they choose when they had no story." Thus, "the story of freedom has now become our fate."[2]

In turning toward Walzer and Levinas's evaluation of the liberal tradition we initially find a similar pattern of critique. With respect to Walzer—an acclaimed political theorist who also works within the same kind of communitarian tradition as MacIntyre and Hauerwas—we find him attacking the same latent tendencies toward social and historical Gnosticism recognized by MacIntyre and Hauerwas.[3] "Moral philosophy," he states, "is usually understood as a twofold enterprise that aims, first, at providing a foundation for minimalism and, second, at building on that foundation for a more expansive structure" (*TT* 6). And once again, because reflection about such principles in the course of normal, everyday conversation among actual people in actual sociohistorical contexts is imbrued with their limitations and ethnocentricities, "what we require for the sake of truth is a hypothetical...conversation whose protagonists are protected against both bad agreements and bad disagreements" (CPC 184).

In other words, liberalism, in order to be rational and objective, needs to design an interpretative framework whose "crucial requirement...is that it eventuate in agreement" (*ISC* 10). Thus this ideal conversation will either, à la Rawls, require "ideal speakers [who] know that they have interests and values of their own and that they will want to assert them," or, à la Habermas, "ideal speakers [who] have full self-knowledge but are internally committed to assert only those interests and values which can be universalized" (CPC 186). This is to ensure that a foundational rule or principle that the ideal conversationalists "invent" "serves no particular interest, expresses no particular culture, regulates everyone's behavior in a universally advantageous or clearly correct way" and "carries no personal or social signature" (*TT* 7). Moreover, it ensures that critical political and moral discourse is a rational and phlegmatic enterprise, a "matter of calm deliberation" and not one which is swayed to and fro by the fickle vagaries of affective passion which "presses inexorably toward violent resolutions."[4] Hence the appropriate analytical posture that liberal theory assumes is one of "radical detachment," both emotionally insofar as "critics must be...wrenched loose from the intimacy and warmth of membership: disinterested and dispassionate," and intellectually insofar as critics must also be "wrenched loose from the parochial understandings of their own society (standardly taken to be self-congratulatory): open-minded and objective" (*ISC* 36).

There are major shortcomings, however, both conceptually and functionally, to this interpretive approach Walzer identifies. With respect to critiquing its conceptual deficiencies, Walzer takes an argumentative tack similar to that of MacIntyre and Hauerwas by asserting that liberalism's foundational claims to objectivity and universality are in reality little more than the epistemological equivalent of a Rorschach test. For if one scratches hard and long enough at the epidermis of tabula rasa, invariably the blood of social and historical particularity will begin to flow. As Walzer cogently explains in *Thick and Thin:*

> The thin morality is already very thick—with an entirely decent liberal or social democratic thickness. The rules of engagement constitute in fact a way of life. How could they not? Men and women who acknowledge each other's equality, claim the rights of free speech, and practice the virtues of tolerance and mutual respect, don't leap from the philosopher's mind like Athena from the head of Zeus. They are creatures of history; they have been worked on, so to speak, for many generations; and they inhabit a society that "fits" their qualities and so supports, reinforces, and reproduces people very much like themselves. They are maximalists even before they begin their rule-governed discussions. (*TT* 12–13)

Thus, as Walzer concludes, the "moralities we discover and invent always turn out, and always will turn out, remarkably similar to the morality we already have," which means that "philosophical discovery and invention" are always "disguised interpretations" (*ISC* 20–21). But these conceptual flaws, while certainly morally and politically deleterious in their own right, still seem to be less troublesome for Walzer than the more functional or procedural problems to which they are inextricably linked. For while we do not necessarily have to "discover" or "invent" the moral and political worlds we inhabit because they are, as it were, already discovered and invented, we do nevertheless have to answer the more "general" and even the more fundamental question of "what is the right thing *for us* to do?" (20, 23).

A universally abstract and detached discourse about morality and politics, however, maintains Walzer, can only get us so far in answering that question of *ought*. To be sure, such a discourse can provide a framework, but ultimately it is "only a framework, with all the substantive details still to be filled in before anyone could actually live in one way rather than another." "It is not until the conversations become continuous and understandings thicken," Walzer argues, "that we get anything like a moral culture, with judgment, value, the goodness of persons and things realized in detail" (*ISC* 25).

Yet as Walzer contends, "universalization has a theoretical purpose, which stands in sharp contrast to the purpose" of such conversations, which is "to rule out bargaining and compromise (the negotiation of particular interests) and to press the speakers toward a preordained harmony" (CPC 186). But simply foisting a "preordained" and contrived consensus onto philosophical conversation does not, *mirabile dictu*, make it so, any more than does it clarify what that consensus actually means to those who have just passively acquiesced to it. Ultimately, then, foundationalist systems of philosophical enquiry are doomed to fail, believes Walzer, in the exact same way that all other deus ex machinas are doomed to fail, and that is "because the acceptance of a particular discovery or invention among a group of people gives rise immediately to arguments about the meaning of what has been accepted. A simple maxim: every discovery and invention...requires interpretation" (*ISC* 26).

Thus Walzer, somewhat echoing MacIntyre and Hauerwas's critiques, sees liberalism's fixation on preserving conceptual purity (i.e., maintaining objectivity and universality) as effectively silencing the very conversations and discursive practices which are responsible for generating the shared understandings necessary to any society's actual processes of moral discernment and political decision-making. "Men and women who find themselves in the original position or the ideal speech situation," he argues, "will not be able to argue coherently with one another unless they share some understanding of what the world is like and where they are within it" (CPC 192). On the contrary, "they cannot sustain a common life without a set of shared conceptions about the subjects of that life—themselves—and their character, interests, and aspirations," without first engaging in "complex social" processes like "political struggle...negotiation and compromise, law making and law enforcement, socialization in families and schools, economic transformations, cultural creativity of all sorts," processes, that is, that "[produce] consensus and shared understandings" (191–92).

What this means then, for Walzer, is that contra the ahistorical and a-particular presuppositions of liberal moral and political theory, what we actually need is a "political theory, and a politics" that is "as complicated as our own lives."[5] Accordingly, such a politics and theory are not spawned from a speculative thought exercise where we conjecture about what hypothetical interlocutors might or might not say to each other and agree to. Rather, it "takes shape as a conversation with particular other people, our relatives, friends, and neighbors.... They are worked out with reference to an actual, not merely a speculative, moral discourse: not one person but many people talking" (*ISC* 47). Not only does such an approach offer a more realistic, which is to say a more accurate, account of how moral and political discourse is actually engaged in, but it also, says Walzer, contains within itself a vitally important moral check that can potentially stave off "bad agreements and bad disagreements." It is the "continuing argument" itself, he contends, which "provides our only protection" (CPC 194).

In somewhat of a paradox, Levinas's critiques of the Western philosophical tradition begin from an affirmation of one of their primary metaphysical and epistemological tenets—the indispensable uniqueness and necessity of the individual consciousness. In subscribing to the Husserlian phenomenological account of metaphysics, Levinas chides and rejects a naturalistic theory of ontology which stipulates that "in order to exist" reality must "be conceived on the model of nature," where "life must be integrated in causal chains and granted reality only inasmuch as it belongs to them." To conceive of reality and life in such a manner, contends Levinas, is to rob them of any intrinsic and distinctive meaning and therefore to reduce all objective existence to "purely subjective phenomena" (*LR* 12).

Instead, what is needed, maintains Levinas, is an account of reality that "dig[s] deeper, down to the very meaning of the notion of being" and which "show[s] that the origin of all being, including that of nature, is determined by the intrinsic meaning of conscious life and not the other way around" (*LR* 12–13). Levinas believes that Husserl's notion of "intentionality"—the idea that the "question [of] '*what* shows itself?' is put by him *who* looks, even before he thematically distinguishes the difference between being and entities" (*OB* 23)—offers such an account insofar as it demonstrates that "conscious life exists even when it is not an object of reflection" (*TIH* 29).

In other words, contra to the Cartesian dictum of *cogito ergo sum*, the idea of intentionality shows that the existence of an individual consciousness and its perceptual faculties is ontologically antecedent to the intention of wanting to train those faculties upon the external realities they encounter. This is not to say, however, that the reality of external existence is dependent upon its being comprehended by a consciously perceiving subject. Rather, it is to posit that subjective conscious and external realities exist independently but in relation to each other according to different modes of being. External realities exist according to a mode of being which "contain[s] the possibility of [their] not-being," whereas consciousness exists as being "continuously present to itself" (*LR* 24).

Thus, as Levinas explains, "only consciousness can make intelligible to us the meaning of the being of the world which is a certain mode of meeting consciousness or of appearing to it.... But, precisely, because concrete life contains in different manners different regions of objects," he continues, "*to be* does not mean the same thing for each of those regions." Subsequently, Levinas holds that discerning consciousness's "proper mode of being...must become the object of philosophy" and constitutes its "central problem" (*LR* 25).

However, even though he commends Husserlian phenomenology for "successfully isolating the idea of an originary, nontheoretical intentionality from the active emotional life of consciousness (*LR* 78)," Levinas is nevertheless weary of how this understanding of consciousness indirectly reinforces a rapacious form of subjectivity. For in linking the existence of consciousness with a form of intentionality, Levinas sees Husserl as unwittingly underwriting a conception of knowledge that is voraciously objectifying and re-presentational. As he explains, "Husserl, inviting us to question the intentionality of consciousness, wants us also to ask 'worauf sie eigentlich hinauswill' (*What are you getting at?*), an intention or wish which, incidentally, would justify calling the units of consciousness acts. At the same time, knowledge, within the intuition of truth, is described as a 'filling out' that gratifies a longing for the being as object, given and received in the original, *present* in a representation. It is a hold on being which equals a constitution of that being" (79). The last sentence is quite telling because it helps illuminate, metaphorically, what Levinas believes has come to fundamentally signify the Western epistemological enterprise. Knowledge, according to such an enterprise, is "an intellectual activity" characterized by a "way of doing something which consists precisely of thinking through knowing, of seizing something and making it one's own, of reducing to presence and representing the difference of being, an activity which *appropriates* and *grasps* the otherness of the known" (76).

Thus Levinas ultimately believes that "the history of Western philosophy has not been the refutation of skepticism as much as the refutation of transcendence" (*OB* 169). For whether one is considering Plato's Eleatic notion of being, Plotinus's idea of the One, Descartes's dictum of *cogito ergo sum*, Kant's categorical imperative, or Hegel's dialectical system, the one thematic thread which consistently binds these seemingly disparate philosophical epochs together is the underlying idea that the "labour of thought wins out over the otherness of things and men" (*LR* 78). Within such a metaphysical system, the difference of the other does not became the occasion of questioning the subject's own sense of being or even the interruption of being itself, since the two are considered to be one and the same.

Instead, they are viewed by *Reason* or by *History,* or by any other architectonic and procrustean system of abstraction that Western philosophy has constructed, as occasions for dialectical absorption and assimilation and thus reasserting a bloblike miasma of homogeneity and sameness. As Levinas writes,

> Hegelianism, anticipating all the modern forms of distrust of the immediate data of consciousness, has accustomed us to think that truth no longer resides in the evidence acquired by myself, that is, in the evidence sustained by the exceptional form of the *cogito,* which, strong in its first person form, would be first in everything. It has made us think that it rather resides in the unsurpassable plenitude of the content thought. In our days truth is taken to result from the effacing of the living man behind the mathematical structures that *think themselves out* in him, rather than he be thinking them. (*OB* 57–58)

Moreover, such a system cannot help but become solipsistic in nature. For if knowledge is seen as a re-presentation of the other's being to the self, that is, if the self's own cognition of being becomes the epistemological foundation upon which being itself and the being of all others is re-cognized, then this leads, according to Levinas, "to [a] full self-consciousness affirming itself as absolute being, and confirming itself as an *I* that, through all possible 'differences,' is identified as master of its own nature as well as of the universe and able to illuminate the darkest recesses of resistance to its powers" (*LR* 79). Thus, thought becomes a "regal and as it were unconditioned activity, a sovereignty which is possible only as solitude, an unconditioned activity, even if limited for man by biological needs and by death" (77).

In standing back and surveying the broader critical thrusts of Levinas's evaluation of Western philosophy and thought, we are sure to see something reminiscent of Søren Kierkegaard's ethical existentialism and Martin Buber's relational ontology of I and Thou. To be sure, there are certainly elements of Levinas's perspective which suggest a strong correlation with the Kierkegaardian notion that "the single individual, though under the demands of the universal, is higher than the universal" (*FTR* 70) as well as Buber's idea that "the Thou knows no system of coordination" (*IAT* 30). Nevertheless, these similarities notwithstanding, it would be a mistake to read too much into their intersections and thus gloss over the fundamental differences that distinguish Levinas's perspective.

In particular, it is important to notice that Levinas's response to the totalizing and dehumanizing dangers of Western metaphysics and epistemology was not to elevate the role of the single individual and his/her ability to authentically choose. Nor was it to posit that the way to surmount the objectifying and reductionist tendencies of modern rationalism was to conceive the relationship with the "other" as an "idyllic and harmonious relationship of communion, or a sympathy through which we put ourselves in the other's place" (*LR* 43). For the former would only reinforce a Promethean-like egoism while the latter would occlude the realization that the "other" is "not only an alter ego" but "what I myself am not," meaning that the "other" is "other" "not because of the Other's character, or physiognomy, or psychology, but because of the Other's very alterity" (48). In other words, both those ethical responses would still be mired in the centripetal vortex of subjectivity and ontology.

Instead, what Levinas proposes is a response that is premised upon an "otherwise than being" not in the sense of "fail[ing] to recognize being or treat it, ridiculously and pretentiously, with disdain, as the fall from a higher order or disorder" (*OB* 16), but in the sense that the ultimate question that philosophical discourse is to take up is not the metaphysical query of "To be or not to be" but the ethical question of "my right to be." As Levinas asserts, "This is the question of the meaning of being: not the ontology of the understanding of that extraordinary verb, but the ethics of its justice. The question *par excellence* or the question of philosophy. Not 'Why being rather than nothing?,' but how being justifies itself" (*LR* 86).

Levinas believes that the only possible way that one can "respond to one's right to be" is not by "referring to some abstract and anonymous law, or judicial entity, but because of one's fear for the Other." Notice here that Levinas is saying that one's existence is premised not, à la Hobbes, on a fear *of* the other but rather a fear *for* the other. It is a fear that considers "all the violence and murder my existing might generate, in spite of its conscious and intentional innocence"; it is a fear "which reaches back past my 'self-consciousness' in spite of whatever moves are made toward a *bonne conscience* by a pure perseverance in being"; it is the fear, states Levinas by way of refuting Heidegger, "of occupying someone else's place with the *Da* of my *Dasein*; it is the inability to occupy a place, a profound utopia" (*LR* 82). Thus it is a fear suffused with a responsibility "for the Other," a responsibility "for my neighbor, for the other man, for the stranger or sojourner, to which nothing in the rigorously ontological order binds me—nothing in the order of the thing, of the something, of number or causality" (84).

However, is there not an insoluble contradiction here between Levinas's conception of consciousness and its modality of intention and his description of fear for or responsibility to the other which precedes intention? After all, it is the existence of intention that Levinas believes makes the individual subject distinct and unique and not just an epiphenomenal causal chain. "How in consciousness," then, Levinas asks in anticipating this apparent contradiction, "can there be an undergoing or a passion whose active source does not, in any way, occur in consciousness" (*LR* 92)?

In order to answer this question, Levinas points us toward a grammatical declension of cases. In the nominative case, the subject and predicate are linked together, as in "I am here." For Levinas, this grammatical structure is indicative of the Western metaphysic of re-presentation which unites subjectivity and substantiality such that the "ego is an equality with itself, and consequently the return of being to itself is a concrete universality" (*LR* 105). However, if the *I* is put in the accusative case, as in "Here I am," then the *I* still retains its uniqueness, but it does so by literally being accused. And to be accused means that "the oneself cannot form itself," for "it is already formed with absolute passivity." Thus, responsibility to the other does not evade subjective consciousness any more than does it erase its uniqueness. Rather, as Levinas states, "there is expulsion in that it assigns me before I show myself, before I set myself up. I am assigned without recourse, without fatherland, already sent back to myself, but without being able to stay there, compelled before commencing.... It has meaning only as an upsurge in me of a responsibility prior to commitment, that is, a responsibility for the other. There I am one and irreplaceable, one inasmuch as irreplaceable in responsibility" (94). Consequently, "this responsibility for the neighbour, this substitution as a hostage, is the subjectivity and uniqueness of a subject" (112).

In setting MacIntyre and Hauerwas's critiques of the liberal democratic tradition alongside those articulated by Walzer and Levinas, one cannot help but notice the sharing of a similar analytical orientation and sensibility. All are highly suspicious of its philosophical, epistemological, and metaphysical presuppositions and the oppressive social and political practices those presuppositions instantiate and reinforce. Moreover, all recognize that the project of creating a more just politic will require an effort to think outside of the liberal democratic paradigm.

It is on the last point, however, where we see these two sets of thinkers taking a radical departure from each other. For MacIntyre and Hauerwas, the defects of the liberal democratic tradition are so entrenched and pernicious that the only conceivable way to think and work outside its paradigmatic penumbra is to disavow it altogether. As MacIntyre states in *After Virtue,* "If a premodern view of morals and politics is to be vindicated against modernity, it will be in *something like* Aristotelian terms or not at all" (*AV* 118). And Hauerwas says much the same when he opines, "That story [the story of liberal democracy], and the institutions that embody it, is the enemy we must attack through Christian teaching."[6] The choice then for the modern-day religious ethicist or philosopher is as stark as it is simple and mutually exclusive: either a (re)turn to tradition to (re)gain moral and political coherence, or a resigned *fait accompli* to the injustices of liberal democratic compromise.

To frame and characterize the situation in this way, however, is to suffer from the same kind of archetypal distortions which Edward Said identifies within Samuel Huntington's now infamous "clash of civilizations" thesis. As Said observes,

> Anyone who has the slightest understanding of how cultures work knows that defining a culture, saying what it is for members of the culture, is always a major and, even in undemocratic societies, a democratic contest. There are canonical authorities to be selected and regularly revised, debated, re-selected or dismissed.... No culture is understandable without some sense of this ever-present source of creative provocation from the unofficial to the official; to disregard this sense of restlessness within each culture, and to assume that there is complete homogeneity between culture and identity, is to miss what is vital and fecund.[7]

Such a view is in keeping with Jeffrey Stout's claim that "commitment to democracy does not entail the rejection of tradition," but instead "requires *jointly* taking responsibility for the criticism and renewal of tradition and for the justice of our social and political arrangements," and it is also one to which Walzer and Levinas subscribe.[8] For as we shall see, Walzer's and Levinas's grounding in the Jewish tradition in general and talmudic interpretation in particular means that they are not only committed to justice for the sake of preserving democratic discourse, but committed to democratic discourse for the sake of preserving justice.

3

One of the most intriguing discoveries arising to the surface when examining Walzer and Levinas's respective engagements with the Jewish and talmudic traditions is that both men came to a more conscientious and concerted study of those traditions later in their respective intellectual careers. This is not to suggest, however, that one can best understand the evolution of their thought by plotting their political and ethical reflections along an artificial timeline and neatly dividing them into discrete pre-Jewish and post-Jewish categories. Nor is it to suggest that their earlier work is devoid of Jewish influences and references. Indeed, a careful perusal of Walzer's *Obligations* and *Spheres of Justice*, or Levinas's *Time and the Other* and *Totality and Infinity*, reveals a judicious collating of the Torah and Talmud with Hobbes, Rousseau, Hegel, and Heidegger.

Yet, as we have just discussed, their growing concerns and worries about the ahistorical and totalizing tendencies within the liberal political tradition and Western philosophy make Walzer and Levinas acutely aware that any attempt at their correction and reform, while not totally divorced from liberal thought and concepts, will still ultimately require going beyond liberalism's discursive parameters. Walzer says as much when he asserts that it "is a matter of principle that communities must always be at risk," and that the "great paradox of a liberal society is that one cannot set oneself against this principle without also setting oneself against the traditional practices and shared understandings of the society." "If the first communitarian critique were true in its entirety," he continues, "if there were no communities and no traditions, then we could just proceed to invent new ones," but "insofar as the second critique is even partly true, and the work of communal invention is well begun and continually in progress, we must rest content with the kinds of corrections and enhancements — they would be, in fact, more radical than these terms suggest."[9] Levinas echoes with a similar sentiment when he states that "it is then not without importance to know if the egalitarian and just State in which man is fulfilled (and which is to be set up, and especially to be maintained) proceeds from a war of all against all, or from the irreducible responsibility of the one for all, and if it can do without friendships and faces" (*OB* 159–60).

Thus, as Samuel Moyn writes in describing the motivations which prompted Levinas to return to a more concentrated reading of the Jewish tradition, a description which in many ways holds equally true for Walzer, "he came to rely on Judaism in general and the Talmud specifically as a result of an evolving philosophical identity that events placed under considerable stress. So it is not just that Levinas did not come to philosophy from a stable Jewish perspective; he may have returned to Judaism in general and come to study the Talmud specifically out of a philosophical conundrum."[10] In a very important way, then, Walzer and Levinas's immersion within the Western liberal milieu already inculcated them with a keen sensitivity to the necessity of constructing an interstitial interpretive methodology straddling both Jewish and Western thought even prior to their more focused reengagements with their Jewish heritage. For, just like Wittgenstein's fictitious chess player, Walzer and Levinas's intent vis-à-vis solving the liberal conundrum is not to invent a new a-liberal game. Instead, it is to adjust the rules of the liberal game in order to play on, which means that the new set of rules to be constructed must share a family resemblance with those that existed prior to the impasse.

We should not take this to mean, however, that the primary impetus driving Walzer and Levinas's interstitial methodology is a pragmatic concern to create a conceptual rapprochement between liberal theory and Judaism. Rather, as we shall soon see, Walzer and Levinas's reading of the Jewish and talmudic traditions shows that practicality follows what is normative and not the other way around. To develop and illustrate this point, we must first turn our attention toward the specific liberal conundrums that lead Walzer and Levinas back to the Jewish and talmudic traditions. We begin with Walzer.

The vexing liberal problem which prompts Walzer's return to Jewish biblical texts and their accompanying tradition of interpretation is the great temptation he sees as being endemic to all programs of Western political thought, the temptation toward "political messianism" (*ER* 135). Walzer sees the trope of messianic politics as a distorted interpretive offspring emanating from Israel's Exodus experience, an experience that has left an indelible stamp upon Western political consciousness insofar as it has provided a powerful narrative paradigm for thinking about and describing the processes of political change and liberation, processes which Walzer enthusiastically affirms. Thus, Walzer muses on how the Exodus political narrative can be read and appropriated without giving rise to and legitimizing a messianic politics, which he believes is distinguished by three central features.

"The first of these features," says Walzer, "is an extraordinary sensitivity to and something like a longing for apocalyptic events" (*ER* 138). With an apocalyptic mindset comes an urge to see history not as locus of meaningful human action but instead "a burden from which we long to escape, and messianism guarantees that escape: a deliverance not only from Egypt but from Sinai and Canaan, too" (136). Walzer sees modern political ideology as trafficking heavily in apocalyptic waters, as it has "not only dreamt of but actually reached for a kind of secular paradise, the perfection of humankind in a perfect society: unity, harmony, freedom, eternal bliss" (145). It has therefore shown a willingness "to initiate the terrors that precede the Last Days; and hence the strange politics of *the worse, the better;* and hence the will to sin, to risk any crime for the sake of the End" (145). This apocalyptic fixation with ushering in the end of history leads to a second feature of political messianism which Walzer describes as "the readiness to 'force the End'—which doesn't mean merely to act politically (rather than wait for God's mighty hand) but to act politically for ultimate purposes." Consequently, those who "force the End take deliverance into their own hands, and it is not from any particular evil but from evil in general that they would deliver themselves and all the rest of us," thereby "effectively rul[ing] out the requirements of both morality and prudence" (139). Finally, Walzer describes the third feature as "the claim of unconditionality," which forecloses and squelches any possibility of debate, contestation, and compromise since "there is no need to surrender territory for the sake of morality, for morality comes, so to speak, with the territory" (140). Once again, we see resonances, especially in features one and three, of Walzer's criticisms of liberalism's ahistorical universalism and its tendency to arbitrarily silence argument.

We have already addressed the philosophical conundrum of Western metaphysics which drives Levinas back to his Jewish faith, but we will briefly repeat it here, albeit with a different emphasis. Is it possible,

Levinas ponders, to develop an ethical discourse which still uses ontological categories and language but which itself is not ontic? Or, as he states, "Over and beyond being does not a meaning whose priority, translated into ontological language, would have to be called *antecedent* to being, show itself?" (*LR* 168).

Both Walzer and Levinas see a broader reading of the Jewish tradition in general and talmudic interpretation in particular as helping to unravel these conundrums in several key ways. First, both see the giving of the Torah and its extended elaboration and codification in the inscription of halakha, or corpus of Jewish legal and ethical codes, as providing a set of inviolable moral principles which countermands any political or philosophical program that ignores or even sanctions oppression for the sake of achieving some Good, no matter how noble or coveted that Good is or may be. This is the first and the most important lesson of the Exodus story—Israel becomes a liberated nation not by forgetting its experience in Egypt, but only by remembering it.

Walzer elaborates on this point in *Exodus and Revolution* by explaining that YHWH's covenant with Israel has "a complex twofold character: God said, 'I will bring you into a land flowing with milk and honey,' and He also said, 'Ye shall be unto me a kingdom of priests and a holy nation" (*ER* 101). The way to interpret the two facets of this covenantal promise, maintains Walzer, is not to view them as two separate promises, one being territorial and the other ethical, but rather to see the latter as a stipulation of the fulfillment of the former. "Conceived in territorialist terms," he says, "the promise of milk and honey has a temporal end point: sooner or later, the people will cross the Jordan and enter the land." But if "conceived in ethical terms, the promise is temporally uncertain, for its achievement is not a matter of where we plant our feet but of how we cultivate our spirits" (108).

Israel will therefore possess material sustenance not simply because it leaves Egypt and enters into Canaan, says Walzer, but because its "members obey" the political and social precepts ensconced in the "divine law" of Torah and halakha. And "much of that law," he states, "is concerned with the rejection of Egyptian bondage," which means that if Israel is to be a holy nation then it will be one where "no one would oppress a stranger, or deny Sabbath rest to his servants, or withhold the wages of a worker" and it "would be a kingdom without...pharaohs and taskmasters" who would have "the power to 'take...your goodliest young men...and put them to his work'" (*ER* 108–09). "Holiness," then, says Walzer, "makes for liberty and justice, but it is effective only insofar as it describes a way of life, a religious and political culture."

Hence the political importance of reading and remembering the Torah and halakha is not only to know the moral principles they encapsulate but also not to forget the social and political circumstances that precipitated their genesis, lest they be repeated. For to forget Egypt, claims Walzer, is "to return to Egyptian oppression" (115). In contrast, then, to the absolutist politics of Western forms of political messianism, a reading of the Exodus through the lens of Torah and halakha shows that "liberation is not a movement from our fallen state to the messianic kingdom but from 'the slavery, exploitation, and alienation of Egypt' to a land where the people can live 'with human dignity'" (149).

Interestingly enough, we find Levinas referencing the same Exodus tradition to explain how the ethical prescriptions of Torah and halakha create an ethical discourse that is beyond the purview of Western ontology. "The traumatism of my enslavement in Egypt," he states, "constitutes my very humanity, that which draws me closer to the problems of the wretched of the earth, to all persecuted people...as if the love of the stranger were a response already given to me in my actual heart." Thus, whereas before we saw Levinas describing responsibility to the "other" in more generic terms, here we see him both literally and figuratively fleshing that "other" out by situating it within the context of obeying the biblical injunctions to care for the other who is a stranger or the poor or the widow. And it is the act of obeying the "Most High," says Levinas, which makes freedom possible, since "to be free is simply to do what nobody else can do in my place" (*LR* 202).

"This makes me wonder," Levinas then continues, "if many aspects of Judaism might not, equally, point to this type of 'rationality,' a reason far less turned in upon itself than the reason of the philosophical tradition." What Levinas means by this statement is that one of the unique parts of the Jewish tradition of revelation is that YHWH does not call upon Israel to first parse out and explicate the moral content of Torah and the halakha before adhering to them. If that were the case, then the emphasis would be on cognition and apprehension prior to obedience, and subsequently the Jewish tradition would share the same conception of being and rationality held by Western philosophy. However, since the Exodus tradition holds that the Torah is received by Israel prior to its understanding it — "All that the Lord has spoken we will do, and we will be obedient" (Exod. 24:7) — then "the expression for obedience is placed before the expression referring to understanding," and this, says Levinas, "exemplifies, in the eyes of the Talmudic doctors, Israel's greatest merit, the 'wisdom of the angel'" (*LR* 206).

What this demonstrates then for Levinas is that this type of "obedience cannot be assimilated to the categorical imperative, where a universal suddenly finds itself in a position to direct the will." Instead, obedience is shown to derive "from the love of one's neighbour, a love without eros, lacking self-indulgence, which is, in this sense, a love that is obeyed." Thus, just as Walzer finds the Torah and halakha important not only because of the moral principles they enshrine but also because of their call to remembrance, so too do we find Levinas emphasizing the point that obedience to the law not only informs a responsibility to the other, but also that such an obedience points not to "a reason which is solid and positive, with which all meaning beings and to which all meaning must return, to become assimilated to the Same" (*LR* 207), but a reason which "finds its concrete realization in the relationship with the Other" (206).

However, to say that the establishment of a particular set of moral principles and precepts exhaust Walzer and Levinas's interest in the Torah and halakha would be to miss a fundamental component of their analysis. For what both find to be especially instructive about Jewish law is not only its moral content but also the hermeneutical method that has arisen within the Jewish tradition to explain and interpret it. More specifically, both see the rabbinic tradition of midrashic interpretation of the halakha as itself supplying an interstitial framework from which it is possible to creatively and constructively juxtapose liberal moral and political theory with the Jewish tradition.

With regard to Walzer, we find his sympathies with the midrashic mode of interpretation to be especially evident in his idea of reiteration. As Walzer understands and describes it, reiteration is a dynamic and multifaceted process whereby "moral arguments have to be repeated even when they are made in a way that claims to be once-and-for-all." It gains its moral and conceptual traction as it were from the talmudic school of thought that there "can be two different readings of the Law that are equally 'right' (though not equally enforceable)."[11]

To illustrate this point, Walzer refers to the talmudic *germa* or rabbinic dialogue concerning an exposition of Deuteronomy 30:11–14 (*ISC* 31–32). The dialogue involves a halakhic dispute between Rabbi Eliezer and another group of rabbis over whether a reconstructed oven is ritually pure or impure. In order to vindicate his particular interpretation, Rabbi Eliezer invokes numerous miracles, all of which transpire before the astounded group of rabbis with whom he is arguing. Nevertheless, they remain persistent in their disagreement with Rabbi Eliezer, which finally provokes the latter to call upon God to verbally confirm his position as the right one. "Whereupon a voice cried out, 'Why do you dispute with Rabbi Eliezer?' In all matters the law is as he says." This would seem to close the matter, except one of the opposing rabbis, Rabbi Joshua, quotes Deuteronomy 30:12 by saying, "It is not in heaven!"

The point of this talmudic story for Walzer is very much the same point we saw him making earlier with respect to the fallacies of hypothetical philosophical moral discourse: even if an interpretative community claims a common tradition of shared meanings and understandings, this is not in and of itself a guarantor of consensus and agreement. Instead, Walzer asserts, "morality...is something that we have to argue about" (*ISC* 32), which means that "if we disagree with either the confirmation or the challenge, there is nothing to do but go back to the 'text'—the values, principles, codes and conventions that constitute the moral world—and to the 'readers' of the text" (30). The fact that Judaism not only preserves these disagreements about the proper interpretation and application of halakha within its tradition of interpretation, but actively encourages disputation as a mode of exegetical elucidation, means for Walzer that "Judaism...is not found in the text so much as in the interpretations of the text" (*ER* 144).

Thus, the full thrust of the enterprise of reiteration is not subsumed in a simple translation or repetition of moral norms. Of course, some degree of repetition and element of translation is necessary for reiteration, but as Walzer states, the "rightness" of the reiterative activity "is relative to their critical occasions" (*TT* 52). This does not mean that reiteration is relativistic, but only that "those moral principles...that all men and women in near and distant worlds are likely to recognize, and ought to recognize, must be expressed in the idiom of a particular time and place and integrated into a particular world-version," which is another way of saying that our reiteration of moral principles will be circumscribed by the conditionalities of audience and context.[12]

Accordingly, Walzer points to the two modes of social critique respectively exemplified by the Jewish prophets Jonah and Amos to help illuminate reiteration's spectrum of particular to universal, or what he also describes as the continuum running between a thick and thin morality. Jonah's indictment of Nineveh's immorality tends more toward the universal and thin poles of reiteration insofar as "he is not a missionary, carrying with him an alternative doctrine; he does not try to convert the people of Nineveh to Israel's religion, to bring them into the Sinai covenant" (*ISC* 89). In denouncing Nineveh's violence and wickedness, Jonah cannot appeal to Israel's halakha since this is not the legal and moral code to which it subscribes. Nor can he appeal to Nineveh's own halakha since he is just as ignorant of its moral precepts as Nineveh is of his. What Jonah can do, however, is refer to "some moral knowledge to which they can return, some basic understanding that God and his prophet alike presuppose." Of course, Jonah's moral discourse with the inhabitants of Nineveh would be somewhat truncated and "centered on those moral understandings that don't depend upon communal life," which means that it would lack the sophistication of "nuance or subtlety" (78). But it at least facilitates an encounter which allows Nineveh to repent, not in spite of Jonah's criticisms, but because those criticisms somehow resonate with its own understanding of what its moral law demands.

Amos's repudiation of Israel and Judah, on the other hand, is more particular and thick in that it "goes deeper than Jonah's because he knows the fundamental values of the men and women he criticizes.... And since he in turn is recognized as one of them, he can call them back to their 'true' path" (*ISC* 90). Amos is not as bound by the constrictions of language and tradition, for the language he speaks is Israel's and the covenant he invokes is the one it proudly touts as distinguishing it from all other nations. Yet, his prophetic critique is no less an exercise in moral translation than Jonah's. For even though Israel is familiar with the covenant, it has forgotten that the promise of a land flowing with milk and honey is inextricably bound to the promise of becoming a holy nation and a kingdom of priests. Consequently it has forgotten about Egypt and therefore become Egypt. Amos, therefore, must retranslate the covenant back to Israel by suggesting "an identification of the poor in Israel with the Israelite slaves in Egypt and so mak[e] justice the primary religious demand" (89).

To compare and contrast these two prophetic modes, however, is not to imply that one is more necessary than the other. Nor is it to imply that, because Amos's prophetic mode is more thick and particular in character, it is therefore more morally substantial. There is a duality, to be sure, but "we should not try to escape the dualism," maintains Walzer, "for it fits what I am inclined to call the necessary character of any human society: universal because it is human, particular because it is a society." Because there is universal/thin/minimum morality, "members of all the different societies, because they are human, can acknowledge each other's different ways, respond to each other's cries for help, learn from each other, and march (sometimes) in each other's [moral] parades" (*TT* 8). Thus the people of Nineveh can listen to and understand Jonah's pronouncements of divine punishment and repent. And thus can those outside Israel appropriate the Exodus narrative and its message of liberation, since the "tasks of political liberation, social construction, nation-building, and law-making are all of them permanent—literally continuous or endlessly renewed."[13] But there can be no Exodus without an Israel and so there can be no universal/thin/minimum account of morality without the existence of a particular/thick/maximalist morality to begin with. With moral thickness, though, "comes qualification, compromise, complexity, and disagreement" (6), which means that the "text and teaching still need to interpreted, and of interpretation, again, there is no end."[14] Hence Walzer would have us see that it is through a process of reiteration that one can speak in a liberal dialect, albeit with a Jewish accent precisely because that accent is reiterative itself.

Turning toward Levinas, we find a similar attention to and appreciation of midrashic interpretation of the halakha and the interstitial methodology it suggests. Picking up again on the pivotal theme of obedience, Levinas states that "from the outset the Jewish revelation is one of commandment, and piety lies in obedience to it." But this obedience takes on a unique character in that, "while it accepts the practical decrees" of the halakha, it "does not bring to a halt the dialectic which is called upon to fully determine them." What this means, then, according to Levinas, is that the meaning of the halakha "is still under debate" today, and this is important because "the decision it makes cannot, therefore, be strictly seen as a conclusion." Instead, Levinas explains, it is "as if the decision rested with a specific tradition, although it could never have been reached without discussion, and does not nullify that discussion in any way" (*LR* 200).

Thus, midrashic interpretation shows us that even though the meaning of the halakha has a certain integrity that is not infinitely malleable, that meaning is nevertheless not punctiliar and apodictic. There is instead a certain provisional quality that always makes it open to a new set of interpretations as different contexts of application arise. Given what we know of Levinas's concerns regarding the totalizing of ontology, this dialectic of interpretation takes on an even greater sense of importance. For even the halakha, if not accompanied by the Talmud, could turn into a set of general universal principles, "and generous principles," says Levinas, "can be inverted in the course of their application." Hence Levinas sees "the great strength of the Talmud's casuistry" consisting in the "special discipline which studies the particular case in order to identify the precise moment within it when the general principle is at risk of turning into its opposite; it surveys the general from the standpoint of the particular," and this "preserves us from ideology" (*LR* 220).

How, then, we must ask, does Levinas see it possible to translate the particularity of the Jewish tradition into the more universal discourse of Western and liberal thought without it becoming just another ideology? To begin to answer this question, we must first understand Levinas's counterhistorical approach to meaning. "The main thesis of counterhistoricism," writes Moyn, "is that meaning transcends time; and, as the label suggests, it is asserted in opposition to historical tendencies in interpretation that reached their apogee in the twentieth century in the discipline of hermeneutics."[15] What Levinas has in mind here, then, are the hermeneutical methods used by philologists and biblical scholars that sequester and lock the meaning of a particular text to its original context and audience. To be counterhistoricist, then, does not mean that one does not take history and context seriously. Rather, it means, as Levinas states, that the "insights of history" are not "sufficient for everything" (*NT* 5).

He elaborates on this point further in the following passage wherein he describes in more detail his own interpretative approach to reading the Talmud.

> We take the Talmudic text and the Judaism which manifests itself in it as teachings and not as a mythic web of survivals. Our first task is therefore to read it in a way that respects its givens and its conventions, without mixing in the questions arising for a philologist or historian to the meaning that derives from its juxtapositions.... It is only after this initial task of reading the text within its own conventions that we will try to translate the meaning suggested by its particulars into a modern language, that is, into the problems preoccupying a person schooled in spiritual sources other than those of Judaism and whose confluence constitutes our civilization. The chief goal of our exegesis is to extricate the universal intentions from the apparent particularism within which facts tied to the national history of Israel...enclose us.... Our approach assumes that the different periods of history can communicate around thinkable meanings, whatever the variations in the signifying material which suggests them. (*NT* 5)

What we have in this passage is not only a remarkable correlation with the Talmud's own dialectic between the particular and the general but also Walzer's idea of reiterating from the thick to the thin. Levinas acknowledges that there is an irreducible particularity to Judaism that cannot be generalized without running the risk of running roughshod over the historical peculiarities and idiosyncrasies that make its moral law distinctive. However, that peculiarity and idiosyncrasy does not prevent its moral law from being translated into traditions and languages that do not find their home in Israel. Indeed, Levinas thinks translation is necessary.

Judaism and its moral law, argues Levinas, still need "to be translated into that Greek language which, thanks to assimilation, we have learnt in the West." "We are faced," he continues, "with the great task of articulating in Greek those principles of which Greece had no knowledge. The singularity of the Jews awaits its philosophy" (*LR* 287). There are even certain points in Levinas's reading of the Talmud where he seems to intimate that translation of the halakha may not be necessary, since the ethical obligations to the other it prescribes are in some sense anthropologically instinctive. An example of this occurs in his own reflection on the Talmud:

> I have it from an eminent master: each time Israel is mentioned in the Talmud one is certainly free to understand by it a particular ethnic group which is probably fulfilling an incomparable destiny. But to interpret in this manner would be to reduce the general principle in the idea enunciated in the Talmudic passage, to forget that Israel means a people who has received the Law and, as a result, a human nature which has reached the fullness of its responsibilities and its self-consciousness. The descendants of Abraham, Isaac, and Jacob are human beings who are no longer childlike.... The heirs of Abraham — men to whom their ancestors bequeathed a difficult tradition of duties toward the other man, which one is never done with, an order in which one is never free. In this order, above all else, duty takes the form of obligations toward the body, the obligation of feeding and sheltering. So defined, the heirs of Abraham are of all nations: any man truly man is no doubt of the line of Abraham. (*NT* 98–99)[16]

And he states much the same in *Difficult Freedom:*

> A truth is universal when it applies to every reasonable being. A religion is universal when it is open to all. In this sense, the Judaism that links the Divine to the moral has always aspired to be universal. But the revelation of morality, which discovers a human society, also discovers the place of election, which, in this universal society, returns to the person who receives this revelation. This election is made up not of privileges but of responsibilities. It is a nobility based not on royalties [*droit d'auteur*] or a birthright [*droit d'aînesse*] conferred by a divine caprice, but on the position of each human I.... The basic intuition of the majority perhaps consists in perceiving that I am not *the equal* of the Other. This applies in the very strict sense: I see myself *obligated* with respect to the Other; consequently I am infinitely more demanding of myself than of others.... This "position outside nations," of which the Pentateuch speaks, is realized in the concept of Israel and its particularism. It is a particularism that conditions universality, and it is a moral category rather than a historical fact to do with Israel. (*DF* 21–22).

However, to deduce that Levinas is describing the existence of a Jewish natural law from this statement would be to ascribe to him a false universality. For the "essential content" of halakha, Levinas affirms, "cannot be learned like a catechism or resumed like a credo. Nor is it restricted to the negative and formal statement of a categorical imperative." Instead, "it is acquired and held, finally, in the particular type of intellectual life known as the study of the Torah, that permanent revision and updating of the content of the Revelation where every situation within the human adventure can be judged" (*LR* 257). Thus, just as Levinas sees an ethical responsibility to the other as providing a philosophical discourse beyond the ontology of Western metaphysical thought, so too does he see the proper interpretation of that responsibility as specific to Judaism. One does not necessarily have to be Jewish in order to obtain an awareness that one has an ethical obligation to care for the other, but the only way to arrive at that awareness is through a Jewish study of halakha, which means one has to enter into its midrashic tradition of interpretation. As Levinas states,

> We Jews who wish to remain Jews know that our heritage is no less human than that of the West, and is capable of integrating all that our Western past has awakened within our own potential. Let us be grateful to assimilation. If, at the same time, we oppose it, it is because this "withdrawal into the self" which is essential to us and which is so often disparaged is not the symptom of an outmoded phase of existence, but reveals a "beyond" to universalism, which is what completes or perfects human fraternity. In the singularity of Israel a peak is attained that justifies the very perenniality of Judaism. (*LR* 287)

Thus, as Richard Cohen observes, in appropriating and elevating the Jewish tradition, Levinas is not proposing a "religion" relegated and confined to an " 'ecclesiastical' zone or compartment of life," but rather a holistic and integrated "way of life" that extends to all of its "familial, social, civic, economic, and political" dimensions. Furthermore, although this tradition is thoroughly and inescapably Jewish inasmuch it is singularly elected, this election is also open to and incumbent upon all. As such, "the particularity of one's own tradition and the universality of morality and justice need not stand in conflict with one another. Indeed, the reverse is true. The elevation demanded by ethical universality is rooted in the particular, just as the aspiration of particularity requires and demands universality."[17]

Notes

In addition to the abbreviations at the front of this volume, the following are also used: Alasdair MacIntyre, *After Virtue: A Study in Moral Theory*, 2nd ed. (*AV*) (Notre Dame, IN: University of Notre Dame Press, 1984); Michael Walzer, "A Critique of Philosophical Conversation" (CPC), in *Hermeneutics and Critical Theory in Ethics and Politics*, ed. Michael Kelly (Cambridge, MA: MIT Press, 1990); Michael Walzer, *Exodus and Revolution* (*ER*) (New York: Basic Books, 1985); Michael Walzer, *Interpretation and Social Criticism* (*ISC*) (Cambridge, MA: Harvard University Press, 1987); Michael Walzer, *Thick and Thin: Moral Argument at Home and Abroad* (*TT*) (Notre Dame, IN: University of Notre Dame Press, 1994); Søren Kierkegaard, *Fear and Trembling*, ed. C. Stephen Evans and Sylvia Walsh (Cambridge: Cambridge University Press, 2006); Martin Buber, trans. Ronald Gregor Smith (London: Continuum, 2004).

1. John Berkman and Michael Cartwright, eds., *The Hauerwas Reader* (Durham, NC: Duke University Press, 2001), 635–36.

2. Stanley Hauerwas, *Sanctify Them in the Truth: Holiness Exemplified* (Nashville, TN: Abingdon, 1998), 198.

3. For a representative sample of Walzer's capacious thought and work, see Michael Walzer, *Thinking Politically: Essays in Political Theory*, ed. David Miller (New Haven, CT: Yale University Press, 2007).

4. Michael Walzer, *Politics and Passion: Toward a More Egalitarian Liberalism* (New Haven, CT: Yale University Press, 2004), 110–11.

5. Walzer, *Politics and Passion*, 140. Here there would appear to be a substantive departure from Levinas's thinking, insofar as Levinas argues that, though moral norms "are steeped in history," they are "not embarked in history and culture" (*CPP* 101). This speaks of course to Levinas's insistence that the face of the other and the ethical obligation entailed there within are "prior to history." Nevertheless, notwithstanding this line of critique, it also important to note that Levinas neither jettisons the importance of historicity in general nor of the Jewish moral tradition in particular. For, as he writes, "the notion of Israel in the Talmud, as my master had taught me, must be separated from all particularism, *except for that of election*" (*BV* 123; emphasis mine).

6. Hauerwas, *Sanctify Them in the Truth*, 198.

7. Edward Said, *Reflections on Exile* (Cambridge, MA: Harvard University Press, 2002), 577–78.

8. Jeffrey Stout, *Democracy and Tradition* (Princeton, NJ: Princeton University Press, 2004), 152.

9. Walzer, *Politics and Passion*, 161.

10. Samuel Moyn, "Emmanuel Levinas's Talmudic Readings: Between Tradition and Invention," *Prooftexts* 23, no. 3 (2003): 342.

11. Michael Walzer, "A Particularism of My Own," *Religious Studies Review* 16, no. 1 (1990): 194.

12. Ibid., 194.

13. Ibid., 194–95.

14. Ibid., 194.
15. Moyn, "Emmanuel Levinas's Talmudic Readings," 344.
16. For further discussion and reflection on this tensive relationship between the particularity of Judaism and the universality of its ethical precepts, see Levinas's *Beyond the Verse,* trans. Gary D. Mole (Bloomington: Indiana University Press, 1994), esp. 198–201; and *Difficult Freedom: Essays on Judaism,* trans. Seán Hand (Baltimore: Johns Hopkins University Press, 1990), esp. 21, 164, 257, and 275.
17. Richard Cohen, *Levinasian Meditations: Ethics, Philosophy and Religion.* (Pittsburgh: Duquesne University Press, 2010), 259.

Otherwise than *Laïcité*?
Toward an Agonistic Secularism in Levinas
Mark Cauchi

LEVINAS AND SECULARISM

Along with the so-called "return of the religious" in contemporary Western philosophy and politics, there has been a renewed effort in recent years to rethink secularism, the political doctrine of the separation of religion and politics.[1] It would not be difficult to show that Emmanuel Levinas has been a substantial force in the resurgence of interest in religion among philosophers, but his impact on thinking about secularism is less evident. Part of the reason for this uncertainty, and part of the reason it is not taken up by scholars, is doubtless the fact that Levinas's conception of secularism is difficult to discern.[2] Although he often discusses religion, politics, and even their relationship, he rarely addresses the question of secularism directly. He certainly uses the term *laïcité*, and, especially in *Difficult Freedom*, often discusses both the place of Judaism in secular society and what he calls the "Christian atmosphere" of modernity, but he never articulates, either here or elsewhere, a complete account of the concept.

In addition to the paucity of Levinas's writings on secularism, a further difficulty is that what Levinas does say about secularism can often seem contradictory and unclear. Consider, for example, his view of the most basic issue of secularism: the separation of church and state. Is such a separation wholly compatible with Levinas's thinking? On the one hand, Levinas is unambiguous about his endorsement of the separation. He writes in "How Is Judaism Possible?" (1959) that the separation "is the citadel that protects us [French Jews] against injustice," and therefore that "we must beware of tampering with it." And yet, as he will immediately add, the "luminous and incontestable formula" separating church and state must be given "its best content," as if in its common understanding it does not possess its best meaning (*DF* 245). This specific double move, where he simultaneously endorses and criticizes the separation of church and state, is indicative of Levinas's more general attitude from the 1950s onward toward the whole of the standard liberal conception of secularism.

What I mean by the latter conception will be fleshed out in the following sections, but it can be defined now, in a preliminary fashion, as the entire liberal enterprise of creating a culturally neutral state and public sphere for the sake of protecting the rights and liberties of the individual citizen. Because the individual citizen is defined as possessing the right to, or liberty of, thought, expression, and association — all of which together, in effect, produce freedom of religion, whether explicitly proclaimed or not — the state and public sphere *must* be constituted in particular ways to guarantee these liberties; in particular, they must be culturally neutralized so that any citizen, from whichever cultural background, can participate in public institutions without bias and thus without the violation of their liberties. Such neutralization is achieved by the reciprocal move wherein participants in these institutions — that is to say, individual citizens — are not allowed to bring their cultural frameworks with them into the constitutions and operations of these institutions, leading to the so-called privatization of religion.

Because Levinas criticizes this model of secularism while seeming to endorse some notion of it, what I would like to do in this essay is to determine what is precisely Levinas's criticism of secularism and, in addition, what a "Levinasian secularism" might be. My central contention will be that the latter (Levinasian secularism) is not equivalent to the former (his stated views about secularism). The reason for this discrepancy is that Levinas critiques standard liberal secularism on the basis of his more general philosophy of ethical alterity, but then reinstates liberal secularism (or an unspecified version of it) as the best way to protect institutionally ethical alterity. This double movement raises the question, how can ethical alterity at once be consistent and inconsistent with liberal secularism? The question is naturally related to the much-discussed one about the relation of ethics and politics in Levinas's thinking. Levinas's approach to the latter relation is consistently to argue that if we recognize that liberalism needs an ethics beyond itself or "beyond the state," then the liberal state will be just. In the narrower case of secularism at least, I want to argue that this approach is inadequate, as the injustices that Levinas identifies as created by liberal institutions cannot be removed simply by undergirding or overlaying them with Levinasian ethics. The problem here is not with Levinasian ethics; the problem is with Levinas's attempt to square the latter with the institutions he, in another moment, correctly critiques.

In place of this approach, therefore, I set out to articulate what a secularism more consistent with Levinasian ethics would look like, what I shall call, in Levinasian fashion, an "otherwise than secularism." I undertake the latter by concentrating on Levinas's reconception of both *fraternité* (what has always been the most controversial principle of the French Republican motto) and peace (what has usually been taken to be the goal of secularism and tolerance) and by showing that, in Levinas's thinking, they possess an *agonistic* dimension—precisely what gets left out in his endorsement of liberal secularism. Using the work of Chantal Mouffe and William Connolly, both of whom defend "agonistic politics," I try to show that an "agonistic secularism" is more consistent with Levinas's ethical philosophy than the liberal secularism he explicitly endorses. In doing so, however, I cannot offer here a full-blooded defense of agonistic secularism in general, but am merely drawing the connection between it and Levinas's thought in the hope of clarifying what Levinas's thought might offer to current debates about secularism and postsecularism.

LAÏCITÉ AND FRATERNITY

We can get a sense of the reason for and the significance of Levinas's rehabilitation of fraternity if we consider for a moment the development of the modern concept and practice of secularism, which, as we shall see, tends to bracket the whole issue of fraternity. The modern understanding of the "secular" as a nonreligious domain of life only develops beginning in the sixteenth century.[3] Prior to that, in medieval Christendom, *saeculum* referred to the earthly temporal world (the *mundus*) in distinction to the spiritual and eternal world (*aeternitas*). However, we should understand this distinction neither in our modern sense as the separation of the secular and the religious nor as the separation of the profane and the sacred. The doctrine of creation stipulated that even the *saeculum* belonged to, and so was under, God, and thus originates many familiar medieval ideas, such as the great chain of being, the divine right of monarchs and popes, and philosophy as the handmaiden of theology. Beginning in the early modern era, this subordination began to be reordered with the attempt to separate religious authorities (those institutions that mediated one's ties to God, i.e., the Church, theology) from secular authorities (those institutions that were concerned with one's earthly life, e.g., the Monarch, philosophy, the commons). When Hobbes, and then Spinoza, Locke, and Rousseau, argued that the sovereign is authorized by the subjects he or she governs, political power was reconceived as autonomous (giving oneself the law), that is, as not relying on the heteronomous authority of divine right. The autonomy of the state was matched in this framework by the autonomy of the individual subject/citizen. The latter because, according to the terms of the social compact, it was the individual who gave to the sovereign the power and the right to rule in exchange for the sovereign's protection of the individual's remaining powers and rights, that is, the subject/citizen's autonomy. This mutual authorizing of the state's and the individual's autonomy meant, in principle, that what made these two entities—what *constituted* them, that is, their *constitution*—was not grounded in a religious or cultural background. In other words, it was not on the basis of one's belonging to a particular religious or cultural community that one was a member of the state and therefore the state did not derive its autonomy from a religious or cultural community.

With the French Revolution and the ensuing iterations of the Republic, these still philosophical ideas were given political form in the ideological distinctions between *l'ancien régime* and *la Révolution*, between *les deux France* of conservative Catholic France and the liberal Republic, and then in the early twentieth century with the Third Republic's legal separation of church and state in the doctrine of *laïcité*.[4] It is for this reason that, as historian Mona Ozouf has shown, from the beginning of the Revolution in 1789 through to the Third Republic (1870–1940), questions about what should be the motto of the Republic were so troubling. Particularly troubling were those questions having to do with the principle of *fraternité:* should it be part of the motto, what does it mean, and how is it connected to *liberté* and *égalité?*[5] The root of the problem had to do with the fact that liberty and equality were easy to square conceptually with one another and were both based on the rationalist individualism of the Enlightenment, whereas fraternity seemed to imply an affective collectivism that granted importance to human connections that preceded and went beyond purely legal bonds.[6] As such, fraternity was often perceived to be allied with several Enlightenment bugaboos, such as enthusiasm, superstition, and fanaticism.[7]

If we fast-forward now to the dramatic intellectual and political context in which Levinas's thinking took shape, we can see that it is framed by this same problematic. Howard Caygill points out that, when Levinas went to study at the University of Strasbourg in 1923, the city had just five years earlier passed from German administration back to French, and the city and the university were freshly in the process of recommitting themselves to the three principles of the Republic. Moreover, France as a whole, including Levinas's teachers at the university, was still deeply affected by the Dreyfus affair (fully resolved officially only 17 years earlier in 1906), which once again brought to the surface the problem of fraternity: how could someone be denied the legal protections of their liberty and equality just because they came from a perceived different cultural background?[8] National Socialism and the Holocaust would only make more graphic for Levinas the importance of getting right the relationship between politics and fraternity. Hitler's denunciations of modern liberalism and its privileging of liberty and equality were made in the name of fraternity, but a fraternity of the *volk*, a biological fraternity understood to be rooted in the earth.

What is perhaps surprising about Levinas's response to this context, given the horrendous violence and injustice present in it, is that he does not wholly give up on the three principles, but instead undertakes to reconceive them radically. In "Space is not One-Dimensional" (1968), he says that the "trinitarian emblem" (*liberté, egalité, fraternité*) "inscribed on the front of [France's] public buildings" is "moral and philosophical" (*DF* 261), but also cautions in "How is Judaism Possible?" (1959), as I quoted earlier, that the "luminous and incontestable formula" separating church and state must be given "its best content" (245). Thus, similar to his familiar argument about politics more generally—that it is necessary for justice, but in itself is not just—Levinas here suggests that the separation of church and state is a necessary but not a sufficient condition of a just secularism. Before considering what that "best content" would be, we should first understand why he thinks, as he implies here, that the conventional formulation of secularism is not the best one.

The Ethics of Being Political

In order to make some provisional sense of this distinction between a good secularism and a bad one, allow me to suggest that Levinas's conception of secularism works analogously to his conception of politics more generally, which should not be surprising given that secularism is a political institution. In Levinas's thinking of the political, politics is a mode of relating to the world that involves using reason to subsume particular individuals under universal rules, thereby treating them objectively and equally to others, but also thereby ignoring their singularity. For Levinas, there is nothing inherently wrong with this political mode of being. It only becomes a problem when politics is treated as if it were its own ground and end, when the very reason for being political is to subsume others under a hegemon or a collective identity. In contrast to this conception and practice of politics, Levinas argues that politics "is necessary both to protect people from threat and to facilitate ways in which people assist one another," as Michael Morgan puts it.[9] Because, according to Levinas's ethical philosophy, the demands on me are infinite, both because I am absolutely responsible for you and because there are infinite others for whom I am also absolutely responsible, I can never meet those demands fairly or even meet them by myself. Thus, if I want even to consider meeting my (ethical) obligations, then *I will have to* engage in politics. Put even more strongly, we can say that the failure to engage in politics will result in a willful failure to meet our obligations and thus would be unethical. Contrary to the common way of framing the relationship between ethics and politics in Levinas—that ethics is a necessary condition for a just politics—politics is actually, in a different way, a *necessary condition* of justice, even if it is not *sufficient,* even if it must be undertaken in the name of responsibility for the other. In his 1990 preface to his 1934 essay on Hitler, he rhetorically asks whether "liberalism is all we need to achieve authentic dignity for the human subject," to which his implied answer is no, which is *not,* it must be noted, an outright rejection of liberalism by Levinas.[10] The issue for Levinas, as we shall see later, is that something in addition to a pure liberal politics is needed.

Unjust Secularism

Thought analogously to politics, then, secularism—the separation of religion and politics—would be necessary for a just politics, but not sufficient to it. Secularism conceived as sufficient in itself would be an unjust secularism, whereas secularism undertaken for the sake of responsibility would be just. In his 1975–76 lecture course on "God and Onto-theology," Levinas develops this distinction by means of a distinction between what he calls there a "secularization of idolatry" and "an other secularization" (*GDT* 169, cf. 165).[11] In both versions, secularization itself means for Levinas the becoming-worldly of something originally transcendent. The two different kinds of secularization that he identifies take their characteristics from the differences in the transcendences they respectively secularize. Hence, the secularization of idolatry refers back to what Levinas calls an "idolatrous transcendence" (*GDT* 165), whereas the other secularization refers to another transcendence (to be discussed in the next section).

In his description of idolatrous transcendence, Levinas describes a "pagan" world where religion is a mystical and mythical relation to the sacred. In it, the heavens, so far above the earth, are untouchable and therefore sacred and divine, and the only way the human being can encounter the sacred is through an ecstatic and ascetic ascent (*GDT* 163–64). Such a solitary experience is one "which excludes commerce and novelty, and which," he adds, "no stranger disturbs" (164). With the advent of ancient philosophy, this idolatrous transcendence is "secularized," that is, made somehow this-worldly. The disembodied gaze of idolatry, concentrated without distraction on its sacred other-worldly target, is refocused on this world and thereby becomes, with Plato and Aristotle, the comprehensive rationality that serenely gathers together through schemata, categories, and concepts the disparate manifold of the world, subordinating the alterity of the world under "the reign of the Same" (164). While this secularization of paganism is a characteristic of all philosophy, according to Levinas, it reaches its apogee in Heideggerian ontology (165), which, as he spells out in *Totality and Infinity,* subordinates the particularities of all beings to the neutrality of Being, whose most authentic expression is found, for the late Heidegger, in dwelling on the earth.

Levinas does not discuss in these lectures the political implications of this secularized paganism, but we do get a sense of these elsewhere.

In *Totality and Infinity,* he argues that, as a mode of being which imposes a neutral order on the diversity of beings, including the alterity of human beings, secular paganism provides philosophical justification for a pure political rationality, one which unites people in the impersonal universality of the state, making it what he calls "a philosophy of power" (*TI* 46). The state, through the imposition of its force, puts an end to the pre-political violence described by Hobbes as the war of all against all, and protects the individual's right to persevere in its freedom, at least up to the limit of the freedom of the other, who thus serves as a constraint on the freedom of the ego. This mutual constraint of ego and other, enforced by universal law and the state's monopoly on violence, is the source of political equality.[12]

While it is perhaps obvious that, since this politics issued forth from the secularization of paganism, it is a secular politics, it might not be so obvious that it is also a politics of secular*ism,* a politics premised on the separation of church and state. In "The Rights of Man and the Rights of the Other," Levinas suggests that the modern institutional apparatuses of liberalism are not viable or even possible in paganism proper, which is a world that "was felt to be doomed to an arbitrary play of ['natural or supposedly supernatural'] forces," and could only arise with the "flourishing of theoretical knowledge" that, we see Levinas holds, only occurs once paganism is "secularized" in ancient philosophy (*OS* 119). Thus, so long as politics does not fully return to a neo-paganism, as Levinas sees occurring in Heidegger and National Socialism, the modern state and human rights are not rooted merely in a locality, aspiring to merely local gods or local goods. On the contrary, aiming at objectivity and universality, they abide by an a priori logic and, thus, at least in principle, transcend particularism and tribalism. The secular state protects one's right to freedom and equality, irrespective of one's particular background. One of the ways it achieves this goal, as Levinas explains in the same essay, is by ensuring the further rights to freedom of thought, expression, and conscience (120), freedoms which result, in effect, in the separation of church and state.

There will no doubt be those who think there is nothing wrong with this essentially liberal model of secularism and who hold that, in putting an end to pre-political violence, it is actually a social good. But, as Levinas almost always points out in discussions of the political, the nonviolence imposed by the political regime, unless directed to the proper end of facilitating responsibility for the other, imposes its own kind of violence on the individual. Indeed, by setting its citizens in opposition to one another and then attempting to contain the opposition through force of law, the state *builds into society* a low-level competitive anxiety. Moreover, when politics is established with the primary goal of restraining aggression, and not with the goal of facilitating mutual care, the state can only descend into a preoccupation with political machinations, stratagems, and ruses (*OS* 122–23). The inevitability of this social anxiety and this Machiavellian politicking—which occur in liberal states, Levinas says, with "necessities constituting a determinism as rigorous as that of nature indifferent to man" (123) (another reference to paganism)—clearly contradicts the noble, although mistaken goal of ensuring freedom and equality. Because of the totalizing nature of the peace achieved in this pagan secularism, Levinas refers to it as a "bad peace," which is, he concedes, "better, indeed, than a good war," but still not a good peace (122).

We can infer analogously from this last comment that this modern model of secularism is, from a Levinasian point of view, *better* than a particularist paganism that worships local gods to the neglect of other gods and worshippers. But that does not make it a truly good secularism.[13] In his characterizations in *Difficult Freedom* of the places of Judaism and Christianity in modernity, Levinas outlines several of the problems with this bad secularism in a manner consistent with the theoretical sketch I have provided. The fundamental problems pertain to the double-sided consequence of the separation of religion and politics, the often-noted privatization of religion and the assimilation of minorities to the neutrality of public society. Consistent with his view that state nonviolence is itself violent, Levinas points out that these apparently beneficial practices have had detrimental effects on modern Judaism, and—we can infer by extension—on other religious communities.

In "How Is Judaism Possible?" (1959), Levinas takes up the effect on Judaism of the relegation of religion to the private realm. This shift, he says, transforms Judaism in multiple ways. It transforms it variously into (1) "a form of worship that does not extend into other forms of spiritual life," (2) "a confession composed of a single institution," (3) "an academic Judaism that commits itself to no exploits, abusing the supernatural like all the others" (*DF* 249). All of these, Levinas contends, defy the spiritual vitality of Judaism. In "Assimilation Today" (1954) he argues that, at least in the case of Judaism, secularism both succeeded and failed: Jews did relegate their Judaism to the private realm *and* enter the public, but they were always and everywhere treated, as if all Marranos, as not full members of the supposedly secular nation. In Levinas's mind, this mere fact attests to the philosophical weakness of the separation of religion and politics (256), for the distinction fails to account for what he calls the "Christian atmosphere" of the secular state. He writes: "There exists in fact an element of diffuse religion, halfway between the strictly rational order of political thought and the mystical order of belief, in which political life itself swims. One does not think of this religious atmosphere because one breathes it naturally. It does not simply vanish as a result of the juridical separation between Church and State" (256–57). This "diffuse religion" of the secular state—diffuse because neither fully religious nor fully secular, being halfway between both, and so diluted—is a problem, because "Jews' entry into the national life of European states has led them to breathe an atmosphere impregnated with Christian essence," which leads to an "unconscious Christianization" and, ultimately, to an "abdication of Judaism" (257).

Taking as given (1) that Judaism cannot [actually] remain itself within the protection of secularism, and (2) that the secular state remains infused by Christianity, Levinas concludes that, as a result of trying to achieve religious equality, "there is in fact a sense of inequality between Christianity...and Judaism" (*DF* 246). As a result of this inequality, whereby Judaism *and* other non-Christian religions are forced by secularism to remain cloistered in their own communities, while secularized Christians are free to participate fully in the public sphere, secularism effectively encourages a kind of tribalism. Indeed, we might regard the splitting of the world into a private space and a public space, or a religious space and a secular space, as risking forming one of those neo-pagan "attachments to Place" that Levinas describes in the essay "Heidegger, Gagarin, and Us" (1961), attachments which "[split] humanity into natives and strangers" (232). Indeed, as Levinas points out in "Space Is not One-Dimensional" (1968), French Jews did not have to wait for the return of paganism with the Nazis to discover that, to the "native" Christian secularists, the Jews were "strangers." The Dreyfus affair had already made painfully clear that Jews were, in practice if not in principle, not part of the *fraternité* supposed to result from the separation of church and state within the French Republic.

If religious freedom is going to be preserved within the context of pluralism, then from a Levinasian point of view the nature of the separation between religion and politics will have to be reconceived.

Toward a Secularism Otherwise

Levinas's own reconception of secularism is based on a rethinking of the nature of the transcendence that is, as we hear him claim in "God and Onto-theology," the basis of secularization. It will not be a surprise to readers familiar with Levinas that he finds the source of this alternate transcendence, and therefore of this "other secularization" (*GDT* 169), in the Jewish tradition. In his essay "A Religion for Adults" (1957), Levinas argues that Judaism is opposed to and breaks from the conception of the sacred that we heard him outline in his discussion of paganism. After reiterating his understanding of pagan religion, in which human beings are subordinated to the perceived overwhelming majesty and splendor of nature, Levinas says about this pagan conception that it "seems to Judaism to offend human freedom" and to be "a form of violence" (*DF* 14). Instead of pagan transcendence, Judaism locates transcendence—God—in the relationship of responsibility for the other. In a section of the same essay, entitled "The Ethical Relation as a Religious Relation," Levinas puts forward his familiar argument that, in the concrete situation of being responsible for another, one is in relationship to a being whose very imminent needs call one into question, and who therefore exceeds oneself, transcends oneself, allowing one to glimpse in the face of this other a trace of God. He writes: "the Other is not a *new edition of myself*; in its Otherness it is situated in a dimension of height, in the ideal, the Divine, and through my relation to the Other, I am in touch with God," to which he adds, "Ethics is not the corollary of the vision of God, it is that very vision. Ethics is an optic, such that everything I know of God and everything I can hear of His word and reasonably say to Him must find an ethical expression" (17). Thus, in contrast to pagan religion, where the divine was located ecstatically outside of one's mundane experience, here it is located in the very heart of it, or, rather, *as* the very heart of it. This transcendence is one that turns one's attention *to* the world, as Levinas argues in "Place and Utopia" (1950) (see esp. 101), a transcendence that is transcendent in *heightening* one's attention to the world. In turning away from the enchanted world of paganism to the concrete world of human needs, Judaism, Levinas says, echoing Weber's disenchantment thesis, "has de-charmed the world" (14; see also 234). Or, as he puts it in his lectures on "God and Onto-theology," the call to be responsible for the other, what is figured in the lectures as "hunger," is actually "a secularization of the world" (*GDT* 169).

I have noted earlier that, for Levinas, the ethical relation is never sufficient to carry out one's ethical obligations, that one *must* turn to politics, and therefore that it is unethical not to be political. This argument implies that the secularization enacted through Judaic ethics must be politicized: it must become a kind of secular*ism*. But we have also seen that, while Levinas endorses the political institutions of secularism—centrally, the separation of church and state—he also holds that in their common form and understanding these are problematic, and so need to be regrounded and reconceived. This is the significance of his concept of fraternity, which is his attempt to rethink how members of a secular polity can be related to each other. In a section of "A Religion for Adults" entitled "Citizens of Modern States," Levinas declares himself bluntly against neo-pagan nationalisms, which, he contends, will all base their fraternity in some notion of blood or autochthony (being born of the earth), when he says that "Man ... is not a tree, and humanity is not a forest." What unites citizens is not that they share (like a forest) some common biological roots, or that they are all rooted to a common territory. Instead, "modern nations" must be constituted on the basis of the free "decision to work in common" (*DF* 23). For Levinas, this working in common, different from biological or territorial commonality, is motivated by responsibility for the other. He asks rhetorically in "The Rights of Man and the Rights of the Other" whether "the fraternity that is in the motto of the republic [should not rather] be discerned in the prior non-indifference of one for the other, in that original goodness"—that is, in responsibility for the other—"in which freedom is embedded, and in which the justice of the rights of man takes on an immutable significance and stability, better than those guaranteed by the state?" (*OS* 125). For Levinas, fraternity is a way to conceive the commonality among a society of egos, others, and thirds (i.e., other others) in such a way that it does not reduce their separation and their uniqueness, and therefore their responsibility, within the unity of the state. Because each of us, as an ego, is responsible for the other and the other others ("the third"), we end up, *like* one another, as mutually responsible, each of us "a brother among brothers" (*TI* 279). But the critical point about Levinas's notion of fraternity is that this "likeness" or fraternity is produced by the very unlikeness (the separation) of ego, other, and third, because it is unlikeness that ensures that the ego, other, and third do not congeal into the oneness of kinship or ethnicity, which would preclude the possibility of a relation among a plurality.[14]

Notwithstanding Levinas's chauvinistic, flippant comments about non-Western peoples,[15] he always argues that this fraternity otherwise, even though it comes to modern politics from Judaism, is universal and can embrace all peoples. He explains in "Israel and Universalism" (1958) that "a Jew can communicate just as intimately with a non-Jew who portrays morality...as with another Jew" (*DF* 176). This universality derives from the fact that the transcendence of the other consists precisely in her being irreducible to and unconditioned by all conditions, including her ethnicity and cultural background.[16] Indeed, it is because the other exceeds such conditions that Levinas often speaks of the *singularity* of the other: the fact that the other does not belong to a concept, category, or genus, including the genera Jew and non-Jew. Since the otherness of the other precisely transcends his cultural conditions, one's responsibility for the other—for the *otherness* and *singularity* of the other—is likewise a responsibility not to those cultural conditions, but for what transcends them (the other in his singularity). So, the other may be a Jewish or Syrian refugee, but one's responsibility is not called upon by her Jewishness or Syrianness, but by her need. Moreover, one's own responsibility, one's assignation by the other, and so one's own self within responsibility, is rendered singular by this relation, removing one from the totalizing categories of one's own cultural identifiers: one is not responsible *because of* one's Jewishness or Syrianness. Whence Levinas's claim in the same essay that, in responsibility for the other, "the differences between Jew, Greek, and barbarian are abolished" (177). One does not need to be a Jew, Greek, or barbarian in order to be responsible for a Jew, Greek, or barbarian, and, therefore, one does not need to be a Jew, Greek, or barbarian in order to have fraternal relations with Jews, Greeks, and barbarians.

One can see here why Levinas believes his ethical philosophy provides, in his mind, a better ground for secularism, for a secularism otherwise. Through his notion of fraternity he provides a new way to conceive relations within society and clearly does so in such a way that no cultural group remains hegemonic. But one can also see here why, as I suggest, questions about the specific differences between the traditional conception of secularism and his reconception emerge. For even if fraternity is understood by Levinas to be universal, it is critical to observe that it is universal for him because it is neutral (neutral from the Latin *ne* [neither] and *uter* [nor]) — neither Jewish, nor Greek, nor barbarian. As I quoted above, in his conception of fraternity, "the differences between Jew, Greek, and barbarian" — that is to say, cultural differences — "are abolished." Besides being staggering, this claim also means that a state which undertook to fulfill the Levinasian mandate of organizing its citizens around the priority of mutual responsibility would do so around ostensibly neutral citizens. In doing so, however, how would this state's secularism be any different from any traditionally liberal secular state? And would such a state not risk committing the same kinds of violence he criticized modern European states for committing? That is, would it not end up having, on the one hand, to privatize religion, and, on the other, to enforce a kind of assimilation to the "neutrality" of the state and the public sphere?

The concerns I raise here are not purely conjectural, as Levinas's discussion of the state of Israel in "Assimilation Today" attests. Here, Levinas addresses the problem I discussed above regarding the place of Jews within the diffuse Christianity of modern European nations. In contrast to their impoverished situation there, Levinas points instead to "the incalculable value of the young State [of Israel], albeit secular, to the religious future of Judaism." (*DF* 257). Given Levinas's recognition and critique of European secularism, the reason he offers for why secular Israel is of incalculable value to religious Judaism is, frankly, stunning. For it is not because Israel will have configured secularism otherwise to produce some novel and more just institution; it is, rather, because "this time," as he says — that is, within Israel, unlike within those secular states where Jews previously used to live (Europe) — "the element" in which Jewish citizens will "swim" "is Jewish" (257). By "element," Levinas means the "diffuse religion" or "atmosphere" discussed above. In other words, what he is saying is that the great benefit — *for Jews* — of secular Israel is that, unlike the Christian atmosphere of European secular states, it will have a Jewish atmosphere. Jews — secular or religious? — will enjoy in secular Israel the same privilege Christian secularists did in European secular states, which makes it conceivable that non-Jews in secular Israel would be subject to the same disadvantages that Jews were in secular Europe. Levinas here praises the secular state of Israel for the very things he criticizes in European secular states.

The important point for me here is not the problem with Levinas's thinking about Israel per se, nor with his Zionism more generally, although these observations could potentially open up other avenues of discussion in those debates. The point is that even after critiquing liberal secularism and arguing for its regrounding, the secularism Levinas seems to endorse appears no different. If Levinas's conception of secularism would commit the same violences as traditional secularism, then what, one has to wonder, is the point of regrounding it? As he asks in his lecture course on "God and Onto-theology," "What difference is there between institutions arising from a limitation of violence [i.e., liberal institutions] and those arising from a limitation of responsibility?" (*GDT* 183) What difference, indeed? Levinas's reliance on conventional liberal institutions seems to belie his attempt to conceive of a secularism otherwise. A more truly responsible secularism, a more truly Levinasian secularism, will thus require a more fundamental reconception of secularism than Levinas himself provides.

Agonizing Peace

In order to help formulate what a secularism more consistent with Levinasian philosophy might look like, I want to shift the discussion slightly and take up the concept of peace, a concept that plays a prominent role in Levinas's late political thinking and which I've touched upon already. As building upon the historical precedents of the Peace of Augsburg and the Edict of Nantes, both of which declare their objective to be the establishment of peace,[17] secularism aims to institutionalize peace and tolerance within the state.

Traditionally, peace is defined as the cessation of hostilities or as a blissful state of calm. Augustine, for instance, defines peace as "the tranquility of order,"[18] and sets up peace as the goal sought in our earthly world of strife and disorder: "in this [earthly] abode of weakness, and in these wicked days, this state of anxiety has also its use, stimulating us to seek with keener longing for that security where peace is complete and unassailable."[19] As such, peace is conceived *negatively* as nonconflictual and nontumultuous; it is the *absence* of conflict or the *absence* of disorder. This way of defining peace corresponds to what Charles Taylor has recently called the "subtraction story" of secularism, which has its roots in the Enlightenment, and which conceives of secularization as the removal of religion and of secularity as an absence of religion.[20] Neutrality and peace thus have congruent structures.

In "Peace and Proximity" Levinas challenges this traditional conception of peace, what he sometimes refers to as "rational peace" (discussed above). He characterizes it as "peace on the basis of the Truth," by which he means a model of cognitive truth wherein a diversity of elements are subsumed under categories and concepts; in other words, where alterity is reduced to sameness.[21] Consistent with what I said above, he explains that peace conceived on this basis

> commands humans *without forcing them or combating them*, which governs them or gathers them together *without enslaving them*, which through discourse, can convince rather than *vanquish*, and which masters the *hostile* elements of nature through calculation and the know-how of technology. Peace on the basis of the state, which would be a gathering of humans participating in the same ideal truths. Peace which is savored as *tranquility* that guarantees a solidarity—the exact measure of reciprocity in services rendered among fellows: the *unity* of a *Whole* wherein everyone finds their *repose*, their place, their seat. Peace as *tranquility* and *repose!* (BPW 162–63; emphasis mine)

What we see here is that, on this model, peace consists in the evacuation of any kind of conflict—force, combat, enslavement, vanquishing, and hostility—and the instillation of tranquility, repose, unity, and solidarity.

Levinas does not believe such a notion of peace is, in reality, viable. All that it does, according to him, is to displace elsewhere or to delay the force of violence. In Europe, where, Levinas avers, this model of peace has been the dominant one, he finds a history of violence committed not simply in defense of peace—which might be defensible—but *according to* this model of it. He reads imperialism, the world wars, genocides, the Holocaust, and the destructive capabilities of technology not as exceptions to the model of rational peace, but as the outcomes of it. In all of these, there is a prioritizing of unification under universal categories, a prioritizing of the reduction of alterity to sameness. It is critical here to reiterate what I stated earlier: that it is not universal categories per se that are the problem for Levinas, but their prioritizing *over* responsibility for the other; it is by way of this prioritizing that "peace with the other turns into hatred" (*BPW* 166). As a consequence of this history, Europe finds itself in the twentieth century with a "guilty conscience" and "anxiety" (164). This anxiety reveals, according to Levinas, that the legitimacy of the rational peace espoused by Europe is "contested," not only outside Europe but also within, so that we now have a "break" in Europe, a "Europe against Europe" (163). The force that was allegedly disarmed by rational peace thus reappears in the latter's violence toward others and in its consequent self-contestation. Combat has not disappeared, therefore; it has merely reappeared elsewhere.

In place of this evasion, Levinas calls on us to envision what he calls an "ethical peace" (*BPW* 166). This peace is one that is grounded in Levinas's usual concern with responsibility for the other. Rather than focus on the relationship between peace and ethical responsibility (proximity), I want to highlight the contrast Levinas draws between the tranquility of rational peace and his ethical peace, the latter of which, I would like to show, presupposes and preserves at its core a kind of agonistic struggle. To see this agonism, we must bear in mind that responsibility for the other, first of all, ensures that the distance and height of the other are maintained. The other, as Levinas always characterizes it, is in fact not reducible to my gaze. I can never wholly identify with or predict the actions and the reactions of the other. Peace with the other, therefore, cannot be some kind of unity, communing, or atonement (at-one-ment). Any attempts on my part to reduce the other in such manners are always in defiance of its primordial excess over me, which is why such attempts are, for Levinas, the very definition of violence. The other's alterity in a sense issues a command not to violate it ("thou shalt not kill") and, because of that issuance, is paradoxically the *fundamental condition* of violence. "The Other is the sole being I can wish to kill," Levinas writes (*TI* 198). The possibility of violence cannot be removed from the relation to the other and therefore cannot be expunged from peace. For this reason, the alterity of the other is "*at once* the temptation to kill and the call to peace" (*TI* 167; emphasis mine).[22] Given the simultaneity of this temptation and this call, the separation between self and other—which, in fraternity, becomes the separation among *all* of us—is not a pacific separation. It is fraught with tension and contention. Even when one responds to the other responsibly, the peaceful relation is never placid, for both members of the dyad. On one side is the other whose transcendence does not put it in a state of blissful calm, but who is, from the self's point of view, always "nude," "destitute," and "defenseless" (197–201). On the other side is the self, whom the other jarringly "awakens" like an epiphany, demanding that we keep "incessant watch" over it, transforming one's mere consciousness into conscience and conscientiousness (the guilty conscience and anxiety mentioned earlier).[23] In other works Levinas famously speaks of how the other holds the self "hostage," "obsesses" it, and "persecutes" it ("Substitution," *BPW* 87–89). Thus, Levinas's ethical peace is "not a matter of peace as pure rest that confirms one's identity but of always placing in question this very identity, its limitless freedom and its power" ("Peace and Proximity," 167). Even though there is here a kind of disarmament of one's power by the other, this disarmament is initiated through a more primordial *contestation* of one by the other. This contestation is not so much "the unforced force of the better argument" as much as the disarming strike of alterity, which is why Levinas can write in *Otherwise than Being,* in contrast to his claim cited earlier that liberalism imposes a "bad peace," that "responsibility for another" is a "disinterestedness imposed with a good violence" (*OB* 43).²⁴ Levinas tends not to put it this way, but we can see here that, in his ethical scheme, self and other maintain something of an agonistic struggle. The face-to-face relation is also, as it were, a toe-to-toe relation. Both responsibility and violence, then, are structured by this agonism, the difference between the two being that violence seeks to overcome difference by en-forcing identity (rational peace), whereas *responsibility attends to the challenge and trial of this difference* by giving to the other what the other needs to persevere in her alterity. In either case, we have here a response to the *challenge* and *contestation* of and by the other, making this peace itself a kind of trial.

This agonism, while not made central by Levinas to his conception of politics, seems to me necessarily to be a part of it. For if, in his view, we are each responsible for each other, and responsibility is both the temptation to violence and the call to peace, then in society we each contest each other. Society is a contestation of all of us by all of us, each of us contested by and responding to the other. Politics would, then, not be the *suppression* or *pacification* of this contestation and response within the unity of institutions, but *the institutionalization of this contestation.* Levinas only hints at this idea in the final section of "Peace and Proximity" where, in a discussion of politics, he explains that his project is aimed at reminding us that political institutions are grounded in ethical peace and justice, not vice versa, and that the former are "not a natural and anonymous legality governing the human masses, from which is derived a technique of social *equilibrium,* placing in *harmony* the *antagonistic* and blind *forces* through transitory cruelties and violence" (*BPW* 169; emphasis mine). A proper conception of political institutions would not see them as aiming at negative peace (the cessation of hostilities), but at the positive peace of facilitating responsibility for the other. Such a goal, he goes on to suggest, is not accomplished by starting from a "war of all against all," but from an ethical peace, which, as I've argued, cannot be without contention and agonism. Indeed, we might say that Levinasian peace is a peace of all against all, an agonized and agonizing peace.

Agonizing Secularism: Levinas with Connolly and Mouffe

Recognizing this agonistic dimension of Levinas's conception of peace provides us with a new opening for conceiving of a secularism more consistent with his general philosophy, one which does not simply return to the standard liberal model of secularism after having articulated a nonliberal foundation for it. This more truly Levinasian secularism would be one that managed to preserve and foreground the agonism of peace. Steps toward conceiving such an agonistic secularism have, in fact, been taken by two key theorists of agonistic politics, William Connolly and Chantal Mouffe, to whose work I shall now briefly turn.[25]

As both Connolly and Mouffe see it, the fundamental problem with the liberal model of secularism is the concept of neutrality.[26] By "neutrality" is usually meant the idea that in a pluralist democracy the state and public discourse should not embody or reflect any of the conceptions of the good or of the metaphysical worldviews of any particular constituency, but should instead be constituted by a set of principles or procedures derived from no constituency that all constituents can agree on, as, for instance, in Rawls's "overlapping consensus" and the early Habermas's "idealized consensus." There are, in fact, two problems with the concept of neutrality, one descriptive, one normative. The descriptive problem is that the state and the public sphere in modern democracies are, in fact, not neutral. As both Connolly and Mouffe try to show, liberal democracies and their theorists always in reality presuppose cultural backgrounds. Connolly points out, for instance, that Tocqueville noticed how the American "wall of separation" between church and state is feasible only because it is in fact "grounded in a larger Christian civilization," that Habermas's drive to neutral consensus similarly reflects an unconscious "reiteration of...Christian" sensibilities (specifically, the Christian sensibility of wanting to occupy the place of authority), and that Rawls admits that his concept of "reasonableness" "comes from a fortunate cultural tradition that already embodies it."[27] Similarly, in her discussion of

Habermas and Rawls, Mouffe shows how each demonstrates that the other's attempt to achieve neutrality fails: Habermas shows that Rawls is not able to conceive a neutral constitution free of metaphysical and moral worldviews ("comprehensive doctrines"), while Rawls shows that Habermas's model of democratic deliberation cannot be purely procedural and free of substantive (i.e., metaphysical) issues. "That they are unable to maintain the tight separation they advocate"—between politics and comprehensive doctrines, for Rawls, and between procedure and substance, for Habermas—"highlights the fact that the domain of politics...is not a neutral terrain that could be insulated from the pluralism of values and where rational, universal solutions could be formulated."[28] Mouffe and Connolly thus agree that liberal democracy and its theorists are not culturally neutral.

The second problem with neutrality is the normative one that, because all members of a polity always actually belong to a cultural background, the *aspiration* to neutrality of that polity can only be achieved through the forcible exclusion of its citizens' backgrounds. This contention no doubt contradicts the standard description of secularism as inclusive, as creating a political and public place in which citizens of different backgrounds can live together peacefully. It is precisely when cultural backgrounds enter into politics and public discourse that, it is claimed, violence and exclusion become possible. Rawls, for instance, argues that comprehensive doctrines must be bracketed in order to prevent any constituency from violently imposing its views on others.[29] But if no one and no institution can escape their cultural backgrounds, as was explained in the previous problem, and if secularism undertakes to "bracket" cultural norms and to establish neutrality, then the decision to bracket or to negate (again, neutral, from Latin *ne* and *uter*, means "neither-nor") metaphysical assumptions is in fact a decision to exclude, dressed up in the guise of peaceful inclusivity. So, for instance, when avowed secularists refrain from publicly discussing controversial metaphysical or moral assumptions, such as whether a fetus is a human being or not, or whether or not euthanasia is morally permissible, these are attempts, Connolly contends, to "discourage a variety of enthusiastic Christians," but also other religious citizens, we can add, "from doing so in turn."[30] Such an approach no doubt avoids conflict and keeps the peace, at least temporarily, but it does so by attempting to prevent others with different metaphysical and moral assumptions from participating fully in public debate and policy, a move that serves the interests of secularists whose metaphysical and moral assumptions are more closely aligned with public institutions.

In Mouffe's view, exclusions are not avoidable in politics and therefore are not inherently wrong. Indeed, for her, determining what is legitimately included and excluded in a polity is precisely the essence and purpose of politics. The task of politics is to establish what should and should not be instituted in a polity, and for this reason politics always involves power and hegemony, an *us* making a decision that affects *all*, including *they* who do not necessarily agree with *us*.[31] The problem with liberalism, and with its version of secularism, is that it pretends not to be exclusive. The consequence of this pretense is that exclusions take place subliminally, as Levinas observed when he highlighted the "unconscious Christianization" of Jews within secular France (*DF* 256–57).[32] As Mouffe summarizes the point:

> Completely missing from such an approach is "the political" in its dimension of power, antagonism and relationships of forces.... It offers us a picture of the well-ordered society as one from which—through rational agreement on justice—antagonism, violence, power and repression have disappeared. But it is only because they have been made invisible through a clever stratagem.... In that way, exclusions can be denied by declaring that they are the product of the "free exercise of practical reason" that establishes the limits of possible consensus. When a point of view is excluded it is because this is required by the exercise of reason; therefore the frontiers between what is legitimate and what is not legitimate appear as independent of power relations. Thanks to this legerdemain, rationality and morality provide the key to solving the "paradox of liberalism": how to eliminate its adversaries while remaining neutral.[33]

What Connolly and Mouffe are both describing as the deceitful exclusion of others from the supposedly neutral political and public spheres is, in Levinasian terms, a reduction of the other to the Same. The universal space in which all can allegedly reside is achieved only by forcing everyone to conform to a particular set of cultural (metaphysical and value) norms. Neutrality is thereby accomplished by effacing the very real differences between culturally identified citizens. This is why Levinas argues that the neutrality designed to protect us from violence in fact imposes its own form of violence. Indeed, we might say that what is presented in liberalism as a *state* of neutrality is in fact an *act* of neutralization or neutering, a forceful excision of distinguishing markers. This model of the universal is, in Levinas's apt term, the "neuter" (*TI* 298–99).

It is in place of the politics of neutrality and consensus that Mouffe and Connolly each defend an agonistic politics and secularism. Politics and secularism, according to them, must begin with the acknowledgement that citizens and polities are culturally grounded, each bearing within itself a set of metaphysical and value assumptions, including religious ones, and that these cannot simply be bracketed. This starting point presupposes that citizens would then come to the public and political spheres bearing these metaphysical and value assumptions. For many issues of public import, these backgrounds would not be relevant anyway. But for those where they are, rather than asking citizens to check at the door their fundamental ways of relating to the world, Connolly suggests that citizens should be allowed to "bring selective dimensions of their religious, ethnic, sensual, gender, and moral sensibilities into public engagements whenever the issue makes it pertinent to do so."[34] Mouffe similarly holds that, "as long as they act within constitutional limits, there is no reason why religious groups should not be able to intervene in the political arena to argue in favor of or against certain causes."[35] Were the present essay devoted strictly to agonism, I would clearly need to interrogate where Connolly's criteria of selection and Mouffe's constitutional limits come from, but, again, my aim here is not to defend agonism per se as much as to show that a properly conceived Levinasian secularism would have to be agonistic.

Because citizens would thus be participating in public debates openly *from the standpoint of their own cultural backgrounds,* it is likely that, around certain issues, these citizens will hold significantly different positions. Each will see the problem differently and be arguing for taking courses of action which reflect their different outlooks. Each will thus be "partisan," as both Connolly and Mouffe describe the agonistic citizen, although not in the narrow sense in which that term is often used today. While partisans, in Connolly's and Mouffe's sense, do not simply do anything they can to win the present fight, including deploying misinformation, deceit, and the disparagement of opponents,[36] they do fight for and identify with their beliefs and therefore fight *against* opponents. Indeed, this antagonism, they both contend, cannot be eradicated from politics. The liberal attempt to do so by way of secularism, we saw above, simply dresses up the wolf in sheep's clothing. But, as we saw, from a Levinasian perspective this gesture of forcing all wolves (partisans) to be universalist (herd-like) sheep is itself an act of violence, an act that reduces the other to the same. Maintaining antagonism, by contrast, would preserve what Levinas means by separation. It would preserve, in his terms, the ineradicable temptation to murder, yes, but it would also harbor the only possibility of a responsible peace.

In the context of politics, avoiding the possibility of violence inherent in antagonism would involve, according to Mouffe, transmuting (1) antagonism into agonism and (2) the enemy into the adversary, both of which demand regarding one's opponents as "legitimate," as Mouffe says, and with what Connolly calls "agonistic respect." Mouffe explains: "While antagonism is a we/they relation in which the two sides are enemies who do not share any common ground, agonism is a we/they relation where the conflicting parties, although acknowledging that there is no rational solution to their conflict, nevertheless recognize the legitimacy of their opponents. They are 'adversaries' not enemies. This means that, while in conflict, they see themselves as belonging to the same political association, as sharing a common symbolic space within which the conflict takes place. We could say that the task of democracy is to transform antagonism into agonism."[37]

In order for antagonism to be transmuted into agonism and for the adversary to be viewed as legitimate, it is critical that two attitudes be adopted by the partisan. First, as Mouffe argues, the agonistic struggle must not take place on a moral register, wherein the we/they distinction would be experienced as a good/evil distinction.[38] If one regards one's opponent as inherently evil, then one will feel justified in outright rejecting their claims and even in resorting to violence against them. Such moves would, in the end, eliminate agonism. Second, as Connolly argues for the obverse, agonistic respect entails "critical responsiveness," in which one recognizes the contestability of one's own point of view, including elements of one's identity, beliefs, values, judgements, and sensibilities, and is therefore at least open to the possibility of having one's point of view altered through engagement with others.[39]

Behind both of these attitudes, we can discern the Levinasian ethic of being responsible for the other. Mouffe actually disagrees on this point, contending that the ethics of "responsibility for the other and...engag[ing] with difference" implies naively that "violence and exclusion could disappear."[40] But, in the case of Levinas at least, this is a mistaken accusation. At the ethical level of his thought, the temptation to violence and exclusion is, as we have seen, part of the very condition of responsibility and, in fact, always haunts it. This is why, within political society, the social identity does not, in fact, form a neutral, homogenous, and universal harmony, even though certain societies, like Levinas's paradigm case of Nazi Germany, will conceive of themselves in those terms. In such a society, being other is evil, which is why it is justifiable to violate the other. But when self and other are recognized as *separate,* in Levinas's sense, and political society thereby understood to embody and contend with this separation, good and evil then refer differently to how one responds to the other, with violence ("evil") or with responsibility ("good"). A just political society, for Levinas, and therefore a just secularism, would thus be one that did not enforce identity (either by forced assimilation or annihilation of the other) but would protect the other's otherness (her distinct singularity, whether as widow, orphan, or poor, or as Jew, Christian, Muslim, Hindu, Buddhist, or Aboriginal). This does not mean that a just society must simply accommodate the demands of any and all of its constituents—something that Levinas recognizes is impossible. A just society must, as Levinas always insists, evaluate and decide on a course of action not possible to satisfy all its members based on a set of criteria that the society prescribes for itself; it will, as Mouffe says, have to exclude. But this exclusion is not due to the evil of the other and so does not take the form of forced assimilation or annihilation. Nor does exclusion take the form of exile or ostracism. One's adversary is, after all, one's fellow citizen, whether neighbor or stranger. The excluded other remains in one's face; the face-to-face does not go anywhere.

What precisely a Levinasian, agonistic secularism would look like cannot, of course, be specified. Levinas, Mouffe, and Connolly have all taken hits for failing to articulate a political program. But philosophy is not institution building or policy engineering. When Hobbes rejected the theory of the divine right of kings and unwittingly laid the foundations for the theory of republican sovereignty, he could not imagine that his ideas would demand radically new institutions, and so imagined merely a new form of monarchy. This "failing" on Hobbes's part, if we can call it that, does not devalue his contribution. Similarly, we should not be surprised if our recent reengagement with the concept of secularism does not issue immediately in some obvious plan for how we should reconfigure our secular, or postsecular, societies. *Ought* may imply *can*, but it never tells us *how*. Rather than rush with certainty to some putative vision of society or of what Levinasian secularism would look like, we should take a cue from Nikolas Kompridis's recent suggestion about the role of recognition in politics and instead continue to struggle over the meanings and possibilities of secularism and postsecularism.[41] Here I have undertaken to discern what Levinas might offer to such a struggle.

Notes

Aspects of this essay were presented at the Société Internationale de Recherches Emmanuel Levinas, in Toulouse, France, July 2010, and at North American Levinas Society Conference, Duquense University, Pittsburgh, July 28–31, 2013. I am grateful to the participants at both conferences for the questions and comments I received.

1. Throughout the essay I will largely follow José Casanova in reserving the term *secularism* to refer to the political doctrine of the separation of religion and politics, *secularization* for the social and cultural process of transforming a religious culture into a nonreligious one, and *secular* for anything (a culture, an idea, a practice) which is not religious. See José Casanova, "The Secular, Secularizations, Secularisms," in *Rethinking Secularism*, ed. Craig Calhoun, Mark Juergensmeyer, and Jonathan VanAntwerpen (Oxford: Oxford University Press, 2011), 54–74.

2. While the question of politics in Levinas has been taken up by many scholars, and the question of secular*ization* has also been (although to a lesser extent), the more specific problem of secular*ism* in Levinas has, to my knowledge, not been. The secularization of Judaism in Levinas's thought has been taken up most thoroughly in Michael Fagenblat's excellent study, *A Covenant of Creatures: Levinas's Philosophy of Judaism* (Stanford, CA: Stanford University Press, 2010); Ze'ev Levy offers one of the few discussions of Levinas's analysis of Western secularization in "Emmanuel Levinas on Secularization in Modern Society," *Levinas Studies*, vol. 1, edited by Jeffrey Bloechl and Jeffrey L. Kosky, 19–35 (Pittsburgh: Duquesne University Press, 2005); Hent de Vries employs Levinas's thinking to critique the secularization thesis (that modernization leads to secularization), but does not directly address secularism, in his monumental study, *Minimal Theologies: Critiques of Secular Reason in Adorno and Levinas,* trans. Geoffrey Hale (Baltimore: Johns Hopkins University Press, 2005).

3. I have presented a version of this genealogy of the secular in relation to the thinking of Derrida in Mark Cauchi, "The Secular to Come: Interrogating the Derridean 'Secular,'" *Journal of Cultural and Religious Theory* 10, no. 1 (Winter 2009): 1–25. The most thorough attempt to produce such a genealogy is Charles Taylor's *A Secular Age* (Cambridge, MA: Belknap, 2007).

4. For a valuable discussion of the history of secularism in France, see Yolande Jansen, "*Laïcité*, or the Politics of Republican Secularism," in *Political Theologies: Public Religions in a Post-Secular World*, ed. Hent de Vries and Lawrence E. Sullivan (New York: Fordham University Press, 2006), 475–93.

5. Mona Ozouf, "Liberty, Equality, Fraternity," in *Realms of Memory: Constructions of the French Past*, vol. 3, *Symbols*, ed. Pierre Nora, trans. Arthur Goldhammer (New York: Columbia University Press, 1998), 77–114.

6. See Talal Asad, "Trying to Understand French Secularism," in de Vries and Sullivan, *Political Theologies;* Jean-Luc Nancy, "Church, State, Resistance" in de Vries and Sullivan, *Political Theologies;* cf. Ozouf, "Liberty, Equality, Fraternity."

7. For an example, see Voltaire's discussion of fraternities in his *Treatise on Tolerance,* in *Treatise on Tolerance and Other Writings,* ed. Simon Harvey (Cambridge: Cambridge University Press, 2000), 12–13. He acknowledges that fraternities do not always lead to violence, but he does contend that reason and tolerance always lead to peace.

8. Howard Caygill, *Levinas and the Political* (London: Routledge, 2002), 2.

9. Michael Morgan, *Discovering Levinas* (Cambridge: Cambridge University Press, 2009), 24.

10. Emmanuel Levinas, "Prefatory Note," trans. Seán Hand, in *Difficult Justice: Commentaries on Levinas and Politics,* ed. Asher Horowitz and Gad Horowitz (Toronto: University of Toronto Press, 2006), 3.

11. Levinas largely repeats the analysis offered in this lecture in the essay "Secularization and Hunger," trans. Bettina Bergo, in "Levinas's Contribution to Contemporary Philosophy," ed. Bettina Bergo and Diane Perpich, a special double issue of *Graduate Faculty Philosophy Journal* 20, no. 2, and 21, no. 1 (1998): 3–12. There has been very little critical commentary on these two pieces. See Levy, "Emmanuel Levinas on Secularization in Modern Society."

12. See Levinas, "Uniqueness," esp. section entitled "Autonomy of the Reasonable Individual," in *Entre Nous,* trans. Michael B. Smith and Barbara Hershaw (New York: Columbia University Press, 2000).

13. Consider the following historical example. The Edict of Nantes, issued in 1598 to end the Wars of Religion between Catholics and Protestants in France, does *better* than the Absolutist doctrine of *cuius regio eius religio* ("in whose realm, his religion"), reached in the 1555 Peace of Augsburg. But this better Edict of Nantes, even before it was finally revoked in 1685 by Louis XIV, hardly succeeded in establishing a just or lasting peace.

14. We see here, in Levinas's distinction between two forms of secularization and secularism—the pagan model and the biblical model (and, along with these, two forms of fraternity, biological and ethical, respectively)—why Critchley is mistaken in his contention that, for Levinas, "universalistic republicanism is simply the secular translation" of the "strict entailment between fraternity and monotheism." Simon Critchley, "Five Problems in Levinas's View of Politics and a Sketch of a Solution to Them," *Political Theory* 32, no. 2 (2004): 174. Levinas is very clear that French Republicanism, *as it is,* is the translation or secularization of "idolatrous transcendence" into universalism. Its fraternity is the fraternity of neutrality, and the neuter that Levinas wants to overcome and to which Levinas wants to ascribe a better meaning. The secularization of monotheism, Levinas thinks, would lead to a fraternity "otherwise," a fraternity

that, at least in Levinas's account, is nonfoundational in precisely the same way as Critchley wishes it to be.

15. Here I'm thinking of Levinas's justly criticized comments that everything other than the Bible and Greece is "exotic" and "dance" (Raoul Mortley, *French Philosophers in Conversation* [London: Routledge, 1991], 18), or his comments about the "yellow peril" of China ("Dialectics and the Sino-Soviet Quarrel," *UH* 108). In these moments—mostly interviews—in which Levinas is hardly advancing a worked-out political analysis, I don't think we can discern a "test" of the political viability of Levinas's philosophy, as Jason Caro suggests. Jason Caro, "Levinas and the Palestinians," *Philosophy and Social Criticism* 35, no. 6 (2009): 671–84. To do so, one would have to establish that the positions outlined in these comments are deductively derived from the premises of his philosophy, which, I would argue, they are not. Here I follow Critchley in following Derrida, who, it seems to me, takes the correct approach in differentiating between what he refers to as Levinas's "opinions" and his coherently argued analysis of peace, hospitality, and the beyond. Jacques Derrida, *Adieu to Emmanuel Levinas,* trans. Pascale-Anne Brault and Michael Naas (Stanford, CA: Stanford University Press, 1999), 117. This approach does not let Levinas off the hook for these comments; it simply acknowledges that Levinas, like most major thinkers, is not always consistent with his own ideas, especially when political allegiances are involved.

16. I have taken up the concept of the unconditional in Levinas in Mark Cauchi, "Unconditioned by the Other: Agency and Alterity in Kant and Levinas," *Idealistic Studies,* vol. 45, no. 2 (Summer 2015): 125–47.

17. The Peace of Augsburg declares in Article XV that it is "In order to bring peace into the holy Empire of the Germanic Nation" that it enacts its principles. B. J. Kidd, ed., *Documents Illustrative of the Continental Reformation* (Oxford: Clarendon Press, 1911), 363. The Prelude of the Edict of Nantes similarly declares that the strength France shows in overcoming the tumult of religious conflict, enacted in the Edict, will lead to "the establishment of a good Peace." "The Edict of Nantes," accessed Dec. 19, 2015, http://www2.stetson.edu/~psteeves/classes/edictnantes.html.

18. Saint Augustine, *The City of God,* trans. Marcus Dodds (New York: Modern Library, 1993), book 19, chap. 13, 690.

19. Ibid., book 19, chap. 10, 685.

20. Taylor, *A Secular Age,* 22, 26–28.

21. See his association of reason and peace in the preface to the German edition of *Totality and Infinity, EN* 198.

22. At the 2010 "Lectures de *Difficile Liberté*" conference in Toulouse, France, Shawn Thomson delivered a probing analysis of the ineffaceability of "the temptation to murder" in Levinas's thought.

23. See Emmanuel Levinas, "From Consciousness to Wakefulness: Starting from Husserl," *GCM* 15–32.

24. I am grateful to one of the anonymous reviewers for reminding me of this perfectly apt passage.

25. Two points. First, Mouffe sees a difference between her conception of agonism and Connolly's; see Chantal Mouffe, "For an Agonistic Model of Democracy," in *The Democratic Paradox* (London: Verso Books, 2005), 107n31, and Chantal Mouffe, *On the Political* (New York: Routledge, 2005), 131n9. There are, indeed, differences between them, but for my purposes these are not as significant as their similarities, on which I shall be concentrating. Second, neither Connolly nor Mouffe, to my knowledge, make substantive reference to Levinas. In *Why I Am Not a Secularist* (Minneapolis: University of Minnesota Press, 1999), Connolly suggests that Levinas recognizes that universalist moralities elide the resources "from which agonistic empathy for difference is cultivated" (155–56). Mouffe, by contrast, suggests that Levinasian ethics, among other ethics of the Other, elides "the moment of 'decision'" central to her conception of agonistic politics (*Democratic Paradox*, 129–30). My discussion above of Levinas's awareness of how *laïcité* excludes Judaism should indicate why this is perhaps an over-hasty conclusion by Mouffe.

26. To be clear, neither Connolly nor Mouffe is totally opposed to liberalism or secularism. Both of them construe their projects as revisionary ones, even if radical revisions. On Connolly's "critical liberalism," see Connolly, *Why I Am Not a Secularist*, 10; on how Mouffe situates herself vis à vis liberalism, see Chantal Mouffe, *The Return of the Political* (London: Verso, 1993).

27. Connolly, *Why I Am Not a Secularist*, 24, 38, 64.

28. Mouffe, "For an Agonistic Model of Democracy," 92.

29. See John Rawls, *Justice as Fairness: A Restatement*, ed. Erin Kelly (Cambridge, MA: Belknap, 2001), 34 and 84.

30. Connolly, *Why I Am Not a Secularist*, 37.

31. See "Politics and the Political" in Mouffe, *On the Political*.

32. Connolly concurs. According to him, the discrepancy between secularism's stated aims and its actual practice leaves it open to the charge of hypocrisy, since it openly espouses the value of secularity but "secretly draws cultural sustenance from the 'private faith' of constituencies who embody the European traditions from which Christian secularism emerged." Connolly, *Why I Am Not a Secularist*, 91.

33. Mouffe, "Democracy, Power, and 'the Political,'" *The Democratic Paradox*, 31.

34. Connolly, *Why I Am Not a Secularist*, 92.

35. Chantal Mouffe, "Religion, Liberal Democracy, and Citizenship," in *Political Theologies: Public Religions in a Post-Secular World*, ed. Hent de Vries and Lawrence Sullivan (New York: Fordham University Press, 2006), 325.

36. Consider the example of current US politics. The problem here is not that people with significantly different views are arguing for significantly different positions. The problem is that those arguments are conducted in a disingenuous and deceitful manner, full of actively disseminated misinformation, the distortion of facts, and the refusal to accept the legitimacy of one's opponents (as in the attempt, in the United States, to depict President Obama as ineligible for the presidency).

37. Mouffe, *On the Political*, 20.

38. Ibid., 72–76.

39. This argument is not made by Connolly at any one point; it is a general idea recurring throughout *Why I Am Not a Secularist*, although especially in chap. 2. He uses the actual term "critical responsiveness" on p. 62. Charles Taylor makes a very similar point in "Understanding the Other: A Gadamerian View on Conceptual Schemes" in his *Dilemmas and Connections: Selected Essays* (Cambridge, MA: Belknap, 2011).

40. Mouffe, "Conclusion: The Ethics of Democracy," *The Democratic Paradox*, 134.

41. Nikolas Kompridis, "Struggling over the Meaning of Recognition: A Matter of Identity, Justice or Freedom?," *European Journal of Political Theory* 6, no. 3 (2007): 277–89.

Ethical Dwelling and the Glory of Bearing Witness

Hanoch Ben-Pazi

The use of the terms "testimony" and "witnesses" is widespread. It can be found in such disparate fields as literature, art, and historiography. I would like to offer a Levinasian look at the question of witnessing and the absolute responsibility placed on witnesses, and on witnesses to their testimony. According to Levinas, to be a witness means to know another, and to know the otherness of the other, meaning to bear responsibility toward that otherness. The focus of this article is the conceptual meaning of witnessing, and the witness's responsibility for his or her surroundings.

This article considers man's attitude toward his surroundings with regard to the challenge posed to Levinas by Martin Heidegger. My aim here is to reassess the manner in which Levinas responds to and critiques Heidegger, with a focus on a category which, at first glance, may seem a strange choice for discussion: the category of "bearing witness." Through a careful reading of the writings of Levinas and Heidegger we gain an understanding of the notion of "bearing witness" in the philosophical realm—not in the sense of a stranger giving testimony in a court of law but as an integral part of everyday life. Although both Levinas and Heidegger address this category in their writings, they each understand and employ it in very different ways.[1]

The Temptation of Temptation and the Uninvolved Witness

In his famous talmudic reading, "The Temptation of Temptation," Levinas offers the following depiction of the condition of Western man and the manner in which he relates to his surroundings. "He is for an open life," Levinas tells us, "eager to try everything, to experience everything, 'in a hurry to live, impatient to feel'" (*NT* 32). However, although he admires a life of adventure, he is unwilling to assume the risk it involves. Contemporary man, maintains Levinas, wants to be tempted to try everything but prefers to refrain from taking the risk of engaging in it in practice. With this, Levinas constructs one of his most curious concepts—"the temptation of temptation," which he describes as follows: "The temptation of temptation is not the attractive pull exerted by this or that pleasure, to which the tempted one risks giving himself over body and soul. What tempts the one tempted by temptation is not pleasure but the ambiguity of a situation in which pleasure is still possible but in respect to which the Ego keeps its liberty, has not yet given up its security, has kept its distance.... What is tempting is to be simultaneously outside everything and participating in everything" (33–34).

Were we to apply this account to the human condition in present times, we would be forced to acknowledge that the human condition, or at least the condition of Western man, has become even more extreme since Levinas penned the above words. We would consider the fact that contemporary man has most of his personal experiences and acquires most of his information about his surroundings by watching television or sitting in front of a computer screen. Indeed, people today are faced with an infinite number of temptations that are just a click away, inviting them on journeys to faraway lands, to pictures of magnificent landscapes, and to spectacular views of the power of nature. According to Levinas's analysis of the human condition, contemporary man, as a product of Western culture, will remain in the capacity of the tempted, or, to be more precise, that which is tempted by the state of "being tempted." People want to get to know the entire world and to experience the whole of nature but to do so while sitting on their sofa at home or with friends at a local cafe. People today can meet anyone, anywhere in the world. They can talk with whomever they please while sitting at their desk at home, drinking coffee that was delivered to them without their actually having to go outside and venture into the world. It is the temptation of knowing everything without taking risks and without joining the real world. I would like to think about this "Western man" not in terms of "temptation" or "the temptation of temptation" that Levinas used to describe him, but in other terms borrowed from Levinas: that of witnessing and testimony, perhaps even defining Western man as the one who wants to be an "uninvolved witness."[2]

In a theoretical sense, the excerpt regarding the "tempted person" can be read as a description of man as witness. With this, Levinas revives one of the major experiences of modern man, who prefers the role of the "witness" to that of the "participant." But can we truly characterize the tempted individual as a witness? I maintain that we can: the tempted individual is indeed a witness, but one who is willing neither to assume responsibility nor to acknowledge his responsibility as such. Theoretically, a person sits at home and wants to become a witness to something taking place in the world that lies beyond us. Consider, for example, the popularity of all kinds of reality shows. Taking things to the extreme, we can argue that, in actuality, a considerable part of life occurs as if it were taking place on television, as if it were responding to the challenge of the temptation of temptation. A significant portion of the phenomenological analysis proposed in this article relates not only to the category of "bearing witness," but to the mediation that facilitates it, such as the role played by the cameras with which people document their environment and the pictures with which they testify to this fact. One of the most common acts of our time is the act of experiencing reality through the lens of a handheld camera or a smartphone used to record and document. Through this act, we convert direct experience with the technological device that distances us from it and sustains our motivation to preserve, to bear witness, and to document.

The scope and complexity of the discussion before us require us to proceed by way of a number of smaller, more focused discussions that ultimately converge into one conception of the act of bearing witness and the witness's responsibility for his or her surroundings. Specifically, my aim here is to better understand the modern human condition, in which the encounter between the subject and reality takes place through the mediation of technology. To this end, we consider both the philosophy of Martin Heidegger, which concerns itself with the condition of the Dasein, its sense of being out of place in the world, and the authentic manner in which it seeks to overcome this feeling, and that of Levinas, who offers a different perspective focusing on issues of the ethics and responsibility stemming from the encounter between the person and that which lies beyond him. To understand how man uses technology to mediate reality we also consider the enlightening phenomenological and sociological work of Susan Sontag, which, in its exposure of the passion to bear witness, provokes reflection on various aspects of control, curiosity, and involvement. All this facilitates a better understanding of Levinas's conception of bearing witness and the manner in which he demands responsibility and ethicality of the individual, not merely as a witness to reality but also — by virtue of his bearing witness — as a partner to it.

The Phenomenology of Testimony and the Concept of Responsibility

The first segment of our discussion addresses the notion of bearing witness and the responsibility borne by the witness by virtue of this act. Although the Western man described above could possibly be a witness who maintains his distance from reality and his surroundings, a phenomenological analysis reveals his involvement, by virtue of his role as a witness, and the responsibility he bears in this capacity.

In order to clarify the complex investigation of the act of bearing witness, we must first assume what is ostensibly true: that bearing witness is a neutral action of "the third"—a person who is not a participant in the event to which he bears witness but simply happens to observe it. In this sense, from a lexical perspective, the concept of "bearing witness" belongs to the practical semantic field of law, as testified to by most dictionaries and encyclopedias.[3] Bearing witness is an action by which one person observes another person or event and takes note of its occurrence. By the witness's own self-definition, he is an outsider, the Third, observing and after the fact possibly giving testimony. Indeed, the philosophical writing on bearing witness appears to be an incorporation of the legal concept into ethical philosophical discourse, complete with all the difficulties that such incorporation involves. In this sense, we may explore the act of bearing witness and seeming to inquire into the legal authority before which it is discussed, whether it be the law of history or the concrete law of the legal realm. "Bearing witness" is the manner in which the link to reality is presented before the judge and is contingent upon the actual outcome of the testimony and the rules of prosecution.[4]

The phenomenological investigation of bearing witness reveals the witness's involvement in the act and the occurrence that he witnessed. In a certain sense, the incidental witness cannot relate to himself as external but rather must regard himself as part of the event. In scientific contexts today, it is customary to acknowledge the involvement of the witness, as in the case of a researcher conducting an experiment. In legal contexts, the witness is obligated to bear witness.[5] And in ethical contexts, we understand that witnesses become responsible for their testimony. Upon initial consideration, this assertion may be difficult to accept. After all, to what extent does the witness truly bear responsibility for that which he saw or heard? Posed in this manner, the question becomes an ethical concern regarding the relationship between two people, which bears ethical and political implications vis-à-vis the subject's immediate or more distant community, regardless of whether he views himself as belonging to this community or feels out of place within it.[6]

What is testimony and what is the responsibility of the witness? The philosophical thinking I seek to stimulate here shifts the focus of observation from the moment at which a person bears witness, in the sense of giving testimony, to the moment at which he or she actually witnesses an occurrence.[7] In other words, we need to reverse the order of discussion by asserting that the moment at which a person witnesses an event is the moment at which he or she assumes responsibility, and that the presentation of legal or historical testimony is only one possible manner of fulfilling this responsibility. The legal route, moreover, can in some sense be considered a relatively easy option, as it makes use of the law and the legal system to limit the responsibility borne by the witness. From a philosophical perspective, this point of departure is difficult to accept, as it regards the witness as playing a true role in the occurrence he witnessed, and, therefore, as bearing responsibility for his bearing witness.

In this way, bearing witness places immense responsibility on the witness himself, who suddenly finds himself involved in an occurrence in which he had no intention of taking part.[8] According to this argument, a person who witnesses an occurrence and may view himself as no more than a bystander and observer is assigned the unique ethical role of the witness. This role is worthy of interrogation and re-interrogation because it causes the witness to consider the extent to which he or she must abandon the role of the witness in order to function within real life itself. The role of witness also highlights the problematic dilemma of hoping for good in a world in which a witness to evil finds himself involved, against his will, in the creation and articulation of evil, which is an issue to which I will return below.[9] This dilemma highlights the significant challenge of bearing witness, as it gives expression to the witness's fear of the responsibility involved, to the point of shifting his gaze away from being a witness. A person may ask himself or his society what he or it fears most, and in some cases this fear is exposed in precisely those events, places, and strata at which members of society prefer to shift their gaze and "not be witnesses."[10]

Distance and Responsibility: Susan Sontag's Exploration of Photography

Phenomenological methodology teaches us to devote attention not only to concepts and to the things themselves, but also to the mind's intention toward its subjects and to the tools with which it comprehends and analyzes the information at its disposal. This section demonstrates our discussion on bearing witness and man's relationship with his surroundings using Susan Sontag's work on photography. It is important to emphasize that the discussion put forth in this article about Sontag's research is only another tool for understanding the meaning of a person's examination of his environment and the use made of technology for distancing a person from taking responsibility for his environment. Levinas, in contrast, understands the meaning of "being a witness" in terms of taking responsibility, negating the self-distancing and flight from responsibility that a person apparently desires when he places himself "outside the situation."

There are many people today who possess a romantic attitude toward nature and who seek, through their relationship with different landscapes and places, to connect to nature and be part of the experience. Many more, however, prefer to be mesmerized by the power and beauty of nature from a position of alienation involving no risk whatsoever. Consider, for example, nature photographs, in which man stands on the other side of the camera, protected by technology, and, in a certain sense, conquers nature by acquiring and retaining its image. It is an appropriation of nature, yet one that is not achieved by venturing forth into the wild but rather by placing it in a guarded box that is kept at home — a collection of pictures that others photographed that document the phenomena of nature. It is a form of bearing witness that is silent and does not take risks.

In her book *On Photography,* Sontag explores one of the most common activities in the modern world—photography—and the kind of relationship between man and his surroundings that is reflected in this act of documentation. Her analysis of photography goes beyond its cultural significance and considers its ethical and social aspects as well. Some of her more familiar questions pertain to her own photographic work and the power of documentary photography: its boundaries with relation to the technology of photography, the distinctive frame of the photograph, and the context in which the photograph is displayed.[11]

Photography highlights the possessive dimension of knowledge by virtue of the ability it gives man to appropriate things that exist beyond himself, whether that be other people, other landscapes, or even himself, at a different point in time. Photography also highlights the importance of appearance and its preference over reality. Indeed, images in photographs are typically perceived as more realistic than reality itself. "To collect photographs," writes Sontag, "is to collect the world."[12] Through photography, one asserts ownership of the objects he photographs. In the eyes of the photographer or the person in possession of photography's product, photographs represent an extremely powerful type of knowledge. They are perceived as true information and represent man's ability to overcome interpretation—as if they endowed him with the ability to be everywhere and to acquire everything—and give the impression of being "miniatures of reality."[13] Photographs, posits Sontag, bear witness. Even if we have heard or read about something, it is imbued with certainty only after we have seen its photograph. Perhaps the most prominent example of this dynamic is the usage of photographs for legal purposes in policing contexts. Indeed, "a photograph passes for incontrovertible truth that a given thing happened."[14]

But what is so fascinating about photography is the fact that, just as it brings us closer to things themselves and stimulates our desire to document them, it also distances us and offers us protection from them. Man photographs and thereby determines the appearance of reality in accordance with the extent of its "photogenicity." Some maintain that the photographic act itself tempers the discomfort of journeys, farewells, and arrivals to new places. A person who photographs continues to work even when he is on vacation; after all, he is taking the pictures. Photography allows a person to feel as if they belong without taking the risks that belonging truly entails. Those being photographed are the passive objects of the photographing subject, who remains constantly active and in control.

Levinas investigated the significance of the proximity and the deception produced by technology in contexts of communication and the ethical dilemmas raised by the evolution of modern technology. According to Levinas, humanity makes substantial efforts to control its surroundings through the use of modern technology, putting man increasingly in the role of magician and sorcerer. Levinas's questions pertain not only to the human condition but also to the acceptance, or avoidance, of responsibility that clearly emerges from his account. Theoretically, man uses electronics and communications technology merely as a tool to maintain his interpersonal relationships. Theoretically, man is on one end, looking at or listening to another person who can be extremely far away. As he does so, however, he is actually closely guarding this distance. In this way, explains Levinas, while inquiring into the functioning of community in contemporary times, man feels part of global society but is simultaneously both lost and alone. He feels as if he is in contact with "humanity as a whole," thanks to communications media and the scope of the world economy. But, at the same time, his social relationships become less and less human: "With each radio broadcast and each day's newspapers, we admittedly feel implicated in the most distant of events and related to men everywhere; but we also notice that our personal destiny, freedom or happiness, depend on causes which strike with inhuman energy. We notice that technical progress itself—to repeat a commonplace—which relates everyone to everyone else, brings with it necessities which leave men in a state of anonymity. Impersonal forms of relation replace direct forms—'short connections,' as Ricoeur calls them—in a world in which everything is programmed to excess" (*BV* 69).

The Temptation to Bear Witness

One way of denoting the involvement of the witness is by drawing attention to the temptation to bear witness. Recognition that a person is not simply a chance or incidental witness to an event, but that bearing witness to events involves an element of choice and desire to do so, raises questions of legal credibility and ethical involvement. Does man's temptation to bear witness, we must ask ourselves, serve to damage his credibility as such? Does drawing attention to the temptation to bear witness undermine our confidence in the very possibility of reaching the truth?

Consider, for example, the efforts by nonprofessionals to document in photographs different events, be they of marginal or central importance in their lives or the lives of others. This matter-of-fact, seemingly benign description becomes more complicated in the context of the psychological temptation to bear witness not only to everyday events but to the harsher and more brutal events of life. In this context, we might consider the unique role of the documentation of brutality, the documentation of pornography, and perhaps even films containing violence and crime.[15] Here, we are making an intolerable leap of major proportions, for if bearing witness also means encountering the limits of the person, and if there is something personally arousing in the brutal manner in which the witness watches, then we also recognize that the very act of bearing witness leads to acts of cruelty. It is the question of the neutrality of the media in the current era, or the voyeurism of the television or the internet which we currently face. The very existence of a witness creates a new relationship between the I and the Other. Knowledge of the existence of a witness may have a moderating effect and define the law — whether the law of shame or of what is appropriate, or the laws of religion and conscience. However, the awareness of the existence of a witness can itself also be the true cause of human cruelty.

In the world in which we live, we need look no further than the phenomenon of terrorism, the phenomenon of pornography, and the phenomenon of reality television programs to reach the conclusion that an awareness of a witness's existence, involvement, and deep identification can encourage the doing of evil.[16] This almost banal statement, which shifts events from the reality of the occurrences themselves to their documentary representations, introduces difficulties to our discussion of bearing witness in that it charges the witness with responsibility not only for what he saw but for the occurrence of the event itself.[17]

What is important in this description, according to Levinas, is not the description of the temptation to be a witness, but the attention paid to the subject's desire to address what is beyond the present. As we will explain further on, for Levinas the temptation to be a witness is not just the temptation to maintain one's distance and control, but also a person's temptation toward what is beyond himself, toward the infinite. This is also the source of the responsibility imposed upon the subject toward the good that is beyond being.

BETWEEN "OUT OF PLACE" IN THE WORLD AND "FEELING AT HOME"

Levinas devotes an important chapter of his well-known book *Totality and Infinity* to the subject of "dwelling," in the sense of "home."[18] Levinas explains: "Habitation can be interpreted as the utilization of an 'implement' among 'implements.' The home would serve for habitation as the hammer for the driving in of a nail or the pen for writing.... And yet, within the system of finalities in which human life maintains itself the home occupies a privileged place" (*TI* 152). His thinking on the subject highlights the unique dimension of hospitality—that is, the manner in which the subject feels at home precisely when he is making room for the Other. Levinas's dialogue is conducted first and foremost vis-à-vis Heideggerian phenomenology. According to Heidegger, a person's sense of being out of place or, alternatively, of feeling at home is related to the authentic manner in which he or she accepts his or her belonging to existence. But, for Levinas, "Man abides in the world as having come to it from a private domain, from being at home with himself, to which at each moment he can retire....

He does not find himself brutally cast forth and forsaken in the world" (152).

This is no coincidental discussion of the case of the private person, of how he, specifically, feels in the world, the extent to which he views himself as a guest in the world, and the extent to which he feels at home.[19] Heidegger's description begins with the Dasein, which links time and being as embodied in the human being.[20] Time is not simply another realm in which man takes part, as in the comparison between the category of time and the category of space. Time, according to Heidegger, is the way in which people live. The action of time—*Zeitigung*—is the principal consciousness of time. Or, in his words, "temporality is the essence of Man's being."[21] Time is what links man and being, Dasein and *Sein,* as Heidegger's thinking regarding Dasein portrays man as being continuously situated in a process of coming into being, at the point of connection between being (*Sein*) and time (*Zeit*); or, to be more precise, the temporality of Dasein.[22] The way in which man—Dasein—relates to the different tenses of time is linked to the extent of the authenticity of his existence and his being. From an ontological perspective, the meaning of Dasein is the unity of the states of authenticity that are built on the different states of time.

The significance of the past for the Dasein lies in the manner in which man understands himself in the world around him. Heidegger refers to this state as "uncanniness" (*Unheimlichkeit*), or feeling out of place. Man feels out of place in the world—like something that fell or was thrown into it. The image used by Heidegger is one of a stone thrown in space. The Dasein finds the factual existence of the world as absolute and foreign to him. The difficulty of its being is rooted in its fundamental experience of feeling out of place in a world into which it was thrown. According to Heidegger, an authentic attitude toward the past is the acceptance of this fact, and dealing with it in an authentic manner facilitates a change in the Dasein's attitude toward the world and its surroundings. The Dasein can transform its uncanniness by being part of the world into which it was thrown.

In juxtaposition to this concept of "uncanniness" stands Heidegger's concept of "homeliness" (in the sense of feeling at home).[23] Uncanniness means being anxious and worried, quite literally the feeling of being "not at home." Homeliness is the authentic manner in which the Dasein feels part of the world around it, into which it has fallen: "In anxiety," writes Heidegger, "one feels uncanny...uncanniness also means not being at home" (*BT* 233). Uncanniness, in Heidegger's lexicon, is the juxtaposition of feeling part of things, involved, family oriented, and friendly.

Levinas is interested precisely in this point, not as a critic of the phenomenological account but rather of its ethical significance. Heidegger seeks to overcome this sense of being out of place in order to be part of the world. Levinas characterizes Heidegger's view as a pagan approach to the ritual of nature and land with which man seeks to overcome his sense of feeling out of place in the world. Indeed, Levinas acknowledges, it is extremely tempting to desire to be part of the world, and there is an element of enchantment in Heidegger's depictions of nature and the sense of belonging to nature they describe. Just before critiquing it, Levinas offers the following account of Heidegger's position, replete with agreeable words and romantic imagery:

> One would like man to rediscover the *world*. Men will lose the world.... To rediscover the world means to rediscover a childhood mysteriously snuggled up inside the Place, to open up to the light of great landscapes, the fascination of nature, and the delight of camping in the mountains. It means to follow a path that winds its way through fields, to feel the unity created by the bridge that links the two river banks and by the architecture of buildings, the presence of the tree, the chiaroscuro of the forests, the mystery of things, of a jug, of the worn-down shoes of a peasant girl, the gleam from a carafe of wine sitting on a white tablecloth. The very *Being* of reality will reveal itself behind these privileged experiences, giving and trusting itself into man's keeping. And man, the keeper of Being, will derive from this grace his existence and his truth. (*DF* 231–32)

But this sense of feeling at home, asserts Levinas, is also manifested in the arrogance of natives toward strangers and immigrants and the arrogance of the I toward the Other: "The possibility for the home to open to the Other is as essential to the essence of the home as closed doors and windows" (*TI* 173). Man's sense of "being a stranger on earth" is what enables him to adopt an ethical approach in his treatment of others, whereas a "native" consciousness splits humanity into locals and citizens on the one hand and immigrants and the detached on the other. The religious ideal of being "a stranger on the earth" (Pss. 119:19) is what makes man's willingness to assume responsibility possible. And, as Levinas wrote, "The relationship with the Other is not produced outside of the world, but puts in question the world possessed" (173).

Seeking the authentic approach toward nature and land means seeking the land as a "homeland," which is not merely a neutral account of the territory or land on which a person happens to live but rather a reference to his "home," his "homeland"—the close bond to the country *in which* he was born and to the land *of which* he was born. This understanding is also indicative of the unique power and energy of the relationship between people and their land or country: that is, their homeland. On this issue, Levinas places an emphasis on his modern scholarly opponent, Martin Heidegger, as man's quest for overcoming his sense of being out of place in the world through authenticity and naturalness with regard to the land leads to acts of extreme brutality toward the foreigner and the stranger.[24]

The important philosophical question, maintains Levinas, is one of language, or the different ways in which language is used. One kind of language stimulates man based on his sense of connection to nature and his quest for nature's first language. Another human language observes and distances itself from nature. The modern model spoke of the educated man who emerges from nature, and viewed the arts as a deviation from it. This romantic account regards human splendor and radiance as part of nature and rooted within it: "Myth announces itself within nature. Nature is implanted in that first language which hails us only to found human language. Man must be able to listen and hear and reply. But to hear this language and reply to it consists not in giving oneself over to logical thoughts raised into a system of knowledge, but in living in the place, in being-there. Enrootedness" (*DF* 232). The language that is enrooted in place is the "first language," that which is part of nature and that is heard by man and responds to him—hence its vitality. The return to nature is a return in the sense of "enrooting," and therefore expresses the return to authentic speech. It is a language replete with emotion and fragility and is described using clear, rooted terms. Indeed, the language of nature presents a great temptation that Levinas refers to as "Heideggerian temptation," the "temptation of the mythos," and the "temptation of paganism," which can only be anti-humanity.[25] And, to use the words of Levinas, behind the mystery of things lies "the source of all cruelty towards men" (232).

Levinas's argument may very well be relevant for all discussions of mythos. However, the focus of discussion here is the mythos of territoriality, or belonging to the land. The mythoi that establish belonging to the land depict man as a native, as someone who was born of the land. These mythoi are a source of violence and brutality because of their explicit definition of who belongs and does not belong to a particular place, which amounts to "the very splitting of humanity into natives and strangers" (*DF* 232). Levinas uses the term *autochtone* to distinguish between citizenship based on nativeness—that is, people born of the land—and those who came to the land from outside. This terminology is extremely significant and leads us back to the platonic myth containing the account of the native of the land. Those who are born on the land belong to it, and those who are not are strangers within it. It is the "homeland" from which they emerge and to which they return: "Men seek one another in their incondition of strangers. No one is at home" (*HO* 66). Man's recognition of himself as a stranger on earth enables him to recognize in all people not only foreignness but also the necessary sense of brotherhood.

According to Levinas, a person's sense of himself as out of place is closely tied to the responsibility and commitment toward others that he is willing to assume. As Levinas says, "The familiarity of the world does not only result from habits acquired in this world, which take from it its roughnesses and measure the adaptation of the living being to a world it enjoys and from which it nourishes itself.... The intimacy which familiarity already presupposes is an *intimacy with someone*" (*TI* 155).

Bearing Witness to Existence and Bearing Witness to Responsibility

We now return to our discussion of the concept of bearing witness as a category of belonging, participation, and assumption of responsibility. Refocusing our observation on man as subject and witness enables us to resume inquiring into his attitude toward his surroundings. Heidegger effectively examined the concept of bearing witness in his major work *Sein und Zeit*, in which he sought to understand the different linkages between man and reality — between Dasein and *Sein* — manifested in the act of bearing witness. Theoretically, the very use of the terms of bearing witness to relate to the Dasein is an act of distancing reality and a distancing from man's authentic mode of existence. Heidegger's investigation regards bearing witness as the act of revelation of the Dasein. According to Heidegger, what is authentically revealed by means of the Dasein is being itself. In a profound sense, Heidegger signifies the possibility of understanding the Dasein as testifying to existence through its own authentic existence. In this way, he rouses the concept of bearing witness from its slumber as external to the issue and turns it into the realm of the exposure of existence. The bearing witness to which the Dasein testifies is actually its own existence and its own coming into being.

We now return to the analysis of bearing witness proposed above — based on Sontag's investigation of photography — for reconsideration. We do so because the manner in which man chooses to use the camera in defining himself as a witness assumes more complex significance, ranging from noninvolvement, cooperation, and possessiveness of external reality to a reversal of roles in which the photographed picture is more real than reality itself and the person photographing it prefers bearing witness over taking part in reality.

Heidegger's quest for bearing witness is a quest for an involved, authentic bearing witness that can express the Dasein's exposure to the *Sein,* that is, to existence itself. Heidegger seeks the presence of the Dasein as it is in itself, and in its connections to reality itself—as opposed to meaninglessness—he contends with the major issue of authenticity. The existential question regarding the Dasein concerns the modes in which the Dasein exists: "being within the world," "being with," or "being itself." Does the Dasein, in its modes of existence, give expression to its own self or the meaningless self? Man's ability for authentic existence is closely related to his ability to face his temporality—the fact of his own death. The "being-toward-death" of which Heidegger speaks is the ability of the Dasein to face the fact of its own finitude, which gives meaning to the temporality of his life. Here, we must take note of the fact that the existence of the Dasein is the existence of being within temporality. The consciousness of the Dasein is born at this moment of the Heideggerian connection, as it is at this point that we can speak of the emergence of the question of bearing witness, or what Heidegger refers to as an "authentic potentiality for being" (see *BT* 247–67). The existential structure of the authentic potentiality for being, Heidegger concludes, is witnessed in the consciousness.

We cannot, in my view, disregard the ethical significance of Heidegger's discussion on this point, as it is an issue that elicits the existential significance of being named, of guilt, and of concern, which are all existential phenomena of everyday life that are worthy of ethical discussion. It is unclear whether the feeling of guilt should be seen as a product of ethical being. It is clear, however, that the existential dimension of a man bearing guilt has ethical implications. In a deep Heideggerian sense, it is the possibility of ceasing a meaningless existence and embarking on an existence of meaning. But about whom is the witness bearing witness in his attestation of being? It is with this question, which is of great concern to Heidegger, that he begins.

"We are looking for an authentic potentiality-of-being of Dasein," writes Heidegger, "that is attested by Dasein itself in its existentiell [*sic*] possibility" (*BT* 247).

The Witness's Responsibility according to Levinas

The next segment of our discussion concerns the meaning of bearing witness, as Levinas understands it, and the path of "infinite responsibility" embarked on by the witness by virtue of his being a witness. The legal and cultural discourse on the subject informs us of the witness's involvement in the events he witnessed and his partial or full responsibility for their occurrence, and Sontag's work on photography causes us to reconsider the subject's own desire to bear witness. Heidegger's quest for authenticity conceives of the witness as one who facilitates the exposure of being through his own existence. Levinas, who recoils from the notion of man's belonging to nature or to a homeland due to its ethical implications, identifies the human feeling of being out of place as the act of facing the other and accepting responsibility.[26] And, finally, the phenomenological investigation informs us of the infinite dimension of responsibility, which redefines the subjectivity of the subject while he is bearing witness. The witness is not faced simply with the event and historical judgment (which desires good), but with an infinite dimension that penetrates being and bears infinite responsibility: "The Witness testifies to what was said by himself, for he has said 'Here I am!' before the Other; and from the fact that before the Other he recognizes the responsibility which is incumbent on himself, he has manifested what the face of the Other signified for him. The glory of the Infinite reveals itself through what it is capable of doing in the witness" (*EI* 109).

The Benefit and Disadvantage of Bearing Witness

The following account relates to the analysis of bearing witness advanced in "God and Philosophy." In this essay, which forms part of

Of God Who Comes to Mind, Levinas considers whether it is beneficial for the subject to assume responsibility toward the Other. After all, he points out, "to be good is a deficit, a wasting away and a foolishness in being" (*GCM* 69). This assessment calls into question the role of the subject and the witness. The moment we acknowledge the witness's own desire to bear witness, we are in fact charging him with responsibility for the evil and brutality to which he is exposed.

Our accounting assigns the witness responsibility for the brutality that takes place before him. It is not at all certain, however, that the witness wants to discover his internal lust for evil and brutality. In a certain sense, being presents us with this revealing element, as desire emerges as "of another order than those characteristic of affectivity and hedonic or eudaimonic activity wherein the Desirable is invested, attained, and identified as an object of need, and wherein the immanence of representation and of the external world is rediscovered" (*GCM* 67).[27] But Levinas proposes understanding the temptation to bear witness, and the desire for the emotional stimulation that doing so reveals, in a different, more profound manner: as the subject's desire for that which lies beyond him: "The negativity of the *In-* of the Infinite—otherwise than being, divine comedy—hollows out a desire that could not be filled, one nourished from its own increase, exalted as Desire—one that withdraws from its satisfaction as it draws near to the Desirable. This is a Desire for what is beyond satisfaction, and which does not identify, as need does, a term or an end. A desire without end, from beyond Being: dis-inter*estedness* [*sic*], transcendence—desire for the Good" (67).

Levinas's account of this observation is only sufficient in terms of form. That is to say, the very existence within the subject of that which is external to him reveals his attitude toward that which is beyond being. Indeed, Levinas himself acknowledges that it is possible to make do with this account and to understand it in terms of pattern alone, even if only in the abstract. Nevertheless, he asks us to take another step by using this form-related pattern of bearing witness to learn about the necessity of the external that lies beyond man, as well as the ethical significance of the approach to bearing witness. How does the account of the infinite that is not contained within the identical become the bearer of ethical significance? This occurs when thinking regarding the infinite becomes an obligation toward the other. That is to say, the concepts of responsibility borne by the witness appear on initial consideration to be impossible to implement and impossible to accommodate. The responsibility borne by the witness goes far beyond his ability as a responsible subject. Bearing witness itself is an act in which the subject faces elements that are increasingly greater and broader than he, ad infinitum. According to Levinas, we can also learn about the meaning of the responsibility borne by the subject by virtue of his bearing witness from the feeling of avoidance that accompanies this responsibility. Hypothetically, the witness tells himself the following: because I cannot take on all the responsibility that is imposed on me, I am better off relinquishing its implementation in practice.

Levinas explains the transformation from bearing witness to responsibility as a change that takes place within the subject at precisely the point that he is unable to accommodate his bearing witness. As long as the subject is engaged in receiving and processing information, his understanding and perception can accommodate the phenomena he observes. As long as it is a question of receiving limited, finite information — even information consisting of multiple pieces provided simultaneously as presence before the subject — they can be comprehended. It is only when the subject faces that which he cannot accommodate, when he is shocked by that which he cannot take upon himself, that he becomes aware of the infinite dimensions of responsibility, and that which lies beyond the infinite becomes an ethical imperative: "The abstraction is nevertheless familiar to us beneath the empirical event of obligation to the other and as the impossible indifference — impossible without avoidance — to the misfortunes and faults of the neighbor, as an irrecusable responsibility for him. A responsibility whose limits are impossible to fix, whose extreme urgency cannot be measured" (*GCM* 70). And, as Levinas describes the concept of witnessing in *Otherwise than Being*, not as "the third" person, but as the responsible person. The witness is defined in Roman law as a "third party"; Levinas's research imposes on that third party full responsibility for being a third party:

> The order that orders me does not leave me any possibility of setting things right side up again with impunity, of going back from the exteriority of the Infinite, as when before a theme one goes back from the signifier to the signified, or as when in a dialogue one finds in "you" a being. It is in prophecy that the Infinite escapes the objectification of thematization and of dialogue, and signifies as *illeity*, in the third person. This "thirdness" is different from that of the third man, it is the third party that interrupts the face to face of a welcome of the other man, interrupts the proximity or approach of the neighbor, it is the third man with which justice begins. (*OB* 149–50)

In this sense, Levinas achieves a shift in the point of view of bearing witness. The subject who views himself as a judge of the event, as processing the information and determining the meaning of the event taking place before him, finds himself trapped within an act of witnessing that he is incapable of accommodating. One problematic aspect of bearing witness is the fact that a witness knows neither the extent to which he caused the event he witnessed nor the extent to which he bears responsibility for it. However, when the subject is not the judge of the event but rather maintains his status as a witness to the event, his bearing witness is first and foremost the bearing of responsibility that is forced on man. In such instances, the judgment which the subject imposes on the situation serves to solve or limit his responsibility: "To reflection, this responsibility is astonishing in every way, extending all the way to the obligation to answer for the freedom of the other, all the way to being a responsibility for his responsibility, whereas the freedom that would require an eventual engagement, or even the assumption of an imposed necessity, cannot find for itself a present that encompasses the possibilities of the other" (*GCM* 70).

As if the ethical significance of his words is not enough, he continues onward and asserts that by virtue of his responsibility toward the Other, the subject is never actually a sufficient subject. Indeed, this responsibility is attestation to the infinity that stems from his standing on the side as a subject that is never neutral or indifferent: "as a responsible I, I never finish emptying myself of myself. An infinite increase in one's exhaustion, wherein the subject does not simply become aware of this expenditure, but is its site and its event, and, if we may say this, its goodness. *The glory of a long desire!* The subject as hostage has been neither the experience nor the proof of the Infinite, but the witnessing of the Infinite, a modality of this glory, a witnessing that no disclosure has preceded" (*GCM* 73).

Thinking about witnessing in Levinas's own language is a provocation. Yet it is not the manipulative sense of provocation, but in the most inner sense, because it is a provocation that does not leave the person in his tranquility. It is a call that forces a person to be awake and aware. The responsibility isn't a product of the interpretation and of the thematization of justice that are incumbent upon the court and the law, or in an understanding of the human situation. It is a call that precedes all calls, a passivity beyond passivity, that is the subjectivity of being for the other: "Glory is but the other face of the passivity of the subject. Substituting itself for the other, a responsibility ordered to the first one on the scene, a responsibility for the neighbor, inspired by the other, I, the same, am torn up from my beginning in myself, my equality with myself. The glory of the Infinite is glorified in this responsibility. It leaves to the subject no refuge in its secrecy that would protect it against being obsessed by the other, and cover over its evasion" (*OB* 150).

Levinas's interpretation of bearing witness changes the face of the phenomenon, as truth is neither found nor revealed through unveiling or exposing the truth. On the contrary, truth lies in the act of bearing witness itself, which neither compromises the independence of the Other nor seeks to completely comprehend. Levinas, perhaps fearing the loss of his lofty words regarding the infinity of bearing witness and the glory and the ability to absorb, insists on guiding ethics toward the concreteness of everyday life. In doing so, he draws attention to the moment at which the witness tells himself, "it was nothing," signifying this avoidance of responsibility.

Sincerity and Witnessing

The complex description offered here of the idea of testimony and the responsibility incumbent upon the witness comprises aspects that appear to be mutually contradictory: the subject's hesitancy to be involved in what is beyond him, the subject's desire to be a witness to what is beyond him, a person's foreignness and separateness in the world alongside the Heideggerian desire to be part of the world, a person's sense that being a witness means being external alongside the responsibility incumbent on a person by dint of his being a witness, and, perhaps beyond all these aspects, the search for the first language, whether the language of authenticity according to Heidegger or the language of responsibility that precedes every other language according to Levinas. In one of the most impressive passages, in my opinion, in the analysis of the idea of testimony in *Other than Being*, Levinas says this: "This witness is not reducible to the relationship that leads from an index to the indicated. That would make it a disclosure and a thematization. It is the bottomless passivity of responsibility, and thus, sincerity. It is the meaning of language, before language scatters into words, into themes equal to the words and dissimulating in the said the openness of the saying exposed like a bleeding wound. But the trace of the witness given, the sincerity or glory, is not effaced even in its said" (*OB* 151). Levinas exposes the most profound meaning on the passivity of the subject, which is revealed precisely in his openness to the other, his openness to the infinite, and in the responsibility that is his. Levinas formulates this in that ever so meaningful expression of his, "sincerity." That may be the most concrete expression of the responsibility placed upon the witness.

On this basis, we can understand Levinas's use of the connection between sincerity and witnessing. Why must a person be sincere with himself during the act of witnessing? The answer to this question is revealed gradually in the course of Levinas's analysis of the act of bearing witness, as there are many ways for a person to evade the responsibility with which he is charged by virtue of this act. It is not the economic fraternity that makes bearing witness important — not the calculation that informs a witness that it is worthwhile for him to assume responsibility so that one day, when he needs someone to bear witness on his behalf, that person will agree to do so. It is not the fraternity of Cain, for in the subject's bookkeeping with himself, the desire for good may put him in deficit. Bearing witness causes man to see himself as torn beneath the weight of the infinite burden of responsibility. Man articulates the infinite without being capable of containing it, and articulates his willingness to bear witness without being capable of bearing full responsibility for doing so: "The glory of the Infinite is the anarchic identity of the subject flushed out without being able to slip away. It is the ego led to sincerity, making signs to the other, for whom and before whom I am responsible, of this very giving of signs, that is, of this responsibility: 'here I am.' The saying prior to anything said bears witness to glory" (*OB* 150).

Levinas writes carefully in order to prevent his words regarding the infinity that reveals itself in the course of bearing witness from assuming religious or ideological meaning. It is important, he tells us, that "in sketching the contours of prophetic witnessing... we have not entered into the moving sands of religious experience" (*GCM* 76). Saying to the face of the other carries significance, because saying is a sign that signifies to the other the sign itself: "This is a Saying bearing witness to the other of the Infinite, which tears me open as it awakens me in the Saying" (74). It is a process by which fraternity is not defined by the fraternity of Cain — of two free men — and in this sense it is an economic fraternity in which the good may end up in deficit. The fraternity proposed here is based on that which precedes my freedom: the Other. "As witnessing, Saying precedes every Said" (74).

In the world of today, Levinas tells us, we live in constant suspicion that philosophy and all philosophical statements are nothing but instruments of ideology. This suspicion emerges not from philosophical discourse itself but from elsewhere:

> And in the transcendence of the Infinite, what is it that dictates to us the word Good? In order that disinter*estedness* [*sic*] be possible in the Desire for the Infinite—in order that the Desire beyond being, or transcendence, might not be an absorption into immanence, which would thus make its return—the Desirable, or God, must remain separated in the Desire; as desirable—near yet different—Holy. This can only be if the Desirable commands me [*m'ordonne*] to what is the nondesirable, to the undesirable *par excellence;* to another. The referring to another is awakening [*éveil*], awakening to proximity, which is responsibility for the neighbor to the point of substitution for him. (*GCM* 68)

Similar to this description is Levinas's account of bearing witness and responsibility, as manifested in questions of sociality, communication, and technology. The illusion created by modern technology, by man's encountering the world via technology, leads us to a renewed encounter with reality by means of the concept of "responsibility." The profound accounting of responsibility we sought to analyze here reveals the responsibility imposed on man by virtue of his bearing witness:

> This must also signify that my responsibility stretches to the responsibility that the other man can assume. I always have, myself, one responsibility more than the other, for I am still responsible for his responsibility. And, if he is responsible for my responsibility, I am still responsible for the responsibility that he has for my responsibility: *en ladavar sof,* "it is never-ending." Behind the responsibility attributed to everyone for everyone, there arises, *ad infinitum,* the fact that in the society of the Torah I am still responsible for this responsibility! It is an ideal, but an ideal that implies the humanity of mankind. ("The Pact," *BV* 85)

Notes

In addition to the abbreviations at the front of this volume, the following is also used: Martin Heidegger, *Being and Time* (*BT*), trans. Joan Stambaugh (Albany: State University of New York Press, 1996).

1. Many studies of Levinas make reference to the two large corpuses he produced: the Jewish corpus, embodied in his talmudic readings, and the Greek corpus, embodied in his "phenomenological writing." My approach takes into

account the two corpuses of Levinas's writings as part of a larger project that is primarily a philosophical one. On the relationship between the two corpuses of Levinas, see, for example: Ze'ev Levy, "L'hébreu et le grec comme métaphores de la pensée juive et de la philosophie dans la pensée d'Emmanuel Levinas," *Pardès* 26 (1999): 89–99; Ephraim Meir, *Levinas's Jewish Thought: Between Jerusalem and Athens* (Jerusalem: Magnes, 2008); Danielle Cohen-Levinas and Shmuel Trigano, eds., *Emmanuel Levinas, philosophie et judaïsme* (Paris: Pardès, 2002); Catherine Chalier, *La trace de l'infini: Emmanuel Levinas et la source hébraïque* (Paris: Cerf, 2002).

2. Levinas's consideration of the topic of testimony that I wish to relate to appears in few of his books: see *OB* 142–52; *TI* 201.

3. In religious discourse (the biblical or Christian and the Muslim), the witness plays a different role in his attestation regarding divine truth. However, in this context as well, the theological philosophical effort is to interpret the action of the *shahid* ("witness" in Islamic context), the martyr (in Christian context), or the *mikadesh hashem* (in Jewish context) as a semi-legal act testifying to the existence and righteousness of god.

4. That is to say, when I wish to discuss a person's testimony, I am first required to address the validity of the testimony before the court: that of an eyewitness, a hearsay witness, a witness basing his testimony on the eyewitness testimony of another, etc. We, a sovereign such as the state, or a court operating under the auspices of the sovereign, require people to testify when they are capable of doing so in order to enable us to conduct a proper trial under the rules of law.

5. The ethical complexity lies in the question of the witness's responsibility to intervene in practice in order to change the situation as it is occurring.

6. Bearing witness became the subject of renewed philosophical interest during the second half of the twentieth century in the wake of World War II and the extermination of the Jews during the Holocaust. Bearing witness holds immense importance in the context of the Holocaust due to its perception as a fundamental basis of a world of meaning and belonging. See Adi Ophir, *The Order of Evils: Toward an Ontology of Morals* (Cambridge, MA: MIT Press, 2005).

7. Shoshana Felman considers this question with regard to witnesses testifying about the Holocaust. See Shoshana Felman, "The Return of the Voice: Claude Lanzmann's *Shoah*," in *Testimony: Crises of Witnessing in Literature, Psychoanalysis, and History*, ed. Shoshana Felman and Dori Laub (New York: Routledge, 1992), 204.

8. Although we as a society may charge a person with the responsibility of being a witness, people also sometimes find themselves playing the role of witness in an official or unofficial capacity.

9. For me, one of the most surprising aspects of this philosophical discussion has been my finding that the more I apply it to different professional contexts, the more I learn about the feasibility of the notion of bearing witness as a philosophical category (in various areas, including psychology and psychoanalysis, education, literature, medicine, and other fields).

10. Ariella Azoulay proposes an analysis of the ethical significance of photography in the modern era as a tool that also creates an obligation toward those who view themselves as uninvolved. See Ariella Azoulay, *Civil Imagination: A Political Ontology of Photography* (Tel Aviv: Resling, 2010), 67–73, 87–95 (Hebrew), also published in English under the same title (London: Verso, 2012). Azoulay also proposes a political analysis of visual testimony as reflected in the official photographs from the period of Israel's War of Independence preserved in the Israel State Archive. See Ariella Azoulay, *From Palestine to Israel: A Photographic Record of Destruction and State Formation, 1947–1950* (London: Pluto, 2011).

11. See also Walter Benjamin, "Kleine Geschichte der Photographie," in *Gesammelte Schriften,* ed. Rolf Tiedemann and Hermann Schweppenhäuser (Frankfurt am Main: Suhrkamp, 1977), 2:368–85.

12. Susan Sontag, *On Photography* (New York: Farrar, Straus and Giroux, 1977), 3.

13. Ibid., 4.

14. Ibid., 5.

15. See Susan Sontag, *Regarding the Pain of Others* (New York: Farrar, Straus & Giroux, 1977).

16. In this manner, for example, Andre Glucksmann (as cited by Sontag in *Regarding the Pain of Others,* 110) has maintained that war is dependent on the mediation of the media, and that, from an historical perspective, we have grown accustomed to the maxim that the outcome of war is dictated not by what happens in the war itself but by its representation in the media.

17. Parenthetically, we must also note the researcher's own influence on the actual subject of research (of course, acknowledging all the reservations required by such an assertion), even in fields such as quantum mechanics or theoretical astrophysics.

18. An extended discussion of the concept of *demeure*—"dwelling"—is undertaken by Levinas in "The Dwelling," *TI* 152–74. This chapter is of very great importance, because through it Levinas develops the basic meaning of the relations between subject as ego and subject as turning toward the other. On the meaning of dwelling and Levinas's relation to Heidegger, see Cecil L. Eubanks and David J. Gauthier, "The Politics of the Homeless Spirit: Heidegger and Levinas on Dwelling and Hospitality," *History of Political Thought* 32, no. 1 (2011), 125–46; and Guillaume Fagniez, "Levinas et Heidegger, côte à côte et face à face: Sur la question de l'habitation," *Revue Philosophique de Louvain* 106, no. 4 (2008), 747–70.

19. It is also fitting in this context to make reference to the following excerpt from Martin Buber: "In the history of the human spirit I distinguish between epochs of habitation and epochs of homelessness. In the former, man lives in the world as in a house, as in a home. In the latter, man lives in the world as in an open field and at times does not even have four pegs with which to set up a tent." Martin Buber, "What Is Man (*Was ist der Mensch?* 1938)," in *Between Man and Man* (New York: Routledge, 2004), 150.

20. See especially *BT* 49–58; and Martin Heidegger, *Metaphysische Anfangsgründe der Logik im Ausgang von Leibniz*, Gesamtausgabe part 2, vol. 26 (Frankfurt am Main: V. Klostermann, 1978), 260–62.

21. On the concept of time in the philosophy of Heidegger, see *BT* 219–46; Martin Heidegger, *History of the Concept of Time: Prolegomena*, trans. Theodore Kisiel (Bloomington: Indiana University Press, 1992); William D. Blattner, *Heidegger's Temporal Idealism* (Cambridge: Cambridge University Press, 1999); R. J. Dourtal, "Time and Phenomenology in Husserl and Heidegger," in *The Cambridge Companion to Heidegger*, ed. Charles B. Guignon, 141–69 (Cambridge: Cambridge University Press, 1993); and P. Hoffman, "Death, Time, History: Division II of Being and Time," in *The Cambridge Companion to Heidegger*, 195–214.

22. See A. Mansbach, *Existence and Meaning* (Jerusalem: Magnes, 1998), 54.

23. Heidegger returns to this issue repeatedly in *Being and Time*. See, for example, *BT* 188–90, 276–96.

24. On the different uses observed by Heidegger of this sense of being thrown into the world, see *BT* 20–24, 371–84.

25. In this context, Levinas regards the danger of this absence of humanity as exceeding that of the anti-humanity of technology. "And in this light technology is less dangerous than the spirits [*génies*] of the *Place*" (*DF* 232).

26. We should pay attention to the radical meaning of "passivity" that Levinas deals with in his book *Other than Being*, because of the infinite responsibility placed upon the subject, and what Levinas calls "passivity more than all passivity." I refer to this notion in the beginning of this article, and the way in which Levinas establishes responsibility as a basic characteristic of the subject as witness.

27. See above on the question of being tempted to be a witness.

About the Contributors

Deborah Achtenberg is professor of philosophy at the University of Nevada, Reno. She is author of *Cognition of Value in Aristotle's Ethics* and of *Essential Vulnerabilities: Plato and Levinas on Relations to the Other*. Her current writing project is on Jacques Derrida's *Monolinguism of the Other*.

Hanoch Ben-Pazi is assistant professor, Department of Jewish Philosophy, Bar Ilan University, Ramat-Gan Department of Jewish Culture, Kibbutzim College of Education, Tel-Aviv. His most recent books are *Emmanuel Levinas: Educational Contract: Responsibility, Hopefulness, Alliance* and *Interpretation as Ethical Act: The Hermeneutics of Emmanuel Levinas*.

Jeffrey Bloechl is associate professor of philosophy at Boston College. He has published widely in contemporary European thought and philosophy of religion, most recently on positions taken by Girard, Jankelevitch, and Kierkegaard. He is currently working on book-length studies of philosophy of religion in the wake of Heidegger and some implications of Freud's late work. Bloechl is the founding series editor of *Levinas Studies: An Annual Review*.

Nicholas R. Brown received his doctorate in Christian ethics from Fuller Theological Seminary. He currently teaches at Loyola Marymount University and lives in Los Angeles with his wife, Audrey, and their three sons, Jonah, Davin, and Nathanel. His monograph *For the Nation: Jesus, the Restoration of Israel and Articulating a Christian Ethic of Territorial Governance*, is forthcoming.

About the Contributors

Mark Cauchi is assistant professor in the Department of Humanities at York University, Toronto. He has published articles and chapters in continental philosophy, philosophy of religion, social and political thought, and aesthetics. He is coeditor of the forthcoming book *Accursed Films: Postsecular Cinema between "The Tree of Life" and "Melancholia."*

Akos Krassoy received his PhD from the Institute of Philosophy, University of Leuven. He has published various articles in English and Hungarian on Levinas's ethical-critical problematic of art, the phenomenology of literature, and the democratic project of the modern novel. His current research focuses on the communicational capacities of art in contrast with those of the public sphere, through the prism of ethical phenomenology (Levinas and Sartre).

Jack Marsh is a doctoral student in philosophy at SUNY Binghamton. His work has appeared in *Philosophy Today, Cahiers d'études lévinassiennes,* and *Philosophy and Social Criticism.*

Cathrine Bjørnholt Michaelsen is a PhD fellow in the Department of Systematic Theology at Copenhagen University. She is currently part of a multidisciplinary research project on self-understanding and self-alienation, working across the disciplines of philosophy, psychology, and psychiatry. Her main areas of research are deconstruction, phenomenology, and psychoanalysis.

Roberto Wu is professor of philosophy at Federal University of Santa Catarina (UFSC), Brazil, and organizer of the Hermeneia International Symposium. He has published several articles in the areas of hermeneutics, phenomenology, rhetoric, and philosophy of art. Much of his research deals with the work of Heidegger, Gadamer, Husserl, Ingarden, Levinas, Aristotle, Quintilian, Cicero, and Dostoevsky.

INDEX

Abbahu, 144
accusative case, 135n11, 167–68
acoustics: art and, 131–32; *il y a* and, 116–17, 130–31; "listening eye" concept and, 119, 129–30; in *Otherwise than Being*, 116, 122–23; resonance and, 120, 125, 127–33, 136n23; silence and, 116–21, 127–33, 136n23; subjectivity and, 120; in "Transcendence of Words," 120–21. *See also* hearing; sound
Acts of Religion (Derrida), 43, 48, 53, 57, 58, 61, 62, 69
Adieu to Emmanuel Levinas (Derrida), 47, 57, 58, 62, 71n1
aesthetics: ambiguousness of Levinas on, 2–4; ethics and, 33n8; phenomenology and, 29–30; in "Transcendence of Words," 17. *See also* art
agnosticism, 189
alterity: absolute, 67, 68, 92, 94, 95–96, 110n11, 111n17; art and, 17, 18, 22, 24, 27, 33n8, 36n23, 40n42; categories and, 103–04; discourse and, 18, 24, 27, 85; ego and, 54, 100; ethics and, 33n8, 36n23; in *Existence and Existents*, 40n42; face and, 110n11; freedom and, 17; good and, 68; illeity and, 55, 64, 66; *il y a* and, 55, 64; intellectual role of, 82; interruption and, 63; in Lacoue-Labarthe, 76n50; "listening eye" and, 129; nonhuman, 111n18; Other and, 166; peace and, 206; responsibility and, 59, 69; self and, 102–03; substitution and, 54, 74n33; theory and, 99; totality and, 22; in *Totality and Infinity*, 99; vision and, 18. *See also* Other
ambiguity: art and, 2–4, 6–7, 12; transcendence and, 64–65, 66–67, 76n46
"And God Created Woman" (Levinas), 137–54
animals, 111n18
apocalypse, 172
Aristotle, 96, 112n25, 194

art: alterity and, 17, 18, 22, 24, 27, 33n8, 36n23, 40n42; criticism and, 12–21, 24–25, 37n26, 41n47; discourse and, 18, 21–22; ethics and, 6–7, 11, 12, 36n23; in *Existence and Existents*, 3, 4, 5, 12; expression and, 26–27; irresponsibility and, 12–13; knowing and, 21–22; light and, 118; literature and, 6–8; manifestation and, 19; meaning and, 10–11; ontology and, 18–19, 31n4, 32n7; Other and, 16, 39n35, 39n38; in *Otherwise than Being*, 10, 32n7, 35n22; phenomenology and, 5–6; plasticity and, 3, 8, 9, 11, 22, 23, 26, 32n7, 36n23, 37n29, 39n35; poetry and, 9; reality and, 5, 13, 14, 16, 20, 21, 26, 30, 31n4, 40n42, 67, 118; in "Reality and Its Shadow," 2–3, 5, 11–12, 13, 15–16, 30n1, 118–19; referential connections to, 3–4; in Sartre, 8, 34n17; silence and, 131–32; totality and, 22–23; transcendence and, 31n4, 39n35; in "Transcendence of Words," 18; vision and, 19–20. *See also* aesthetics
"Assimilation Today" (Levinas), 202
Augustine, 203–04
Azoulay, Ariella, 247n10

Basic Philosophical Writings (Levinas), 48, 76n48, 204, 205–07
bearing witness. *See* witness
Beast and the Sovereign, The (Derrida), 45–46
Bell, Aaron, 111n18
Bergo, Bettina, 111n17
Bernasconi, Robert, 79, 80, 108n9
betrayal, 64
Blanchot, Maurice, 6–7, 8, 9, 13, 33n14, 34n15, 76n47; *Space of Literature, The*, 33n12; *Step Not Beyond, The*, 70; *Writing of the Disaster, The*, 73n37
breathing, 126–27
Bruns, Gerald L., 116
Buber, Martin, 165, 166, 247n19

Cain, 243, 244
camera, 223–24
Captive, The (Proust), 3, 41n46
Caro, Jason, 217n15
Casanova, José, 214
categorical imperative, 175
categorical intuition, 85
categories, alterity and, 103–04
Caygill, Howard, 191
Celan, Paul, 7, 8, 9, 10, 35n20
church and state, separation of, 188, 197

circularity, of *Totality and Infinity*, 83, 105–06
Cohen, Richard, 38n33, 41n45, 183
command, 123–24
communitarians, viii, 170
computer screens, 222–23
conditionality, 98–99, 156–57
Connolly, William, 189, 208–15, 218n25, 218n26, 218n32, 219n39
constitution, 89, 96–99
constructivism, 87
"content overflowing concepts," 90–91
creation, 89, 113n30, 144
Critchley, Simon, 76n43, 216n14, 217n15
criticism, 12–21, 24–25, 30, 33n9, 37n26, 41n47
Crowell, Stephen, 81–82, 107n6, 110n11

de Boer, Theodore, 80, 81, 82, 108n9, 112n26
deception, 144–45, 147–48
deconceptualization, 120
deformalization, 96–98, 100
democracy. *See* liberalism
Derrida, Jacques, vii, xiv–n5, 112n26; Freud and, 71n7; justice in, 43–44; responsibility in, 69, 75n38, 77n52; sound in, 115; substitution in, 61; *Totality and Infinity* method in, 107n6; trauma in, 45–46
Derrida, Jacques, works by. *See specific titles*

Descartes, René, 73n18, 163, 164
diachrony, 68, 73n18, 124, 126–27, 128, 131, 133
Difficult Freedom (Levinas), 182, 187, 188, 192, 196, 197, 198, 200, 201, 202, 210, 233, 235, 248n25
discourse: alterity and, 18, 24, 27, 85; art and, 18, 21–22, 27; morality and, 159–60; objectivity and, 25, 40n39; reality and, 24; transcendence and, 17, 24
distance, 227–29
documentation, 223–24. *See also* photography
Drabinski, John, 81, 108n9
Dreyfus affair, 191–92, 198
dualism, 23, 178–79
"Dwelling, The," 247n18

Eaglestone, Robert, 41n47
eating, 88
echoes, 121, 122–27
Edict of Nantes, 203, 216n13
ego: alterity and, 54, 100; face and, 86, 100; freedom and, 87–88, 195; in Heidegger, 112n28; *il y a* and, 127; infinity and, 88; Other and, 48, 200, 247n18; sound and, 135n11; temptation and, 222; totality and, 105; witness and, 222
enjoyment, 89–90, 93–94, 100

equality, 191
ethics: aesthetics and, 33n8; alterity and, 33n8, 36n23; art and, 6–7, 11, 12, 36n23; deformalization and, 97; in Derrida, 43–44; language and, 16; literature and, 10; ontology and, 173; of political action, 192–93; politics and, 192–93, 199–200; secularism and, 192–93; sexual, 152–53; witness and, 239–41; women and, 137, 153. *See also* morality
Ethics and Infinity (Levinas), 86, 238
evil: witness and, 226–27, 239
Existence and Existents (Levinas), 116–17, 119, 128, 134n7, 136n23; alterity in, 40n42; art in, 3, 4, 5, 12
Exodus and Revolution (Walzer), 171–72, 173
expression: art and, 26–27

"Fable, The" (Lacoue-Labarthe), 76n50
face(s): alterity and, 110n11; in animals, 111n18; communicative dimension and, 95; as derivative, 109n9; discourse and, 86; ego and, 86, 100; fraternity and, 101; in Husserl, 111n16; infinity and, 100; in Levinas, 80, 81–82; meaning of, 81; methodological status of, 79–80; ontology and, 93, 103–4

fact, Other as, vs. idea, 83, 85
Fagenblat, Michael, 215n2
Fear and Trembling (Kierkegaard), 166
"Force of Law: The 'Mystical Foundation of Authority'" (Derrida), 43
fraternity, 101, 189, 190–92, 200–01, 216n7, 216n14, 243, 244
freedom: alterity and, 17; egoism and, 195; liberal democracy and, 158–59; morality and, 158–59; norms and, 87. *See also* liberty
French Revolution, 191
Freud, Sigmund, 45, 71n7
"Freud and the Scene of Writing" (Derrida), 69
Friedman, Randy, 110n14

Gadamer, Hans-Georg, 103
Gallagher, Shaun, 109n10
gender: hierarchy, 153; humanity and, 137–38; norming, 153. *See also* women
givenness, 116
glory, 73n36
Glucksmann, Andre, 247n16
God: creation by, 113n30; idolatry and, 148–49; infinity and, 101–02; liberal democracy and, 157; messianism and, 172; Other and, 199; transcendence and, 67, 169, 199; women and, 146
God, Death, and Time (Levinas), 52, 60, 62, 64, 66, 68, 194, 199

"God and Onto-theology" (Levinas), 194, 198, 203
"God and Philosophy" (Levinas), 38n33, 238–39
Goncharov, Ivan, 3
Gorgias (Plato), 130

Habermas, Jürgen, 159, 208, 209
habitation, 231
Hägglund, Martin, 44, 74n33
halakha, 173–83
Hamlet (Shakespeare), 72n10
Hart, Kevin, 37n29
Hauerwas, Stanley, 155–56, 156–69, 168
hearing: in Derrida, 115; Other and, 122–24; silence and, 132–33; in *Totality and Infinity*, 115. *See also* acoustics; sound
Hegel, Georg Wilhelm Friedrich, 9, 164, 165
Heidegger, Martin, 89; categorical intuition in, 85; ego in, 112n28; justice and, 167; out of place in, 231; practice vs. theory in, 90; silence and, 128; time in, 232, 248n21; *Totality and Infinity* and, viii; the uncanny in, 233; witness in, 237–38
"Heidegger, Gagarin, and Us" (Levinas), 198
Hirsch, Emmanuel, 82
historicity, 113n28, 184n5
Hitler, Adolf, 193
Hobbes, Thomas, 167, 190, 214

Hölderlin, Friedrich, 75n43
Holocaust, 192, 246n6
home, 231–36, 247n18
"How Is Judaism Possible?" (Levinas), 188, 192, 197
Humanism of the Other (Levinas), 63, 73n24, 75n41
humanity, gender and, 137–38
Husserl, Edmund, 81, 85, 102, 103, 110n16, 162, 163, 164
idealism: Levinas between, and realism, 85–88; overflow concept and, 89
idolatry, 148–49, 194, 216n14
illeity, 55, 64, 66, 67, 73n28
il y a, 66, 76n46; alterity and, 55, 64; Other and, 135n14; silence and, 136n23; sound and, 116–17, 127–33
inequality, women and, 146–47
infinity, 68, 85–86, 100, 101–02
insomnia, 119, 130
intentionality, 163
interlocutor. *See* Other
interruption, 63, 121
"In This Very Moment in This Work Here I Am" (Derrida), 71n1
irresponsibility, 12–13
"Is Ontology Fundamental?" (Levinas), 116, 118

Jay, Martin, 129
Judaism, 153–54, 169–76, 181, 182–83, 188, 196, 197–98, 202–03, 246n6
justice, 166, 193–98

Kant, Immanuel, 65, 81, 90, 103
Katz, Claire, 137
Kavka, Martin, 79, 81–82, 108n6, 109n10
Kierkegaard, Sören, 165, 166
Kompridis, Nikolas, 214

Lacoue-Labarthe, Philippe, 75n43, 76n50
laïcité: use of term, 187. See also secularism
language: as being, 128; ethics and, 16; formal structure of, 86–87; nature and, 234–35; Other and, 6–7, 10, 15, 18, 26, 51–52, 86; poetry and, 9–10; reference systems in, 129; in *Totality and Infinity*, 16, 86; transcendence and, 28; as violence, 85, 95
Leiris, Michel, 116
Levinas, Emmanuel, works by. *See specific titles.*
liberalism, xi–xii; communitarianism and, 170; discourse and, 159–60; dispute resolution and, 157; fraternity and, 192; freedom and, 158–59; Hauerwas and, 155–69; in Hitler, 193; MacIntyre and, 155–69; messianism, 171–72; morality and, 157–58; neutrality and, 211; objectivity and, 160, 161–62; ontology and, 162–63; paganism and, 195; peace and, 206–07; secularism and, 188, 189, 196, 210; theism vs., 157; transcendence and, 156
liberty, 191. *See also* freedom
light, 115, 116, 118
"listening eye," 119, 129–30
literature, 6–8, 31n4, 41n47. *See also* art
Locke, John, 190
love, 147
Lyotard, Jean-François, vii

MacIntyre, Alasdair, 155–69
Maimonides, Moses, 113n32
makeup, 144–45, 147–48
manifestation, art and, 19
materiality, 133
maternity, 137
meaning, 10–11
"Meaning and Sense" (Levinas), 118
Meditations (Descartes), 73n18
Menasia, Simeon ben, 144
messianism, 171–72
methodology: face in, 79–80; overflow concept and, 88–96; theory and, 99–102; in *Totality and Infinity*, 80; transparency and, 106
morality: discourse and, 159–60; freedom and, 158–59; liberal democracy and, 157–58; Other and, 95; reality and, 102; universalization and, 161; in Walzer, 160–61. *See also* ethics
Moran, Dermot, 108n7, 110n13
Morgan, Michael, 79–80, 193

Mouffe, Chantal, 189, 208–15, 218n25, 218n26
Moyn, Samuel, 170–71
myth, 234–35

nature, 234–35
neutrality, 208–11, 216n14
Nietzsche, Friedrich, 28
Nine Talmudic Readings (Levinas), 139, 141, 142, 143–46, 147, 148, 150, 180–81, 182, 222
norms, 87, 94–95

Obama, Barack, 218n36
obedience, 122–24, 175, 179
objectivity: art and, 21–22; conditionality and, 157; discourse and, 25, 40n39; *il y a* and, 131; liberal democracy and, 160, 161–62; politics and, 195
Oblomov (Goncharov), 3
Of God Who Comes to Mind (Levinas), 50, 51, 106, 238–39, 240, 241, 242, 244, 245
On Escape (Levinas), 73n31
Oneself as Another (Ricoeur), 134n5
On Photography (Sontag), 228
ontology: art and, 18–19, 31n4, 32n7; ethics and, 173; face and, 93, 103–04; hearing and, 132; naturalistic, 162–63; Other and, 16, 48; overflowing and, 92; reality and, 162–63; secularism and, 194; violence and, 95, 113n33
originality, 92–93

Other: alterity of, 166; art and, 16, 39n35, 39n38; discourse and, 24, 27, 40n39; ego and, 48, 200, 247n18; as fact vs. idea, 83, 85; God and, 199; hearing and, 122–24; *il y a* and, 135n14; language and, 6–7, 10, 15, 18, 26, 51–52, 86; morality and, 95; norms and, 94–95; ontology and, 16, 48; originality of, 92–93; as other, 67; overflowing concept and, 91–92; peace and, 205–06; in Proust, 41n46; respect for, 95; responsibility and, 59, 61–62, 82, 167; responsibility for, 82, 123–24; in Sartre, 37n29; separation and, 100–01; signification and, 20; subject and, 20; temporality and, 48; in *Totality and Infinity*, 52, 59–60, 83, 100–01; transcendence and, 201, 206; trauma and, 48; violence and, 206; vision and, 134n5; witness and, 240. *See also* alterity
"Other in Proust, The" (Levinas), 41n46
Otherwise than Being (Levinas): acoustics in, 116, 122–23; art in, 10, 32n7, 35n22; betrayal in, 64; *il y a* in, 130–31, 136n23; "listening eye" in, 119, 129–30; peace in, 206–07; responsibility in, 49–50, 67; silence in, 117, 128; solitude in, 60; sound in, 117–18; subject in, 49, 76n50;

subjectivity in, 47–48; trauma in, 46; witness in, 240–41, 243; women in, 137, 153
out of place, 231–36
Outside the Subject (Levinas), 51, 66, 67–68, 117–18, 121, 195, 196, 200
overflowing, 88–96, 97–98, 116–21
Ozouf, Mona, 191

paganism, 194–95
participation, 104
passivity, 51, 168; photography and, 229; subject and, 248n26; subjectivity as, 135n11
paternity, 101
peace, 203–07
"Peace and Proximity" (Levinas), 204, 206, 207
Peace of Augsburg, 203, 216n13, 217n17
Perpich, Diane, 137, 151
persecution, 126
phenomenology: aesthetics and, 29–30; art and, 5–6; in reading of Levinas, vii–viii; of testimony, 224–27
photography, 223–24, 227–29, 236–37
plasticity, art and, 3, 8, 9, 11, 22, 23, 26, 32n7, 36n23, 37n29, 39n35
Plato, 130, 164, 194
poetry, 8, 9–10, 33n14
"Poet's Vision, The" (Levinas), 7
political theory, vii, viii
Politics and Passion (Walzer), 184n5

practice, theory vs., 90
Proper Names (Levinas), 10, 43, 67, 76n49
Proust, Marcel, 3, 41n46
provocation, 242
proximity, 130
"Proximity of the Other, The" (Levinas), 135n10
Pseudo-Dionysus, 113n32

"Question of Subjectivity, The" (Levinas), 128

Rawls, John, 159, 208, 209
realism, 85–88
reality: art and, 5, 13, 14, 16, 20, 21, 26, 30, 31n4, 40n42, 67, 118; consciousness and, 163–64; constitution and, 111n16; discourse and, 24; eating and, 88; of God, 101; in Heidegger, 233, 236; morality and, 102; ontology and, 162–63; photography and, 228; representation and, 65; responsibility and, 245; rhythm and, 120; theism and, 112n28; theory and, 99; totality and, 105; witness and, 223, 224–25, 236–37
"Reality and Its Shadow" (Levinas), 118–19; art in, 2–3, 5, 7, 11–12, 13, 15–16, 30n1, 65; criticism in, 30, 33n9, 37n26; Sartre and, 34n18; "Transcendence of Words" and, 116
reality television, 223, 231
recording, 223–24

"Religion for Adults, A" (Levinas), 198, 200
resonance, 120, 125, 127–33, 136n23
respect, for Other, 95
responsibility: art and, 12–13; for claims, 106; in Derrida, 69, 75n38, 77n52; for Other, 82, 123–24, 167; out of place and, 235–36; peace and, 207; photography and, 227–29; reality and, 245; secularism and, 213–14; substitutional, 53–61; testimony and, 224–27; third and, 200, 241; traumatic, 49–53; undecidable, 61–68; witness and, 224–27, 236–38, 240–41
rhythm, 119–20
Ricoeur, Paul, vii, 103, 134n5, 229
"Rights of Man and the Rights of the Other, The" (Levinas), 195, 200
Robinson Crusoe (Defoe), 121
Rodin, Auguste, 4–5, 28, 31n4
Rogues: Two Essays on Reason (Derrida), 46
Rötzer, Florian, 82
Rousseau, Jean-Jacques, 190

Said, Edward, 169
Sandford, Stella, 137
Sartre, Jean-Paul: art in, 34n17; eidetic scheme of, 8; "Reality and Its Shadow" and, 34n18; *Totality and Infinity* and, viii
saying, 124–25, 127, 128, 136n15

sculpture, 4–5
secularism: agnostic, 189; agonizing, 208–15; Dreyfus affair and, 191–92, 198; ethics and, 192–93; fraternity and, 189, 190–92, 200–01, 216n14; French Revolution and, 191; history of, 190; idolatry and, 194; Judaism and, 197–98, 202–03; liberalism and, 188, 189, 196, 210; neutrality and, 208–09, 208–11, 216n14; paganism and, 194–95; peace and, 203–07; politics and, 212–13; responsibility and, 213–14; rethinking of, 187; secularization vs., 215n1; and separation of church and state, 188, 197; state sovereignty and, 190–91; in *Totality and Infinity*, 195; transcendence and, 198, 216n14; unclear treatment of, by Levinas, 187–88; unjust, 193–98
secularization, 215n1
"Secularization and Hunger" (Levinas), 216n11
self, 95, 102–03. *See also* ego
separation, 100–01
separation of church and state, 188, 197
"Servant and Her Master, The" (Levinas), 7, 9, 10, 33n14, 35n19
sexuality, 145–46
shadow, 118
Shakespeare, William, 72n10
signification, 10

silence, 116–21, 127–33, 136n23
sincerity, 243–45
social action, vii
social theory, vii, viii
solitude, 60
Sontag, Susan, 224, 227–29
sound: in Derrida, 115; echoes and, 121; ego and, 135n11; *il y a* and, 127–28, 130–31; in *Otherwise than Being*, 117–18; transcendence and, 121. *See also* acoustics; hearing
sovereignty: secularism and, 190–91
"Space Is not One-Dimensional" (Levinas), 192
Space of Literature, The (Blanchot), 33n12
Specters of Marx (Derrida), 43
speech, 95, 115. *See also* language
Spinoza, Baruch, 190
state sovereignty, 190–91
Step Not Beyond, The (Blanchot), 70
subjectivity: antihumanism and, 74n34; art and, 13, 23, 25; breath and, 52; consciousness and, 164; *il y a* and, 55; as passivity, 51, 126, 135n11; sound and, 120; substitution and, 54, 57, 60, 123; trauma and, 46–49, 50–51; witness and, 238
Subject of Philosophy, The (Lacoue-Labarthe), 75n43
substance, 96–97, 112n25

substitution, 49, 52, 54, 62, 69, 74n33, 123, 127, 131, 168, 206, 245
"Substitution" (Levinas), 206
substitutional responsibility, 53–61, 74n37

Talmud, 137, 138–46, 170–71, 180–81
Taylor, Charles, 204, 219n39
technology, 223–24, 229, 248n25
television, 222–23
temptation, 222–24, 230–31, 235
"Temptation of Temptation, The" (Levinas), 222–24
testimony, 221, 224–27, 246n4. *See also* witness
theism, 112n28, 157
theory: methodology and, 99–102; practice vs., 90
Thick and Thin (Walzer), 160
third: face and, 101, 112n19; illeity and, 55, 123; responsibility and, 200, 241; substitution and, 62; witness and, 225
time, 232
Torah, 138, 173, 174–76
totality: art and, 22–23; breaching of, 104, 105; creation of, 104–05; violence and, 113n33
Totality and Infinity (Levinas): alterity in, 99; art in, 7; circularity of, 83–84, 105–06; constitution in, 89, 96–99; discourse in, 21–22; enjoyment

as concept in, 89–90; ethics in, 17; face in, 80, 81; hearing in, 115; home in, 231, 234; language in, 16, 86; methodology in, 80; neutrality in, 211; Other in, 52, 59–60, 83, 100–01; overflowing concept in, 88–96, 97–98; as response to Heidegger and Sartre, viii; secularism and, 195; separation in, 100–01; subjectivity in, 46–48; theory in, 99–102; transcendence in, 65–66; vision in, 19–20, 118; women in, 137, 153

transcendence: ambiguity of, 64–65, 66–67, 76n46; art and, 10, 31n4, 39n35; betrayal and, 64; breathing and, 126–27; diachrony of, 126–27; discourse and, 17, 24; experience and, 81; God and, 67, 199; idolatry and, 194, 216n14; infinity and, 88, 91; language and, 28, 87; liberalism and, 156; of literature, 8; Other and, 201, 206; overflowing and, 91; poetry and, 33n14; refutation of, 164; secularism and, 198, 216n14; sound and, 121; substitution and, 54; witness and, 239

"Transcendence of Words, The" (Levinas), 16, 17, 18, 19, 20, 29–30, 116, 120–21

"transcendental/empirico-metaphysical puzzle," 80–81, 83

transparency, in method, 106

trauma, responsibility as, 49–53; and subjectivity, 46–49; and temporality, 45–46

"Typewriter Ribbon" (Derrida), 45

universalization, 161, 182

violence: art and, 19, 25, 39n38; ego and, 18; evil and, 70; good and, 68; ontology and, 95, 113n33; Other and, 54, 61, 63, 206; speech as, 95; subjectivity and, 57; totality and, 113n33

"Violence and Metaphysics" (Derrida), 71n1, 107n6, 112n26

vision: art and, 19–20; limitations of, 118; "listening eye" concept and, 119, 129–30; Other and, 134n5; in *Otherwise than Being*, 119; in "Reality and Its Shadow," 119; in *Totality and Infinity*, 19–20, 118

Visker, Rudi, xiv–n4

Voltaire, 216n7

Vries, Hent de, 215n2

Wahl, Jean, 66

Walzer, Michael, 156, 159, 160–62, 168, 170, 171–78; *Exodus and Revolution*, 171–73; *Politics and Passion*, 184n5; *Thick and Thin*, 160

What Is Literature? (Sartre), 8

witness: ego and, 222; ethics and, 239–41; evil and, 226–27, 239; to existence, 236–38; fraternity and, 243, 244; in Heidegger, 237–38; Holocaust and, 246n6; Other and, 240; phenomenology of, 225–26; photography and, 227–29, 236–37; provocation and, 242; reality and, 223, 224–25, 236–37; responsibility and, 224–27, 236–38, 240–41; responsibility of, 238; sincerity and, 243–45; technology and, 223–24; temptation and, 222–24, 230–31; third and, 225; transcendence and, 239; uninvolved, 222–24; use of term, 221

Wittgenstein, Ludwig, 171

women: deception and, 144–45, 147–48; ethics and, 137; God and, 146; humanity of, 137–38; inequality and, 146–47; as inferior, 137–38; love and, 147; makeup and, 144–45, 147–48; as mothers, 137; in *Otherwise than Being*, 137, 153; prohibitions against, 146–47; sexuality and, 145–46; in Talmud, 137–46; in *Totality and Infinity*, 137, 153

Wood, David, 109n10